WE WHO SPEAK ENGLISH

We Who Speak English

AND OUR IGNORANCE OF
OUR MOTHER TONGUE

By

CHARLES ALLEN LLOYD

THOMAS Y. CROWELL COMPANY

PUBLISHERS   ::   NEW YORK

Printed in the United States of America

CONTENTS

AN
AMAZING
SITUATION

I

THROUGH the radio, which has made the power of the spoken word greater than ever before in history, multitudes of people are becoming daily more sensitive to the use of English and more imbued with the desire to use it correctly. Yet the sad fact is that frequently those who set out to improve their speech are led astray by false guides and spend much time and energy in training themselves to avoid perfectly innocent expressions and thoroughly good pronunciations, while at the same time they are entirely unaware of many genuine errors of the gravest sort that crop out repeatedly in their daily conversation.

The amount of misinformation that is continually being poured out on the subject of English is amazing. A striking instance is found in a recent issue of a popular magazine, which gives what purports to be a test of the reader's knowledge of our language in the shape of twenty-five sentences on whose correctness he is asked to pass judgment. After doing so he is to turn to another page, where the proper answers are supposed to be printed, and compute his score. Here is the first sentence:

During the reign of his father the Prince of

Wales, now Edward VIII, visited the United
States.

Can you find an error in the sentence? I sincerely hope
not, for as a matter of fact there is none. It is not exactly
a literary masterpiece, but it is correct as far as grammar
and the use of words are concerned. Yet, behold, the anonymous author of the test tells us that the very first word is
wrong. "During," so he says, means "as long as the act or
existence of," and since the Prince was not in the United
States for the entire duration of his father's reign, he insists
that it should be "in the reign" and not "during" it. I
wonder—oh, how I wonder—why it did not occur to him
to look into a dictionary before he perpetrated a piece of
nonsense like this. If he had opened the new *Webster* or
the *Century,* he would have found that the first meaning
given for "during" is "in the time of." And this is likewise
the second meaning recorded by the *Oxford* dictionary, the
leading British authority.

To be sure, "during" may also mean what the author of
the test says it does, but the other meaning is now more
common, and when we want to show that something went
on during the entire time that something else was going on,
we frequently say "all during" or something similar. Edgar
Allan Poe, for instance, perhaps as great a master of English prose as ever lived, begins his wonderful story *The Fall
of the House of Usher* in this way: "During the whole of a
dull, dark, and soundless day in the autumn of the
year . . ." If "during" meant only what the magazine
writer says, it would have been needless repetition for Poe
to say "during the whole." But I cannot help thinking that
Poe knew more about the English language than our anonymous friend.

"Each other" and "one another"

And here is another sentence from the test:

When the shot was fired, the three of us looked
at each other in consternation.

"Ah," some of you are saying, "I know what's wrong there; the English book I studied in high school taught me that 'each other' should be used only for two, and that for more than two 'one another' is the correct form." The author of the test must have studied an English book of the same sort, for he criticizes the sentence on exactly that ground. But John Keats seems not to have studied one of these books. Do you recall the lines from that famous sonnet in which he describes his feelings on first reading Chapman's translation of Homer?

> Then felt I like some watcher of the skies
> When a new planet swims into his ken;
> Or like stout Cortez when with eagle eyes
> He stared at the Pacific—and *all his men*
> Looked at *each other* with a wild surmise—
> Silent, upon a peak in Darien.

Now I would not for an instant rest a point of English usage solely upon the words of some author, even as great a one as John Keats. But in this instance the very highest authorities I can find agree with the poet, not with the magazine writer and the English books. The new *Webster* says that some people have sought to restrict the use of "each other" to two, but that the rule is not observed by literary men. The *Century* defines "one another" as meaning "each other," and the distinguished British authority Fowler says that the distinction which some try to make between the two expressions has neither historical backing nor present utility. Of course, anyone has the right, if he chooses, to limit his own use of "each other" to two only, and to use "one another" for three or more, but the views of these high authorities being what they are, he certainly has no right to say that others are wrong who do not see any gain in observing such a distinction.

What does "intriguing" mean?

And now just one more of these so-called errors. How does this sentence impress you?

Shirley Temple has the most intriguing dimples.

The author of the test finds great fault with this use of the word "intriguing," which according to him means only "puzzling," or "plotting," and hence cannot be used to describe dimples. But the editors of the new *Webster* say that one meaning of the verb "to intrigue" is "to arouse the interest, desire, or curiosity of," and they add as an example the expression "an intriguing smile." If a smile can be intriguing, why not Shirley's dimples?

Altogether in the list of answers in the magazine twenty-one sentences are condemned as being incorrect. Yet in seven of these—exactly one third—the usage condemned is supported by one or more of our leading dictionaries. In other words, our anonymous public examiner has hardly passed his own test. Surely there is no subject in the world other than the use of the English language in regard to which such a situation would be possible.

Ending a sentence with a preposition

Yet as we proceed with our discussion we shall encounter still more amazing, well-nigh incredible, things. How many of you who read these words, for instance, are certain that it is unquestionably a gross error in English to end a sentence with a preposition? Probably ninety per cent at the least, I should say. But you are entirely wrong, if you will pardon my saying so in this blunt manner. To end an English sentence with a preposition may be, and often is, an excellent use of our language. There is probably not an English-speaking person alive who does not do so many times a day. "What were we talking about?" "There goes the man we spoke of." "What are you laughing at?" Is there anyone who wishes to contend that such sentences are not examples of good English? Would it not sound dreadfully stilted to say, "About what were we talking?" "At what are you laughing?" and so on?

"Oh," some of you are saying, "no doubt the prepositional ending might pass in ordinary conversation, but surely it is out of place in formal, dignified writing." Well, Milton was probably as formal and dignified as any English writer who ever lived, but he ended sentences with prepositions; the translators of the King James version of the Bible were exceedingly dignified, and they did likewise; Shakespeare is generally conceded to be the greatest English writer— perhaps the greatest writer in any language—and he did not hesitate to end sentences with prepositions. The truth is that the majority of our leading literary figures from Chaucer down to the present have placed prepositions at the end whenever in their judgment it was advisable to do so.

These things being true, are you asking why you were taught in school that you must not under any circumstances place a preposition at the end of a sentence? The answer to this question brings out another amazing fact; namely, that no present-day text-book teaches any such doctrine, and if it was taught to you—unless you are over fifty years old—the chances are that your teacher took it not from the book you were studying, but from the recesses of his own mind, where it was likely implanted in his youth. All modern authorities are agreed that whether a sentence shall end with a preposition or not is a matter to be decided by the taste and judgment of the speaker or writer, and that those grammarians of fifty years ago or more who taught that such an ending is wrong were themselves mistaken. It is not that the rule has changed, but that there never was any such rule —at least not in the past five hundred years.

Who makes the rules of English, anyway? Not the grammarians, not the writers of dictionaries, but the great mass of intelligent English-speaking people. At least, that is what the grammarians and the lexicographers say themselves. Every one of them will tell you that it is his business simply to record what the people say—educated and cultured people, of course, for they naturally set the styles. The best English is that which is most likely to please educated and cultured people whose native tongue is English. That is all there is to it.

Now, I take it that no English-speaking person is offended

by such a sentence as "What are you looking at?" unless he has been artificially taught to be so. For there can be no doubt that that is our natural way of asking such a question, and futhermore, it has likewise the approval of the large majority of our great writers. What more is needed to make it good English?

Yet it must be admitted that it would not be good French, good German, or good Latin. The word "preposition" itself comes from the Latin and means "something placed before." It was doubtless this name and the Latin custom which induced the poet Dryden to go over all his works and change all prepositions which he had orginally placed after their objects to a position before them, thus giving rise to the notion that the preposition at the end is incorrect. From his day to the present the superstition has flourished in spite of all that can be said against it by those who truly understand the spirit of the English language. Not, of course, that any English-speaking person really observes such a rule in his actual speech. Only one of superhuman will-power could do that. But nine-tenths, at least, of literate speakers of English cling tenaciously to the notion that the rule exists, even though nobody obeys it.

There may be times, of course, when the prepositional ending is exceedingly awkard. To take an extreme instance, consider this sentence: "What do you bring such a book for me to be read to out of for?" Here it is obvious that a revision is sadly needed to turn it into something like "Why do you bring such a book to read to me from?" (Incidentally, it may be remarked for the benefit of those interested in the subtleties of grammar that "from" in the foregoing sentence is an adverb rather than a preposition, and hence does not violate even the imaginary rule we have been discussing.) Yet "what . . . for" cannot always be changed to "why." It does not mean "why" in the simple question, for instance, "What is this for?" And that, by the way, is another instance in which it is extremely difficult to avoid ending with a preposition. Would anyone propose that we should say, "For what is this?" I hardly think so.

And consider likewise this sentence: "That depends on what it is wrapped in." Who would wish to say, "That depends on in what it is wrapped?" Surely no one who retained his common sense.

Common sense—how characteristic it is of the English language and how strange that so many fail to recognize its value to our speech and seek by artificial rules to do away with it! They want apparently to bind English, to tie it down, to restrict its freedom and confine its vigor, to do away with its simple directness, and all for no reason at all except perhaps that they may rejoice in their supposed superior knowledge and find fault with those who speak naturally. It is amazing that the great body of intelligent English-speaking people have bowed down before their pseudo-scholarship for so long. It is high time they were learning that English makes its own rules and that their attempts to impose others upon it reveal only their own ignorance.

The use of "each," "every," "any," etc.

But let no one imagine for an instant that English is *without* rules, that each of us is free to speak or write as he pleases without suffering for it. Consider the sentence you have just read, for instance. I might have worded it, " . . . that each of us *are* free to speak just as *we* please . . . ," but if I had done so, I should have broken a rule of English—a rule, to be sure, that is very frequently broken in such expressions in ordinary conversation, and sometimes even in print, but one which really ought to be observed. "Each" is singular; that is, it refers to one person (one at a time, so to speak), and consequently it must be followed by "is," not "are," and must be referred to later in the sentence by "he," not "we." A little thought will, I believe, make it clear to anyone that the only logical way to put it is to say, " . . . that each of us is free to speak just as he pleases," and, furthermore, that that sounds best.

These words are troublesome: *each, each one, everyone,*

everybody, anyone, anybody, someone, somebody, no one, nobody. All of them are singular, although in meaning they seem to be plural very frequently, when the thought of the sentence as a whole is considered. For instance, "Everybody was at his post," means almost exactly the same as "All of them were at their posts." Nevertheless, I don't believe that anyone would think of saying, "Everybody were . . ." No, even the illiterate person will instinctively say, "Everybody was." Yet an amazing number of educated persons will go on and say, "Everybody was at *their* post," making the word "everybody" singular as far as the verb "was" is concerned and plural with regard to the pronoun "their," which refers to it. The reason for this remarkable confusion of numbers is that "their" may be both masculine and feminine, whereas "his," so they think, refers exclusively to males. Yet the truth is that according to the rules of English the word "his" may mean "his or her" in sentences such as we have been discussing. In like manner "he" may stand for "he or she," and the courts have actually upheld these meanings when interpreting the law, having ruled on more than one occasion that statutes containing the words "he," "his," and "him" apply to women just as to men unless there is other evidence in the wording to show that only males are referred to.

The strange case of *"none"*

Some of my readers are doubtless wondering why "none" was not included in the list of the words that are always singular. The answer is simple: it does not belong there. "None" may be either singular or plural, in spite of the fact that an amazing number of sticklers for good English do not know that its use in the plural has the sanction not only of the great mass of the people, but that of the highest authorities. It is correct to say either, "None of the children *is* at home," or "None of the children *are* at home," though the present day preference is for the latter. Let readers who are skeptical consult any dictionary. To be sure, "none" comes from the old Anglo-Saxon negative *ne* and the word "one," so that in derivation it is practically the equivalent of "no one," which is always singular. Nevertheless more than a thousand years ago, in the year 888, to be exact, King Alfred used "none" as a plural in the sense of "not any," and ever since that time it has been good English to use it in that way. Indeed, most present-day speakers use "not one" rather than "none" in a singular connection. "*Not one* of the children is at home," is the usual form of the sentence, rather than "*None* of the children is at home."

But it would be a mistake to think that it was King Alfred who made it correct to use "none" as a plural. In spite of the common phrase, "the King's English," kings have had little or nothing to do with making the rules of English. It is correct today to follow "none" by "are" because to many millions of educated and cultured English-speaking people during the past thousand years it has seemed good to do so. Indeed the chances are that in so doing Alfred was simply following the cultivated usage of his time, for his use is merely the first recorded instance that the editors of the *Oxford* dictionary have been able to find.

It is the people who have made the English language, and we who speak English are making it today. For it is not complete, and it will never be complete till it is dead, like Latin. But, far from being dead, it is changing, living, growing year by year, becoming a finer, a more responsive instrument for the expression of our thoughts and feelings. No language is more thoroughly under the control of the great mass of the people who speak it, and to no people has a greater privilege been given. It is ours to guide this growth and change, to have a share in the perfecting of the speech that has come down to us from our forefathers. But how shall we guide it, how shall we perfect it, how shall we measure up to our privilege and our responsibility if we are ignorant of the rules, the spirit, the history, the achievements, and the marvelous possibilities of our mother tongue?

MORE
FALSE
TEACHINGS

II

Not long ago, in a well known and widely syndicated newspaper feature devoted to the exploitation of the marvelous, there appeared the remarkable statement that there is no such word as "unsanitary." The explanation given the next morning was that the proper form is "*in*sanitary." Now, the author of this feature takes great pains to be strictly accurate, offers to present proof of any statement to readers who ask for it, and some time after this statement appeared, made the claim in a magazine article that he had never been guilty of an error in his feature. Yet the simple fact is that the statement is false. The word "unsanitary" is listed in all four of the leading English dictionaries: *Webster's New International*, the *New Standard*, published by Funk and Wagnalls, the *Century*, and the great British authority, the *Oxford*. Furthermore there is nothing in any of these dictionaries to indicate that the word is in any way inferior to "insanitary," which, of course, they also list. The truth is that the form with "un" is more common, though there are careful speakers who prefer the other.

How a man who prides himself on accuracy could have given such wide currency to a statement so easily disproved is almost beyond comprehension, yet the situation is not without parallel. A recent writer in a magazine devoted entirely to the use of the English language declared that *Webster's* does not sanction the use of "secure" in the sense of "obtain," as in the sentence, "He secured a good position." But the truth is that *Webster's* does give "obtain" as one meaning of "secure," as the author could easily have seen if he had taken a glance at that dictionary during the preparation of his article.

Another instance of the same kind lies in the fact that there are many people who pride themselves on their knowledge of English who insist that the expression "a grammatical error" is a misuse of words. Their contention is that "grammatical" means "in accordance with the rules of grammar" and that therefore no error could be grammatical, since it is actually a violation of one of those rules. Having delivered themselves of this wonderful piece of reasoning, they put on a wise look and evidently expect to be praised for their marvelous acumen. But the really marvelous feature of the whole affair is that it has apparently never occurred to them to see whether the dictionaries support their contention. If they should do so, they would find that "grammatical" has two meanings. The other one—and the more common of the two—is "pertaining to grammar," and that, of course, is the sense in which the word is used in "a grammatical error." Indeed the very expression is given in the *Century* as an example of the proper use of the word "grammatical" in this sense.

And so it goes. People who really ought to know better are continually making very definite statements about the use of English that find no support with the real authorities. Yet they utter them with an air that would imply that they are setting forth universally admitted truths. If they wanted to argue the matter, to oppose the authority of the lexicographers, it would be different, for, after all, the men who write our dictionaries, while able and distinguished, are not infallible, do not always agree with one another, and recognize themselves that the language is in a state of change, so that what is correct at one time may be incorrect a few years later. But the people I am speaking of are usually those who regard the dictionaries as divinely inspired, so to speak, and would not think for a moment of opposing them.

And yet, I think our dictionaries are sometimes to blame in not making their information as readily available as it might be. Let us consider, for instance, a very remarkable matter of pronunciation.

The pronunciation of "ask," "last," "past," etc.

There is in the English language a group of about a hundred words of which the following are conspicuous examples: *ask, last, past, class, master, after, bath, chance, vast.* The large majority of Americans use exactly the same sound of *a* in these words that they use in the word "fat." A considerably smaller number, living mostly in New England, New York, or Virginia, use in them the *a* of "father," frequently called the broad *a*, or the Italian *a*, the *a* in "fat" being known on the other hand as the short or flat *a*. And another comparatively small number, living largely in New York City and New England, utter them with a sound midway between these two, known as the short Italian, or intermediate, *a*. Strange to say, most educated Americans have been taught and firmly believe that this intermediate sound is the only correct one for this group of words, in spite of the fact that it is the most difficult of the three, is the least used, *and has no more dictionary authority than the other two.*

Some of my readers are no doubt eager to question that last statement. Aren't the words of this group all marked with a single dot over the *a* in our dictionaries, they are asking, and doesn't that mean that they are to be pronounced with the intermediate *a?* The answer is yes and no. They are marked with a single dot over the *a*, but that doesn't mean that they are necessarily to be pronounced with the intermediate *a*. It means that they may be pronounced with *either* the flat, *or* the broad, *or* the intermediate *a*. But to find out this very interesting and important fact, you will have to search carefully in the fine type of the introductions to the dictionaries. If you look in that of the *Century*, for instance, you will come upon the statement that the marking of the *a* in this fashion should be regarded "as pointing out the varying utterance here described (from *a* in 'far' to *a* in 'fat'), rather than imperatively prescribing any shade of it." The *Standard* makes a similar statement, but conceals it rather carefully, while *Webster's New International* (the new second edition) refers the reader in the case of all such words to section 83 of the article on pronunciation in the introduction, where after reading through two or three columns of fine type he will come once more to the vital information that as far as these words are concerned, the three sounds of *a* stand on the same footing.

But this is a new departure for *Webster's*. Until the new second edition appeared, in 1934, this dictionary stood out stoutly for the intermediate *a* as being the only correct sound in these words of the "ask" type, and it is largely due to its influence that millions of Americans have striven valiantly and mostly unsuccessfully to acquire what to them was a highly unnatural utterance, under the pitiful delusion that their natural short *a* was either incorrect or uncultured.

The attitude of the *Oxford Dictionary*, the great British authority, upon this point is very interesting. Most Americans think that all British people say "lahst," "ahsk," "pahst," and so on, using the broad *a*. This is indeed cultivated Southern British usage, but in the north of England it is usual to hear the same short-*a* sound that is used by the majority of Americans. The *Oxford* recognizes this difference by adopting a special symbol for the *a* in its pronunciation of words of this group, to indicate either the short or the broad *a*. It does not recognize the intermediate *a* at all.

There is no reason, then, why one who does not naturally use the broad or the intermediate *a* in these words should adopt either of them. Indeed such a one who does so is likely to make himself extremely ridiculous. In the first place, unless he has the gift of the actor, he can never make his utterance of the acquired sounds seem natural. And then he is almost sure to use them in the wrong words or to fail to use them in the right ones. There is a story current of a lady who was desperately trying to acquire the broad *a*, who concluded the narration of a comic incident with these words: "And, my dear, do you know it all seemed so very funny that I just sot thar and lahffed."

This story may be apocryphal, but I know a very fine and deservedly popular speaker on the radio who says "ahsk," "lahst," "everlahsting" and "ahfternoon," but at the same time pronounces "answer," "clasp," "pass," "vast," "master," and "fast," with as short an *a* as do the great majority of his fellow Americans. And I heard one good Middle Western lady say she was "glahd" to see me, and another speak of "thaht mahn" for "that man." Such affectations are equally repulsive to those who use the broad *a* and those who do not.

What shall we call our aunts?

The word "aunt" has been the source of a great deal of trouble and much misunderstanding. The new *Webster* classes it with the group of which we have been speaking, indicating thereby that it may properly have any one of the three sounds. Yet there are those who contend that it should always be called "ahnt" to distinguish it from "ant," the insect. The idea seems to be that when some one says, "An ant bit me on the leg a while ago," for instance, his hearers may not know whether he means an insect or his father's sister, for of course aunts do sometimes get angry enough with their nephews to bite them. It would, indeed, be sad to leave the matter doubtful like this. Yet what are we to do? There are millions and millions of Americans who would rather die than call their aunts their "ahnts." Yes, believe it or not, New Englanders and Virginians, the pronunciation "ahnt" for the word "aunt" is just as repulsive to them as "ant" is to you. In this impasse, all I can suggest is a compromise. Let the pronunciation "ahnt" be used by two classes of people: (1) those who use it naturally and have done so from their youth; (2) those who have difficulty in distinguishing their female relatives from insects. The rest of us would do well to continue to say "ant" for both words. And for the benefit of those timid souls who feel the need of dictionary support for their pronunciations, let me add that such a course is authorized not only by the new *Webster*, but also by the *Standard*.

The words that end in "-ary"

The editors of the new *Webster* have done one thing for which everyone who believes that Americans should talk like Americans ought to be profoundly grateful. I refer to its marking of the pronunciation of the "-ary" words, such as "dictionary," "military," "library," "missionary," and so on. The natural American pronunciation for these words and the one still used by the vast majority is that in which a secondary emphasis is put on the next to the last syllable, just as if they were spelled "dictionerry," "militerry," "librerry," and so on. In England all the accent is put on the first syllable and the rest of the word is required to look out for itself. The result is that the next to the last syllable is usually lost in the confusion and the words sound as if they were spelled "diction'ry," "milit'ry," "libr'ry," and so on. Most amazingly, about twenty years ago many high-school and grammar-school teachers conceived the remarkable notion that the British mode of utterance is correct and the American consequently wrong. Just when or by whom or why this notion was first conceived nobody seems to know, but it swept over the country like a prairie fire. East, west, north, and south, teachers began the weird task of forcing American boys and girls to talk like their English cousins, at least in this respect. There were—and doubtless still are—schools in which pupils were not allowed to consult the dictionary unless they called it a "diction'ry," or to go to the library unless they made it a "libr'ry." Strangly enough, with many teachers these two words, "dictionary," and "library," have been the only ones involved, and they have gone on their blithely incongruous way, pronouncing them in the British style and insisting that their pupils do likewise, while at the same time they continue to utter all the other "-ary" words—*necessary, temporary, secretary, literary, missionary, January, February*, and many others—in good American fashion.

However the fad started, there is no doubt that it was greatly helped by the fact that no American dictionary marked the secondary accent in these words, though it was evident to those who knew how to interpret their markings that they were intended to indicate the regular, almost universal American pronunciation. They might easily have made it clearer, and should have done so, but as things were, when the advocates of "diction'ry" were challenged and the dictionary itself was consulted, they were able to exclaim in triumph, "See there, there is no secondary accent!" and the weight of authority seemed to be against America. But when the new *Webster*, the second edition, appeared in 1934, behold, it had the American pronunciation in first place, with the secondary accent plainly marked, as it should be. It gives also very properly the British utterance, but marks it, likewise very properly, as being "especially British." So hereafter there is surely no excuse for an American teacher's forcing a British pronunciation on an American child.

Rather curiously, however, there are some Americans who apparently actually prefer the British pronunciation wherever there is a difference. Many of these belong to a highly cultured group of people living on our Eastern seaboard, but they have their imitators in all parts of the country. It is the tradition of the stage to speak with a British accent, and we very frequently encounter the odd situation of American actors performing for American audiences, but talking like Englishmen.

Now, I do not question for a moment the right of any American to talk like an Englishman if he wishes. Indeed my theory is that each of us has the privilege of selecting his pronunciations just as he selects his clothes. But most people, surely, would like to speak in a way that will be pleasing to those with whom they most frequently come in contact, and to the large majority of Americans the British accent sounds unutterably affected when they hear it from the lips of a fellow countryman. In an Englishman it merely seems quaint, or even attractive, but in an American—oh well, you that have heard it know the feeling it inspires. I do not know how to put it into words.

Is British English the standard?

But there are many Britishers and doubtless some Americans who argue with seeming logic that if what we speak is the English language, the correct way of speaking it must be the way in which it is spoken in England by the English. American English, they hold, is only a base corruption of the pure and genuine language which is to be found only in the mother country. Let us examine that contention for a few moments and see whether it is as reasonable as it sounds.

In the first place, the present generation of Englishmen has had no more to do with the making of the language than the present generation of Americans. Nor can it make the claim of having preserved it in its pristine purity, for the truth is that in very many instances American speech is nearer to that of our common ancestors of the seventeenth century than the British is. One of the instances is the pronunciation of the "-ary," words about which we have just been speaking. How Shakespeare pronounced them will be evident from this line from *Hamlet:*

Nor customary suits of solemn black.

It is impossible to read the line and make poetry of it without putting a secondary emphasis on the next to the last syllable of the word "customary," just as is done in the usual American pronunciation.

It would be natural to think that the great influx of non-English-speaking people into the United States has had some effect on American English. But the truth is that it has not, or at most that the effect is negligible. What has happened is that these alien people have learned English and that their children and grandchildren speak it as idiomatically as Americans of English descent, and without a trace of foreign accent, except in the few spots in our large cities or elsewhere where foreigners have clustered and preserved their native tongue and customs.

The fact is simply that American English has developed in one way and British English in another, and that neither can rightly lay claim to being the original tongue or to being intrinsically superior to the other. But the American version has at least one advantage; namely, that it is the speech of about two thirds of the English speaking world. It is a startling fact that there are about twice as many speakers of English in the United States as in Great Britain and all the vast British Empire together. Furthermore, American English is far more uniform than that of England. It is a source of amazement to Englishmen who visit this country that they can travel from Maine to California, from Florida to Oregon, and find no real difficulty in making themselves understood or in understanding when dealing with the masses of the people. On the other hand, in England the differences of dialect are sometimes so great as to make the speech of the common people of one section almost unintelligible to those of another.

The situation in America is unique. There has never been another instance in the history of the world when so many millions of people scattered over so wide an area spoke the same language in substantially the same way. Such a fact cannot be ignored. Whether our British cousins like it or not, whether we Americans understand and appreciate our great privilege and responsibility or not, it must be evident to thoughtful observers that in our hands rests very largely the future of our mother tongue.

STILL MORE
FALSE TEACHINGS
AND SOME HISTORY

III

NEXT to the groundless notion that it is incorrect to end an English sentence with a preposition, perhaps the most wide-spread of the many false beliefs about the use of our language is the equally groundless notion that it is incorrect to begin one with "but" or "and." As in the case of the superstition about the prepositional ending, no textbook supports it, but apparently about half of our teachers of English go out of their way to handicap their pupils by inculcating it. One cannot help wondering whether those who teach such a monstrous doctrine ever read any English themselves. They need only pick up a newspaper, a magazine, or a book at random to find numerous sentences beginning with one of the two words.

But it is not simply ordinary, everyday, contemporary writers who begin their sentences with "but" and "and." The very best do it. What writer of English prose, for instance, is superior to Macaulay in brilliancy and clearness of style? Yet Macaulay uses "but" at the beginning of his sentences so frequently that it almost becomes a mannerism. And Edgar Allan Poe, celebrated among American writers for his artistry in words, begins eleven sentences with "but"

and thirteen with "and" in the twelve pages of his masterpiece *The Masque of the Red Death*. Yet a pupil of mine,
who was struggling to be a writer, told me that she had been
taught not to begin a sentence with "but" if it could be
avoided, and hundreds of others have quoted their teachers
as ruling it an absolute error to begin with either of the two
words. Can it be that the English-speaking people, including their greatest writers, do not know how to speak or
write English?

Now, it is quite true that young children in the lower
grades of school will frequently turn what should be a compound sentence into two simple ones, writing for instance:
"The wind blew hard. And the leaves fell," when it ought
to be, "The wind blew hard, and the leaves fell." It is
doubtless to correct such errors as this that teachers tell
them never to use "and" or "but" at the beginning of a sentence, but such instruction simply displaces one error by another equally bad or worse. Whether or not a sentence
should begin with one of these words is a matter of judgment, to be decided by the intelligence and taste of the
writer or speaker, as is true of so many other points in the
use of English.

Readers who are interested in technical grammar—and
I wish I could count on many of that sort—may very properly ask what part of speech "and" or "but" is when it
begins the sentence. The answer is that it is an adverb
grammatically considered, though still a conjunction rhetorically. The new *Webster* lists "but" as an adverb in this
use, and the logic of the situation seems to me inescapable.
The words cannot be conjunctions—grammatically, that is
—because they do not grammatically connect. They do
rhetorically, for they carry the mind back to the preceding
sentence, but that is a different matter. In general, our dictionaries and grammars have never distinguished clearly
enough between the grammatical construction of a word
and its rhetorical use.

What is a superstition?

The term "superstition" appears well fitted to describe false ideas about the use of English such as the notion that it is incorrect to end a sentence with a preposition or to begin it with "and" or "but." If it seems too harsh to some, may I ask what other word is appropriate to describe a false belief tenaciously held with almost religious fervor by millions of otherwise intelligent persons in the face of ample and frequently easily available evidence of its falsity? Education is generally considered the foe of superstition. But in the field of English it seems to intensify and even to originate superstitions. The situation is well-nigh incredible. If a teacher of science should tell his classes that it is bad luck to see the new moon over one's left shoulder, most of them would laugh at it, and if they took it seriously and reported it at their homes, quite a stir would be raised in the community. Yet every school day of the world thousands of English teachers all over the country are teaching their pupils things equally absurd and nobody seems to realize it, much less get excited over it. The teachers, of course, are not wholly to blame. They are merely handing down what was taught to them or what they find in their textbooks, but they would do well to be a little skeptical of what they hear and read.

As matters stand, the only thing necessary to put some wholly correct and long-established expression under the ban as being "bad English" is for somebody to condemn it with an air of authority. When this happens, teachers and all seem to swallow whatever is put forth without stopping to consider whether the one who is doing the condemning knows what he is talking about, or to see what the real authorities have to say on the subject.

In his very interesting book *What Is English?* Mr. C. H. Ward tells of a school superintendent at a gathering of English teachers who talked for twice his allotted time on the terrible misuse of English that was devastating his section of the country. The only examples he gave of this dreadful speech, however, were the phrases "as though" and "all that sort of thing." Now, "as though" is in quite good use with the sense of "as if," as any dictionary will testify, and there is nothing gramatically wrong with the expression "all that sort of thing," though it may be and sometimes is much overworked. Yet as Mr. Ward left the meeting, he asked a friend, "What per cent of the teachers who heard that talk do you suppose accepted it as the gospel and made a mental resolve never to use the condemned expressions again?" "Oh, about eighty per cent," replied the friend.

"Somebody's else" or "somebody else's"?

How many people there are who painfully force themselves to say "somebody's else," "anyone's else," "nobody's else," and so on, because they have been led astray by *somebody else's* false advice! To be sure, the word "else" in this use is an adverb, but expressions like "somebody else" form phrases which are naturally treated as one word, and it is the custom in English to put the possessive sign on the last word of such a group. This is done in order to get it as near the thing possessed as possible. For instance, we speak of "my brother-in-law's house," though when we add the *s* that forms the plural, we attach it to the word "brother." "I have two brothers-in-law," is the correct way to put it.

Or take a phrase like "the King of England." "Did you hear the King of England's abdication speech?" is the way we say it. Now, of course, it was the King's speech, not England's, and yet in the phrase "the King of England's speech," the possessive sign goes on the word "England." If this is not enough to prove that "somebody else's" is the natural, normal, and correct expression, let me add that all the authorities that I am familiar with support it. But that, I suppose, will not prevent some overcareful people from continuing to use the unnatural, abnormal, and incorrect "somebody's else."

Can "that" refer to persons?

A young man, who happened to be a college graduate, said to me once, "I was very much surprised to hear President Roosevelt use some rather bad English the other night."

"That must have been surprising," was my answer, "for the President's English, though perhaps not perfect, is usually excellent. What was his mistake?"

"Why," he replied, "he used the pronoun 'that' to refer to a person—something like, 'These are the men that we can trust.'"

"Well," said I, "what is wrong with that?"

"Oh," he exclaimed, "I was always taught that one of the worst mistakes one can make in English is to use 'that' to refer to a person, rather than 'who' or 'whom.'"

The truth is, of course, that the relative pronoun "that" may correctly be used for either persons or things. "Who" refers exclusively to persons, the only exception being those animals who seem to have almost human intelligence. "Which" is used for animals or things, but "that" may apply to persons, animals, or things. We may say, "Bring me the book which you see on the table" or ". . . that you see on the table." "There goes the man who was here yesterday" or " . . . that was here yesterday." Any dictionary will support this, yet thousands, perhaps millions, of people all over the country believe, like the young critic of the President's English, that it is gross error to use "that" in reference to a human being. When you ask them why they think so, they can only answer, "My teacher taught it to me." But who taught the teacher such a falsity? Another teacher, no doubt, but where and why did it all start?

There was a time in English when "which" was also used to refer to persons, and indeed that time is not very remote. It is so used constantly in the King James Version of the Bible, issued in 1611. In repeating the Lord's Prayer we generally say now, "Our Father who art in Heaven," but the King James Version has it, "Our Father *which* art in Heaven." Incidentally, it ought to be remarked that the version we are speaking of really is the *King* James, not the *Saint* James Version, as many people mistakenly term it. James, who authorized its translation, was king of England, not a saint.

The King James Version, nevertheless, in spite of the fact that much of its language is now out of date, has had a great deal to do with making English what it is today. No other book printed in our language has been so widely circulated and read, and numbers of its expressions have passed into popular speech. We say today that a man is talented, meaning that he possesses unusual gifts in some field like music, painting, poetry, wit. Indeed we have extended the application beyond the field of the arts and may say, for instance, that he has a talent for salesmanship. But a talent was originally simply a certain weight, and our present-day use of the word comes from the parable of the talents told by Jesus and recorded in the New Testament, Matthew 25: 14-30.

The word "talent" is of course originally from the Greek, that being the language in which the New Testament has come down to us, and the one in which it was probably originally written. Many English words come from the Greek, but a great many more are from the Latin. Nevertheless, the view popularly held that Latin forms the basis of English, or that English is a direct descendant from it, is quite mistaken. Latin is the direct ancestor of French, Spanish, Italian, Portuguese, and Roumanian. Indeed these five languages are called, in recognition of that fact, the Romance languages, that is to say, the languages derived from the Roman, since it was, of course, the Romans who spoke Latin. But the case is different with English.

The origins of English

English is a Teutonic, or Germanic, language. It originated, believe it or not, in Germany, though perhaps it would be more accurate to say that we find it spoken in Germany at the dawn of history. Other Teutonic languages are German, Dutch, and the four Scandinavian tongues—Norwegian, Swedish, Danish, and Icelandic. All these and English are believed by the scholars to have descended from one language, usually known simply as Teutonic.

But we can go further back than this, at least in theory. If we examine the various languages now spoken in Europe, we find that they are more or less alike in vocabulary and grammar—all, that is, with the exception of three: Finnish, Hungarian, and Basque. Furthermore, Persian and Sanskrit, the language of ancient India, likewise resemble this European group. Now, to the one who has not made a special study of linguistics, these resemblances may seem to have no special significance. Indeed, many people who have studied only one or two foreign languages, such as French, Latin, Spanish, and German, finding them to be somewhat similar to English and to each other, have very naturally jumped to the conclusion that all languages are alike. This, however, is not true, as will at once be evident to one who undertakes to master a language like Chinese or one of the tongues of the American Indians or Hebrew, any one of which he will find to be made in an entirely different fashion from our own or any other European language. To the scholar, when language A resembles language B, one of three things is always indicated: (1) language A came from language B; (2) Language B came from language A; (3) language A and language B both came from another, which we shall call language C.

When we find a whole group of languages resembling one another, the natural inference is that they have come from a common ancestor. Consequently the scholars feel certain that the European languages, with the three exceptions of Finnish, Hungarian, and Basque, are descended from a language to which they have given the name of Indo-European (sometimes called also Indo-Germanic), and, of course, that Persian and Sanskrit likewise come from this source. They have found no relics of this original Indo-European language, but believe that of its descendants Sanskrit most nearly resembles it.

According to the theory, the ancestors of the people who now speak the Indo-European languages once lived together in some spot of Europe or Asia, speaking what we now call Indo-European, though what they called it we naturally do not know. In the course of time, however, they separated, one group after another going off to settle in various parts of Europe and Asia, losing contact with the original body and the other groups, and therefore changing considerably the forms of their words and to some extent the ways of putting them together; likewise, of course, picking up new words from other peoples with whom they came in contact. We have therefore today eight branches of this Indo-European family: the Teutonic, to which our own language belongs, as I have already stated; the Italic, which includes Latin and its descendants, the five Romance languages; the Greek; the Slavic, including Russian, Polish, and so on; the Celtic, the language of the early Britons and the ancient Gauls, from which come the highland Scotch, the Welsh, the language of Brittany in France, and modern Irish, now the official language of the Irish Free State, which has become Eire; Indo-Iranian, including Persian and Sanskrit; Albanian; and finally, Armenian.

An example of the kinship of some of these tongues may be seen by comparing their various words for "father." In German it is *Vater*, in Latin, *pater* (from which comes the French *père*, the Spanish *padre* and the Italian *padre*), in Greek, *pater*, in Old Irish, *athir*, in Persian, *pidar*, and in Sanskrit, *pitar*.

English, then, is a member of the Teutonic branch of the great Indo-European family of languages. The people whom we first find speaking it in Germany are generally known as the Anglo-Saxons and their language is by some scholars called Anglo-Saxon, by others simply Old English. But the English language was not spoken in England till after the year 449, when the Anglo-Saxon invasion of that island began. Let me repeat that *the Britons, the early inhabitants of England, did not speak English*, but spoke a variety of Celtic, another branch of the Indo-European family, not

similar enough to Anglo-Saxon, however, to be understood
by the invaders. History says that the Anglo-Saxons drove
the Celtic Britons into Scotland, Ireland, and Wales. This
is probably not entirely true, but it is an amazing fact that
the Celtic language of the Britons had scarcely any perceptible effect upon the English of the Anglo-Saxons.

French and Latin in English

But a great change was in store for English. In 1066
William the Conqueror came over from Normandy in
France, made good his claim to the throne of England by
force of arms, and settled down as ruler along with thousands of his French-speaking followers. For a long time
then the two languages were spoken side by side in the little
island, French in general being the official language spoken
by the ruling class, English the language of the common
people. But little by little English prevailed, as it always
has. Yet in so doing it picked up a large number of
French words and managed to absorb much of the clearness
and grace that are characteristic of French.

French itself, as we have said, is simply a corruption of
Latin, and hence this bit of history explains how a great
many Latin words eventually got into English. But it does
not account for all. For hundreds of years Latin was the
language of scholarship all over Europe, and of course in
England as well. It naturally happened, then, not infre-
quently that when a learned Englishman was writing in his
native tongue and found himself at a loss for a word to
express a certain idea, he would borrow one from the Latin.
The result is that in many instances we cannot be sure
whether a Latin word came to us directly from Latin itself
or indirectly from the French. Sometimes we got it in both
ways. "Fragile," for instance, is from the Latin *fragilis*,
"frail" from the French corruption of *fragilis*, and, we may
add, "breakable" is the original Anglo-Saxon for essentially
the same idea.

The question may well be raised why, if more than half

of English words come directly or indirectly from Latin, it is not considered a Romance language rather than a Teutonic one. The answer is two-fold: first, a language is primarily a way of putting words together rather than a collection of words, and in this respect—that is, in its grammar —English is Teutonic, Germanic, not Latin; second, though there are more Latin words than Anglo-Saxon in the dictionary, it is the Anglo-Saxon that are the most used. For instance, in the two preceding sentences of this paragraph I have used a total of seventy-nine words, of which only twelve, or slightly more than one seventh are from the Latin. These are: *question, directly, indirectly, considered, language* (twice), *primarily, collection, respect, grammar, dictionary,* and *used.* Notice, incidentally, that most of them are rather long in comparison with the Anglo-Saxon words such as *in, is, a, and, than,* and so forth, and that the Latin words are of the sort usually found in books, or in the speech of educated adults, rather than in ordinary conversation or the speech of children.

There is one point which should be made clear just here concerning the method by which Latin words came into our language. The Romans controlled England and maintained garrisons there for a period of about four hundred and sixty-five years, that is, from 55 B.C. to 410 A.D. It would be very natural to think that during this long occupation many Latin words crept into English. But the fact is that scarcely a one entered at that time. Those who have read this chapter carefully will, I believe, be able to say why. The simple reason is that when the Romans were in England, the English language was in Germany, and that consequently there was very little contact at that time between Latin and English.

But the story of English would not be even roughly complete without mentioning that we have borrowed words from a great many other languages, chief of which is Greek. Scientific and medical terms, such as *thermometer, pneumonia, biology, zoology, telescope, phonograph,* and *megaphone* are among our numerous and important borrowings from that language. "Automobile" is a mixture of Greek and Latin, while "speedometer" is a blending of Anglo-Saxon and Greek, and though objection has been offered to each of these words because of its hybrid nature, they are apparently here to stay.

English has a way of grasping eagerly at words that meet its needs from any language under heaven with which it comes in contact. But I trust this rough and hasty summary of two thousand years of its history has made it clear that broadly speaking, it is a fusion of elements characteristic of two leading languages of the modern world and the two leading ancient languages. The strength and directness of the German, the clarity and grace of the French, the sonorous beauty of the classic Greek and Latin are all welded into one harmonious instrument in our mother tongue.

SOME
INTERESTING
SPECIMENS

IV

To ONE who is interested in points of English the newspapers and the radio offer more than an ordinary amount of entertainment. The news dispatches from Washington, for instance, told us not long ago that President Roosevelt had vetoed a bill to change the name of the Chemical Service of our army to the Chemical Corps. The reason given was that the service deals mostly with the production of poison gas, which the president hopes before long to see outlawed from use in war, and since a corps is a large and permanent division of an army, such as the Marine Corps, for example, he did not feel that the name would be appropriate.

I take it that most of my readers are aware that this word "corps" is pronounced as if it were spelled "core" and comes to us from French, which in turn took it from the Latin word *corpus*, meaning "body," the same word from which the English "corpse" ultimately comes. Indeed, "corpse" is nothing but "corps" with an added *e*, and the *p* and the *s* pronounced. Oddly enough, the *s* on the end of "corps" is sometimes pronounced—that is to say, when the word is plural. We may speak of one army corps or of two army corps, but though the singular and the plural are

30

spelled exactly alike, the one is pronounced "core," the other "cores."

Corpus delicti

There is an interesting use in English of that Latin word *corpus*. You may be familiar with the fact that before an accused man can be found guilty of murder, it is necessary to establish what our lawyer friends call the *corpus delicti*. These two Latin words mean literally "the body of the crime," which most people think is the same as "the body of the murdered person." Actually, however, the phrase means simply definite proof that a murder has been committed. The finding of the dead body would of course be quite a step in the establishment of the *corpus delicti*, but it would be necessary also to prove that the dead person had met death through a criminal agency.

"Tread" and "trod"

But let us leave this rather gruesome subject and consider for a while the newspaper account of how a nineteen-year-old girl in New York swam four miles to shore in order to get help for her three companions after their boat had capsized. Even in the story of such a thrilling incident we may find a secondary interest in a discussion of some points of English. Here is a sentence from a newspaper dispatch:

> An expert swimmer, she tread water until a wave tossed her high enough so that she could see the lights of Rockaway Beach.

How many readers can see two errors in the sentence? It should read:

> An expert swimmer, she *trod* water until a wave tossed her high enough *to see* the lights of Rockaway beach.

"Trod" is the past tense of "tread," and "enough" should be followed by the simple infinitive "to see" rather than by "so that she could see." Notice that the original form is long and awkward, the amended one briefer and more graceful.

It is surprising how many people do not know that "trod" is the past of "tread" and still more surprising that in certain sections of the United States "trod" is used as the present or with "will" to form the future. A woman who was playing the part of a retired actress in a radio play not long ago exclaimed, "Never again will I trod the dear old boards." It should of course have been, "Never again will I tread . . ."

The mention of treading water brings to mind another verb whose past tense is a matter of some confusion—the verb "dive." The prevailing usage in the South is to say, "I dived." In the North, however, a great many people will say, "I dove," and this form even sometimes creeps into newspapers and magazines. Rather strangely, the dictionaries support the South on this point, all stating that "dived" is the proper or at least the preferable form. Some of them record "dove," but call it "colloquial," a term which means that the word so marked is suitable for ordinary conversation, but should not appear in dignified or formal speech or writing. Those who say "dove" probably are influenced, though perhaps unconsciously, by the verb "drive," whose past is, of course, "drove."

"Themselves" or "himself"?

Here is a slip taken from a very prominent weekly news-magazine:

> Many a politician in Washington, including some of Franklin Roosevelt's loyal friends, privately expressed themselves as more than content at his defeat.

Now, while "many a politician" is exactly equivalent in thought to "many politicians," it is singular, not plural, and consequently the wording should be "privately expressed *himself*." What misled the writer was, no doubt, the word "friends," though that really has nothing to do with the matter. In striking contrast with this rather slipshod wording, let me present a passage from a recent radio play. The hero was a man of sober middle age and the heroine likewise past her early youth. In attempting to persuade her to agree to their marriage, he spoke as follows:

> We wouldn't be getting married because each of us thought *he* was getting a package of pink popcorn with a prize in it.

Notice that "he" is used here correctly, as I have previously stated, to mean "he or she." The careless writer would have made it "because each of us thought *they* were getting," and the one a shade less careless would have said, "because each of us thought *we* were getting," and the over-careful one, "because each of us thought he or she was getting," which would indeed have been correct, but is needlessly awkward. And I am willing to leave to my readers the question whether the sentence does not sound better as it was spoken than in any of the three ways in which it might have been.

Some dreadful examples

And here is a dreadful example of English taken from a newspaper advertisement:

> John Jones announces that due to increased business it has made it necessary for him to double his present place.

I like to speculate as to the mental processes through which a man goes before writing such a sentence. Here is probably what happened. The author of the dreadful specimen had two sentences in mind. One was, "John Jones announces that increased business has made it necessary for him to double his present place," the other, "John Jones announces that due to ('because of' would have been better than 'due to,' but let that pass for the present) increased business it has become necessary for him to double his present place." He attempts to write both at once, and, as always, the attempt ends in disaster for him and the English language.

Fortunately, such sentences as the one above are rare even in hastily worded newspaper advertisements. But here is one taken from an article on aerial warfare in a very popular magazine, which sounds almost as bad when we consider its source. Referring to the United States, the author says:

> Our natural security is *relatively less absolute*
> than it was in the earlier days of aerial navigation.

Now, "absolute" means "not relative, not dependent on anything else, entire, complete." Strictly speaking, if a thing is absolute, it cannot be any more or less absolute. But I have never been one to insist on mathematical accuracy in the use of words, and should not be inclined to consider the expression "less absolute" a serious fault if this were all. It might be interpreted as meaning "not so nearly absolute," just as we sometimes speak of a thing as being "more perfect" or "less perfect," though strictly speaking, perfection is perfection, and there is no more or less about it. But why does the author say *"relatively* less absolute"? What added meaning does "relatively" give? Judging from its use several times in the remainder of the article, it is merely a cautious word that the author inserts every now and then, to keep his statement from sounding too sweeping. What he apparently means is simply that our safety from aerial attacks is not absolute, as it once seemed to be, and it would be better if he had been content to say it.

Many years ago a weekly magazine commented unfavorably on a passage in the speech of a supposed expert at a conference on South American trade, which ran something like this:

> It is evident that if broad economic bases exist
> for our trade with South America, we are in for a

period of prosperity in that trade. But if such broad bases do not exist, we shall meet with disaster, unless we have seen our danger and avoided going too far.

All of this is about like saying, "If we go up the hill, we shall reach the top and stay there, unless we come down."

"New beginner"

Though, as I have indicated, mathematical accuracy of speech is not necessary, there are certain common expressions wherein the idea is repeated, which careless speakers seem to delight in and careful ones avoid. Such an expression is "new beginner." It would be possible, I think, actually to have new beginners. A golf professional, for instance, who was giving lessons might have some beginners one week and the next week some others, whom he might correctly term "new beginners" by way of contrast with his first group. But that is not what most people mean when they use the expression, for they apply it to all beginners, and in so doing are using the word "new" in an entirely needless way.

Another expression of the sort is "a dull thud." All thuds are dull, for "thud" means "a dull noise." Still another is "the true facts." All facts are true, but we are so accustomed to hear things asserted as facts which are not facts that it is difficult to keep from distinguishing facts from assertions by referring to them as "the true facts." But I think the most remarkable example of this useless repetition ("tautology" is the technical name for it) that ever came under my notice appeared in an account written by a popular motion-picture actress of her first appearance on the stage. In describing the feeling of fright that possessed her on that occasion she wrote: "The floor seemed to be undulating in rising and falling waves." This is expressing the same idea in three ways. "Undulating" means moving in waves, and waves, of course, rise and fall, so that "undulating" alone would have been sufficient. As a rule, whatever does not add to the meaning detracts from it and had better be omitted.

Yet this is not always true, and it is easy to go too far with this sort of criticism. Sometimes we are justified in adding an unnecessary word for the sake of emphasis or smoothness of sound, or simply in accordance with long-established custom. We all speak of "falling down" when, of course, it would be rather difficult to fall in any direction except down. It is true that some people who live on one of the upper floors of an apartment house do say, "Drop up and see me," but I fear it would be difficult to take the invitation literally. Nevertheless it is very common among cultured and educated English-speaking people to speak of "falling down," and it is rather absurd to see the expression adversely criticized in a little book on the use of English issued by a prominent publishing house and edited by a man who ought to know better. Another similar expression is "lift up," in which the "up" is not really necessary, but is permitted by ancient custom. Readers will recall the passage from one of the Psalms, "I will lift up mine eyes to the hills."

It might be well to add here that the phrase "consensus of opinion" is *not* tautological; at least, that is the consensus of opinion of the four leading English dictionaries. "Consensus" in this use means something like "general agreement," and as one of the dictionaries points out, there might be a consensus of taste, or of judgment, as well as of opinion.

"Ought"

On the radio not long ago the master of ceremonies of a very popular program, in presenting an actor who had performed in a number of Western pictures, asked him facetiously, "Hadn't there ought to be a horse here?" This master of ceremonies is a college graduate, and yet he had apparently never learned that "had" is not to be used with "ought." The correct way to put the question is, "Oughtn't (or more formally, ought not) there to be a horse here?" The master of ceremonies has been highly honored by his university for the fame he has brought it, but I wonder what his professor of English, if he happened to be listening to the broadcast, thought of the unfavorable advertising the university was receiving through the bad English of its celebrated alumnus. And yet we all know that this particular university was not any more at fault in its teaching—or lack of it—than all the rest of them are.

A very weird idea prevails among many people concerning this word "ought." They seem to think that it is in some way not the equal of "should." On a number of occasions I have made the experiment of writing on the blackboard the sentence, "Everybody ought to do their duty," and asking my classes to rewrite it so as to correct any mistakes in English, but not to make any needless changes. Of course the mistake is in the use of the word "their." It should read, "Everybody ought to do *his* duty," because, as was mentioned in a previous chapter, "everybody" is singular. But invariably a number of pupils ignore this glaring error entirely and make the sentence read, "Everyone should do their duty." Evidently a good many teachers in various parts of the country are putting forth the monstrous doctrines that "ought" is inferior to "should" and "everybody" not as elegant as "everyone."

"Ought" and "should" are both ancient and excellent English words, and both may be used to express obligation. The difference is that the obligation expressed by "should" is limited to that imposed by conventionality or mere propriety, while "ought" may be used both in this weaker sense and in the stronger one of deep moral obligation. In the sentence given, "should" would be far too weak. It would be appropriate to say, "You should be more polite," "You should write a better hand," or "One should cultivate a good speaking voice," but highly inappropriate to say, "You should not steal." "Ought" must be used in a case of this kind, and might be used in the other sentences also, for it is not possible to draw the line always sharply between propriety and moral obligation. People in whom conscience is strong will naturally feel that they "ought" to do whatever they "should" do.

I was once for two hours in the company of a good woman whose early education had been neglected; or who, at least, had not obtained much benefit from it as far as the use of English was concerned. She was a great talker, as women are now and then, and the words came out in a pretty steady stream of bad English. She uttered scarcely a correct sentence during the entire time and made, it seemed, almost every mistake possible—horrible things like "I ain't had no time," "We wuz a-goin'," "I never done it," and so on. She gave only one indication that she was conscious that there is a difference between good English and bad, and that was when she said once, "I ought" and instantly corrected herself and said, "I mean I should." Oddly enough, I once heard a college graduate with a Ph.D. degree, who was a member of *Phi Beta Kappa*, correct himself in the same way. Yet he calmly said "drug" for "dragged," with no apparent consciousness of error. I shall never cease to wonder at the difficulty with which people learn the real rules of English contrasted with the ease—nay, the eagerness —with which they pick up the false ones.

I trust my readers will not think that in presenting these various examples of incorrect English I am attempting to do what a girl asked of Dorothy Dix, according to an article which appeared recently in the *Saturday Evening Post*. "Dear Dorothy," she wrote, "I am a young girl of sixteen, and do not know what is wrong to do. Please tell me everything that is wrong and bad, so I won't do it." I presume Dorothy found the task somewhat difficult, and I think it would be equally difficult to comply with such a request in the field of English. It is a sound principle both in speech and morals that it is better in general to devote one's attention to the attainment of the good than to a study of how to avoid the bad. But the bad has a way of mixing with the good, even of pretending to be the good, and there are times when it needs to be exposed and unmasked. We seem now to be standing at such a time in the history of our mother tongue. It is conquering the world, but millions who have spoken it from childhood are ignorant of its rules, careless of its beauties, and unaware of its possibilities. To rouse them from their lethargy, to open their eyes to the marvels of the heritage they despise, is surely a task worthy of the unremitting effort of all of us who love the English language.

THE VEXING
MATTER OF
PRONUNCIATION

V

Most readers have doubtless noticed, and many have perhaps wondered over the current fad among radio announcers for pronouncing words like "suit," "assume," and "absolutely," with a *y*-sound, which might be represented by spelling them "syuit," "ass-yume," and "absol-yutely." If an announcer were queried as to his reason for adopting this mode of utterance, which seems so peculiar to the large majority of his listeners, he would probably indignantly deny the charge of affectation and contend that he was only following the dictionary and cultured usage.

The sound of "long u"

Neither of these contentions, however, is exactly true. To be sure, the dictionaries do mark the *u* long in these words and most others of the same sort, and the sound of long *u* in English is supposed to be exactly like the name of the letter itself; the spelling "yoo" would correctly represent it as it is heard in words like *use, union, pure, few, view, volume,* and *salutation.* But the most interesting and important information that our dictionaries have to give us about the pronunciation of certain words is often to be found, not under the word itself in its alphabetical place, but in the section of the introduction where the pronunciation of words of that sort is discussed in detail. For instance, if the reader will turn to the discussion of the pronunciation of long *u* in the introduction to the new *Webster*, he will find that cultivated speakers in both England and America often omit the *y*-sound of long *u* after *s* and *l;* that is to say, they pronounce the words we have been discussing as if they were spelled "soot," "assoom," and "absolootly." "Often" is the term the dictionary uses. My own observation is that the very large majority of cultured people in America do not use the *y*-sound of long *u* when it comes after *s* or *l*, except in words like "volume" and "salutation" where the *l* is pronounced with the preceding syllable and therefore does not affect the *u*.

I do not think there is any doubt in the world, though I am perfectly willing for the reader to be his own judge on this point, that to most Americans such pronunciations as "syuit," "ass-yume," and "absol-yutely" sound unutterably affected. They may not always *be* affected, of course, but they might as well be if they seem so to the listener. Take a sentence like this, "The deluded lunatic committed suicide," and read it if you can without laughing, "The delyuded lyunatic committed syuicide."

But there is another group of words containing the sound marked in the dictionaries as a long *u* about which American usage is more evenly divided. These are those in which the sound comes after *d, t,* or *n,* such as *due, duty, tube, Tuesday, news,* and so on. Although teachers of English and of speech nearly always recommend that the "yoo"-sound be used in these strictly, it is very common in all parts of the country except the South to hear them pronounced *doo, dooty, toob, Toosday,* and *noos,* and those who use these pronunciations may be found among the cultured and educated as well as among the uncultured and ignorant. But practically all Southerners of whatever rank or station use the full *yoo*-sound in them—*dyue, dyuty, tyube, Tyuesday, nyews*—and, it may be added, they do so naturally, without training or effort. As long ago as 1795 this fact was noted and commented upon by a Northern writer who was traveling in the South.

More Pronunciation Problems

There is no type of question that comes to a radio lecturer on English more frequently than "What is the correct pronunciation of so-and-so?" And it is a great surprise to many people to find that this is a question which very often has no definite answer. What, for instance, is the correct pronunciation of "advertisement," to take one about which I am often asked. Most dictionaries give two for it: "adVERTisement" and "adverTISEment." They also put "adVERTisement" first, to indicate that it is the better of the two. My own observation is that in America "adverTISEment" is heard more often, and this fact, combined with the fact that it is the one I have been familiar with from early childhood, makes it my personal choice. But there is no doubt that both pronunciations are in good use and that neither can be called the exclusively correct method.

Shall we say "ILLustrate" or "ilLUStrate"? Here again both are given by the dictionaries, with the preference usually for "ILLustrate," though the other is the original pronunciation. But, I hear some one say, if that is the original one, is it not really the correct one and consequently the one we all ought to use? The answer is: Not necessarily. Up to a certain point this is a sound principle; beyond that point it is foolishness. There is scarcely a word in English that now retains its original pronunciation. Indeed we have no entirely certain way of determining just what that pronunciation was. But we are rather sure that if anyone should now begin to pronounce all his words as they were pronounced in the time of Chaucer, about five hundred years ago, he would hardly be understood by anyone else.

Pronunciation is not a matter of mathematics or of morals, but of style and taste. Two and two always were and always will be four. And the present writer is old-fashioned enough to believe that some things, like unselfishness, kindness, and honesty, are eternally right, while others, like cruelty and lying, are eternally wrong. But the rightness or wrongness of a pronunciation is a changeable thing. What is right today may be wrong within a few years, and *vice versa*. (By the way, that Latin phrase is pronounced with the *e* sounded—"vicey," not like the English word "vice.") For instance, not so long ago, people accented the word "balcony" on the second syllable—"balCOny." The first man who called it "BALcony" was wrong. So was the second and the third and the fourth, and the ten thousandth, but after a while the new pronunciation triumphed, and today the man who says "balCOny"—if there is any such man —sounds ridiculous.

Noun and verb accent

There is a decided tendency in English to shift the accent of a noun to the first syllable, as we have done in "balcony." Indeed we sometimes distinguish nouns from verbs by such a shift. "Why do you conDUCT yourself in such a fashion?" we say, but "You should be ashamed of such CONduct." When a new athletic RECord is made, we reCORD it in the books. When something inCREASes, we speak of the amount of its INcrease. And so it goes for many other words that are used both as nouns and verbs. But let no one imagine that this is a *rule* of English, for it is not. It is merely a tendency, and there are few errors that show ignorance more plainly than to allow the tendency to operate in words where the custom of cultured people has not sanctioned it. Andy, of Amos and Andy, for instance, is always asking for a "REport"; it should be a "rePORT." Many people speak of sending a package by EXpress; it should be sent by "exPRESS." When you exchange something, the transaction is not an "EXchange," but an "exCHANGE."

Doubtless some of my readers are bursting to ask "Why?" Why is "INcrease" right and "EXpress" wrong, when both pronunciations are brought about by the same tendency? The only possible answer is that to the majority of educated and cultured English-speaking people "INcrease" has a pleasing sound, while "EXpress" displeases them. Just why this should be I do not know, and it is quite possible that some day "EXpress" will be in their good graces. Yet it certainly is not today, in spite of the fact that some very worthy people may use it.

Accents

The two worst pronunciations of this sort are, I believe, "POlice" for "poLICE" and HOtel" for "hoTEL," though I regret to say that I have heard both used by educated people. Nevertheless, if I should hear a man say "POlice" or "HOtel," and knew nothing else about him, I should conclude that he was either uneducated or had grown up in an uneducated family. I cannot help wondering why so many people say "INsurance" for "inSURance," or "CIGarette" for "cigaRETTE," and I very strongly favor "adDRESS" over "ADdress," "roMANCE" over "ROmance," "reSOURCE" over "REsource," "reSEARCH" over "REsearch," and "magaZINE" over "MAGazine," in spite of the fact that the new *Webster* now lists the second pronunciation as a possibility for each of the last four words. Yet it puts in first place the one with the accent on the last syllable, and I believe that likewise every reader will prefer that one himself if he will only take the time and trouble to compare the two. Consider for a moment this imaginary newspaper article:

> An unusual event occurred at a local hotel yesterday when the police arrested a man who claimed to be an insurance agent from Detroit, as he sat in the lobby smoking a cigarette and reading a magazine. By diligent research and the use of all resources, however, they have established the fact that he is really the insane son of a millionaire in Tennessee.

Now, just how did you read that to yourself? Did you say:

> An unusual EEvent occurred at a local HOtel yesterday when the POlice arrested a man who claimed to me an INsurance agent from DEtroit, as he sat in the lobby smoking a CIGarette and reading a MAGazine. By diligent REsearch and the use of all REsources, however, they have established the fact that he is really the INsane son of a MILLionaire in TENNessee.

If you read it in that way, try this method:

> An unusual eVENT occurred at a local hoTEL yesterday when the poLICE arrested a man who claimed to be an inSURance agent from De-TROIT, as he sat in the lobby smoking a ciga-RETTE and reading a magaZINE. By diligent reSEARCH and the use of all reSOURCES, however, they have established the fact that he is really the inSANE son of a millioNAIRE in TennesSEE.

And now, which did you prefer? Which method leaves the impression of the greater culture? The second one, to my mind, far and away, but let every reader make his own choice.

Many of these words which should have the accent on the last syllable come to us from the French; for instance, *police, hotel, address, romance, resource, millionaire, cigarette, research*, and this fact explains the accent, for it is the French custom to place it on the end of the word—or so it seems to us. The Teutonic languages, of which English is one and German another, are inclined to place it, however, on the first syllable, and herein we have the explanation of our tendency to shift it. But while English is basically Teutonic, it has neverthless a great admixture of French, and the expert speaker of English is the one who is able to combine its German and French elements harmoniously, without overemphasizing either. Incidentally, it may be remarked that when the Germans take a word from the French, they accent it on the last syllable.

French words in English

But these French words in English, while a source of grace and elegance, cause much trouble in pronunciation, because there is no set rule to govern them. Some retain their French pronunciation entirely, others are pronounced according to English ideas, and still others acquire a sort of mixture of the English and French methods. "Machine," for instance, is pronounced practically as the French would pronounce it, but "introduction" has become perfectly Anglicized in pronunciation, as those who are familiar with the French utterance of the same word will recognize. "Garage," is best, I think, in the French manner, "gaRAZH," but sometimes, particularly in England, it is made to rhyme with "carriage." "Chauffeur" started out as "showFUR," but "SHOWfur," seems to be gaining ground. "Route" is by many people called, in the French manner, "root," and this is preferred in the dictionaries. My own observation is that the majority of the American people make it "rout," to rhyme with "out," and could not possibly call it "root" without feeling affected. "Chic" should be "sheek," but we often hear "chick."

One of the most remarkable misunderstandings in the history of languages is concerned with the name of the article of furniture known as a "chaise longue." Please note the spelling of the last word. It is not l-o-u-n-g-e, but l-o-n-g-u-e, being the French word for "long" in its feminine form. "Chaise" means "chair" in French and the whole expression is simply French for "long chair," or to be more accurate, "chair long," as the French prefer to put it, to whom, incidentally, a chair is feminine, whence the feminine adjective "longue." The true pronunciation of the phrase is, as nearly as I can represent it, "shayz long," that is to say, its true pronunciation in English, and close enough to the French method for a Frenchman to understand it. But the spelling of the word "lounge" is so near to that of this French word "longue," that probably the majority of people —even of furniture dealers—confuse the two and call it a "chase lounge," the confusion being aided by the fact, of course, that the chaise longue is intended for lounging.

The word "chaise," by the way, when used to mean a sort of carriage, is correctly pronounced "shayz," just as in the phrase we are discussing, not "chase," as we frequently hear it. And "shay," as used in Holmes's famous poem, *The One-Hoss Shay*, is merely a corruption of "chaise," due to ignorance of the true spelling and the feeling that the word was plural—since it ended in a z-sound—and the singular therefore must be "shay."

Another misunderstanding concerns the spelling of the name of the cloth, correctly known as piqué. I have seen it in newspaper advertisements printed as "P. K." and again as "Pekay." Both these correctly represent the sound of "piqué," but are obviously the product of a mind that is ignorant of French, or at least of the fact that "piqué" comes from that language. Incidentally, when the final accent is left off—that is, properly left off, and not simply because the printer has no accented *e* at hand—the word is pronounced "peek" in both French and English, and is with us either a noun meaning a feeling of offended dignity, or a verb meaning to pride oneself or to stir up.

It is a great pity that ordinary newspapers are not equipped to print these French accents, for their omission often gives us an entirely false idea of the pronunciation of a word. For instance, *exposé*, meaning "exposure," properly has the accent and is consequently pronounced "exposay," not "expose." On the other hand, *impasse* has no accent and is pronounced in English simply "imPASS."

Latin words in English

Latin words are likewise troublesome in English, much more troublesome than they used to be, not so much because the study of Latin has declined as because the so-called Roman method of pronunciation is now universally taught in Latin classes, whereas in the time of our grandfathers the English method was used. Since Latin words and phrases that have become an integral part of our language are correctly pronounced as if they were English, the student of Latin today is more likely to get them wrong than right. A very interesting instance is found in the words "alumni" and "alumnae." By the English method the former is "aLUMnigh," and the latter "aLUMnee," but by the Roman method the reverse is true, and that is probably why so many alumni do not know what to call themselves.

It may be just as well to mention here for the sake of readers not familiar with Latin that "alumni" and "alumnae" are both plural, the singulars being respectively "alumnus" and "alumna." There was a time when one might have assumed that every college graduate was familiar with Latin, but the situation today is well exemplified by the reported remark of a graduate to the president of a college: "You know, sir, I feel pretty strongly about this matter, because I am an alumni of this institution myself."

"Are you really?" replied the president. "That's singular." But of course the alumnus never saw the point.

Another Latin word which is the subject of some misunderstanding is "alias." One good lady is reported to have said that if she should ever have a son, she would never name him "A-LIE-as," for she had noticed that people with that name seemed to be always getting into trouble. The word, however, should be pronounced "AILias," and is Latin for "at another time." "John Smith alias Joe Brown alias Jim Williams" means "John Smith, who at another time was known as Joe Brown and at still another as Jim Williams." Notice, however, that English with its characteristic freedom has turned the word likewise into a noun, and it is now possible to say, "John Smith, who traveled under the alias of Joe Brown."

"Alibi" is another legal term taken from Latin, but it has so passed into common use that practically everybody pronounces it correctly. In Latin it means "elsewhere," and an accused man who offers an alibi presents evidence that he was elsewhere when the crime was committed. But, alas, so many false alibis have been presented in our courts that in the popular speech of the day, "alibi" means usually a false excuse of the nature of those given by Ring Lardner's hero known as "Alibi Ike."

Some difficult pronunciations

Perhaps as troublesome a group of words as any to be found in the language is the one given below, the proper accent being indicated in each case:

ADmirable
LAMentable
inCOMparable
inEXplicable
irREVocable
irREFutable (New *Webster* gives also irreFUtable)
inDISputable (New *Webster* gives also indiSPUTable)
inDISsoluble (New *Webster* gives also indisSOLuble)
irREParable
FORmidable

To many people such pronunciations seem entirely unreasonable. If something is to be laMENTed, they ask, why do we not say it is laMENtable, rather than LAMentable? Their reasoning is good, but the fact remains that the majority of people *who use these words in expressing their own thoughts* accent them in the way I have indicated. With the exception of "admirable" they are all rather unusual and scarcely to be heard except in the speech of persons who are considerably beyond the average in intelligence and education. And the pronunciation "ADmirable" is so well established that only children and uneducated people are likely to say "adMIrable."

But the question may well be asked how such apparently illogical pronunciations ever became established. The an-

swer seems to be that all of them came to us from the French
and were pronounced in a manner corresponding roughly
to the French method, with two accents, as, for instance,
"ADmiRAble," "LAMenTAble," and so on. In the course
of time, however, in accordance with a natural English tendency, the second accent was lost and all the emphasis put
on the first one. It is well to bear in mind that "lamentable"
in English does not come from "lament," but is simply the
French word *lamentable* taken over bodily, and so, of
course, for the others.

All of us come across many words in our reading that we
have never heard pronounced, and instead of looking them
up in the dictionary, we give them a pronunciation which
seems reasonable to us, but which may be widely different
from the correct one. This practice sometimes produces
very ludicrous results when we have occasion to utter the
word aloud and make use of our mental method. A radio
announcer on a nation-wide circuit a few years ago made
this horrible slip. "We will now take you," he said, "to
Indianapolis, where the governor of Oklahoma, AHLfahlfa
Bill Murray, is making an address." He had probably never
heard anyone pronounce the word "alFALfa," not much of
which is grown in New York City, where he had no doubt
been reared, but his pronunciation must have produced
howls of glee from all his rural listeners, particularly in
Oklahoma.

Twice on another national radio system I have heard the
word "awry," pronounced "AW-ry," and a friend of mine
who possesses a Ph. D. conferred by Harvard told me that
he pronounced it in that way for many years, until it dawned
on him that it is simply the word "wry" with "a" before
it, and is, of course, pronounced "a-WRY."

Another word by which many people are misled is this
very one—"misled." I should not be surprised if some of
my readers have read it "mizzled," for that is not at all an
unnatural way to pronounce it. Actually, however, it is
"mis-led," and is the past tense of "mislead."

And now for my more sophisticated readers who may

have learned nothing new to them concerning the words discussed so far in this chapter, and who possibly are beginning to feel a little superior, I have a list of five good English words, non-technical and in general, if not very frequent, use. If they can pronounce them all correctly, I shall be perfectly willing to admit that they are entitled to their feeling of superiority, for I do not believe that more than one in fifty thousand can do so. Here they are:

> vagary
> simony
> swathed
> congeries
> rationale

Be sure to try them before you read the remainder of this paragraph, for here are their pronunciations according to the three leading American dictionaries, there being no difference of opinion among them. "Vagary" is "vaGAry," not "VAgary." "Simony," is "SIMony," (*i* as in *it*), in spite of the fact that it comes from the name "Simon," in which the *i* is long. "Swathed" is "swaythed," not "swah-thed." It comes from the verb "swathe," which is naturally pronounced to rhyme with "bathe." "Congeries" is Latin, not French, and is consequently "conJEE-ri-ezz," not "cawnzheree," as many people imagine. Finally, "rationale" is likewise Latin, not French, and is "rashuNAYlee," not "rashuNAL." And now, are you the one in fifty thousand, or one of the forty-nine thousand, nine hundred and ninety-nine?

The vaGAries of English pronunciation are LAMentable, but not inEXplicable, the composite character of the language being responsible for most of them. The ratioNAle of the matter should become evident to the careful student when he realizes that English is not a mere conGEries, or aggregation of words drawn from many and varied sources, but an ADmirable and inCOMparable fabric for the clothing of thought, woven into a harmonious pattern by the language-making genius of those who speak it.

IS GOOD
ENGLISH
UNNATURAL?

VI

A RADIO listener once wrote me a letter which ran substantially as follows:

"I agree with you that the use of good English is desirable, but some of the expressions required by it sound so stilted that I can scarcely bring myself to use them. For instance, it seems exceedingly awkward to me to have to say 'None is,' or to speak of 'an hotel.' 'It is I' is also quite unnatural, and sounds even affected. What can I do about it?"

As it happens, the dilemma of this listener is created almost entirely by his misunderstanding of what the rules of good English really require. As I have shown in a previous chapter, "none" may be followed by either a plural or a singular verb, despite a wide-spread impression to the contrary among those who ought to know better, and in usage of the present day "none are" is more common than "none is."

There is likewise no rule that requires one to say "an hotel," and though the expression is used more or less in England, it is very rare in America. The rule is that before words beginning with "h" in which the accent is not on the first syllable, "an" *may* be—not must be—used. It is correct to say either "a hysterical woman" or "an hysterical woman," "a hypnotic condition" or "an hypnotic condition." "Hotel," of course, comes under this rule, for its accent should be decidedly on the last syllable, as I have mentioned in another chapter, but remember, the rule is merely permissive, and few Americans seem inclined to avail themselves of the permission as far as this particular word is concerned.

In older English "an" was used before any word beginning with "h," regardless of the position of the accent, the reason being that "h" is not a thorough-going consonant, but only a sort of rough breathing coming before the vowel, and to the minds of our ancestors apparently did not separate the vowel sufficiently from "a" to avoid the unpleasant sound that occurs when two vowels come in succession. We have not this feeling, but we do realize that when the accent does not fall on the first syllable, the "h" is not ordinarily heard very plainly. In rapid speech it is sometimes hard to tell whether one says "historical," for instance, or "istorical," so that the use of "an" does not seem inappropriate in the phrase "an historical novel."

Most people think that the indefinite article is properly "a" and that we add the "n" when the word that follows it begins with a vowel. The reverse is the truth. The word is originally "an," and we drop the "n" before a consonant, or, to be more accurate, before a consonant-sound. People often write to ask whether it is correct to say "an unique event," or "an unanimous opinion," for instance. The answer is no, for "unique" and "unanimous" begin with a consonant-sound, although their first letter is a vowel. The sound of long "u," as has been mentioned in a previous chapter, really begins with a "y," and indeed might be spelled "yoo."

We use "an," of course, before words beginning with a silent "h," such as "honor," "honest," and "hour." All these "silent-h" words came to us from the French, which in turn took them from the Latin. The "h" was sounded in standard Latin, but apparently not by the soldiers and merchants who brought Latin into France. At any rate the French did not sound it, and therefore neither do we. There has been for some time, however, a movement to restore these silent "h's" in English, and in many words today usage varies considerably. I believe the majority of people now say "humble" rather than "umble," and there has been recently a tendency to sound the "h" in "humor," though, in the South at least, most people cling to "umor." "Herb" is sometimes pronounced with the "h," and again as "erb," while one may also hear "homage" and "omage," though to my mind "homage" with the "h" clearly sounded is much to be preferred. There are people who say "uman" for "human," but no dictionary sanctions this pronunciation, though "human" when it came to us was as "h-less" as "honor" and "hour."

"It is I"

But some of my readers may feel that I am trying to avoid the discussion of "It is I." Not at all, and I am perfectly willing to admit that in ordinary careless conversation on trivial topics "It is I" does sound stilted. So much is this true that many college professors of English frequently say "It's me," just to keep from being considered overprecise. A story is told of the president of a college in the days when our educational institutions were small and the man at the head could keep in rather intimate touch with the students. While passing through the campus late one night, he heard outbursts of unseemly mirth coming from a room in one of the dormitories. Making his way to it, he knocked on the door. Instantly the noise ceased, and a voice from the inside called out:

"Who is it?"

"It's me," replied the president.

"Well, who is 'me'?"

"It's the president. Let me in at once," came the answer.

"Oh, go on away," shouted the student in the room.

"You can't fool us. The old sucker would have said 'It is I.' "

The story goes that the president was so humiliated by his bad grammar that he slunk away without any further effort to establish his identity. Yet the mistake was not one of great importance *under the circumstances.* The expression "It's me" may now be said to have risen to the dignity of a colloquialism—that is to say, an expression which may be heard on the lips of cultured and educated people in easy, everyday talk, but which would not be used by them on occasions of formality and dignity.

I feel sure that everyone, including my correspondent, will admit that on such occasions "It is I" does not sound affected or stilted. Take the words of Jesus, for instance, when he said to the disciples, "It is I. Be not afraid." Who would wish to exchange the dignity of this utterance for the version that a small boy gave when his Sunday School teacher asked him to quote the verse, which happened to be the Golden Text for the day: "Don't git scared; it's jest me." But some reader may protest that the boy's version makes other changes than the substitution of "It's me" for "It is I." It does, to be sure. But if we do nothing except to put "me" in place of "I" in the Biblical version, the incongruity will still be strikingly apparent: "It is me. Be not afraid."

Rather oddly, it is a far worse mistake to substitute "I" for "me" than it is to put "me" for "I." A rather well-known song has a line which runs:

The time has come for you and I to part.

It should, of course, be "you and me." No one would dream of saying, "The time has come for I to part from you," and if we cannot say "for I," neither can we correctly say "for you and I." No doubt expressions like this arise partly because as children we acquire the notion that "you and I" is always preferable to "you and me" through being corrected when we say things like, "You and me had a good time, didn't we, Mother?" Mother replies, "Don't say 'you and me'; say 'you and I,' " and in our childish minds the idea becomes fixed that people who speak correctly don't say "you and me." The consequence is that many of us go through life taking a great deal of pains to avoid that combination even where it would be proper to use it.

"But," some reader is doubtless asking, "why is it any worse to say 'I' for 'me' than 'me' for 'I'? After all, a mistake is a mistake, isn't it?" Yes, a mistake is a mistake, but in the field of language some mistakes are nevertheless much worse than others. The man who says "It's me" may not be making an effort to speak correctly, may be fully aware that the rules of English call for "I" in such a situation, but is simply speaking carelessly or purposely avoiding formality. At any rate, the use of "It's me" is not necessarily a sign of ignorance. But the one who says, "Let's take her with you and I," is obviously making quite an effort to speak correctly, but just as obviously doesn't know what is correct. Consequently those who hear him naturally assume that he is ignorant of the simple rules of good English.

A little technical grammar

But perhaps to those reared in these days when the study of grammar is almost entirely neglected in our schools, the rules governing the use of these pronouns may not seem so simple as to those brought up under the old regime. In any event no harm will be done by a repetition of them here. Readers who have studied Latin will recall that in that language nouns and pronouns have five different forms, depending on their use in the sentence. These forms are called cases—namely, the nominative, genitive, dative, accusative, and ablative. German has the first four of these, but modern English has only three, nominative, possessive, and objective, the last corresponding to the Latin and German accusative. In all three languages, the nominative form is used when the noun or pronoun is the subject of a verb and the objective or accusative form when it is the object of a verb or a preposition. In English, however, the objective form of a noun looks exactly like its nominative form—though it was different originally—and it is only in certain pronouns that the distinction between the two cases is kept alive.

Here are these forms:

Nominative—I, we, he, she, they, who, thou
Objective—me, us, him, her, them, whom, thee

There is an old story about a man who heard a woman apparently calling to some ragged and dirty children who were playing near him in utter disregard of her.

"Why don't you answer your mother?" he inquired.

"Oh," replied one, "her ain't a-callin' we; us don't belong to she."

I have always been inclined to doubt that this story is true, for it is difficult to believe that even the most illiterate child would confuse the pronouns in this weird fashion. The person who never heard of the nominative or objective case recognizes instantly by the sound that something is radically wrong. The grammarian says gravely that the child used the objective forms "her" and "us" as the subject of verbs where the rule calls for the nominatives "she" and "we"; and on the other hand that she used "she" as the object of a preposition and "we" as the object of a verb instead of the objective forms "her" and "us," which the rules would call for. But the grammarian did not make these rules. The English-speaking people made them.

A word more is necessary with regard to "It is I." The non-grammatical reader is probably asking why "It is me" is not correct, if "me" as stated in the rule is the form to be used as the object of a verb. Is not "is" a verb? It is indeed, but it is a part of the verb "to be," which from its very nature cannot take an object. Consider for a moment the difference between "This is my new car," and "I wrecked my new car." In the first instance nothing at all has happened to the car, and the verb "is" merely connects this with "new car" and points out that they are one and the same thing. But in the second it is easy to see that "car" is very decidedly the object of "wrecked." After all forms of the verb "to be"—such as "am," "is," "are," "was," "were," "will be," "shall be," "may be," and so on, "have been," "has been," and "had been"—the following noun or pronoun is not an object, but is called a predicate noun or predicate pronoun and naturally takes the same case-form as the subject of the verb. And that is why "It is I" is correct. It seems a rather long explanation and a little complicated, but once more, don't blame the grammarians. Blame the English-speaking people.

Fortunately, in most instances it is not necessary to understand the rule in order to use the correct form. Many people begin a confidence, for instance, by saying, "Now this is just between you and I," where it should be, of course, "between you and me" in accordance with the rule that says that the objective form "me" should be used after the preposition "between." But suppose the speaker does not know the rule, never heard of a preposition and could not tell the objective from the nominative case. In spite of all this he can still get the sentence right if he will use a little common sense. All he needs to do is to drop for a moment the words "you and" and consider whether he should say "between I" or "between me." Since "between," however, naturally implies two persons or things, it might be better to compare, "He stood between I and the wall," with, "He stood between me and the wall." Would any English-speaking person naturally say "between I and the wall?" Why, then, should one say "between you and I?"

But, some say, if the people made the rules, they certainly have the right to change them, and why should we not just agree to use "I" or "me" indiscriminately, as the notion strikes us? Why seek to maintain the notion of case, which has about died out in English anyway? Now this is indeed what the French have done. Their grammarians have nothing to say about nominatives and objectives and they seem to get on very well without them. Perhaps we could do the same thing. But it is worth noting that while the French do not speak of cases, they do have varying forms for their pronouns and rather complicated rules for their use. Where English gets along with the words "I" and "me," the Frenchman needs three forms, *je, me,* and *moi.* And it is just as bad a mistake—or worse—in French to use "me" where the rules call for *je* or *moi* as it is in English to use "me" for "I." We must have some rules, and the simplest thing is to maintain those that we have already. One thing is certain—and this sentence is addressed chiefly to teachers, grammarians, writers of English textbooks, and other such peculiar people—we are going to have to give up entirely the notion of case in English or make a determined fight to retain it. Fowler, the great British authority, says that he believes it is worth fighting for. I cannot help agreeing with him.

Those who have tripped in their use of the pronouns, however, may find consolation in the fact that they have distinguished company. In Shelley's *Ode to the West Wind* occurs the line:

> Be thou me, impetuous one!

The rule calls for "Be thou I," but it must be admitted that it would sound a little odd to phrase it in that way. "Me" seems to fit better into the poetry, perhaps because the use of "I" would give three vowels in succession. Then, too, the thought and its expression are unusual, and even the "Be thou me" of the poet sounds somewhat strange. We are forced to admit that the line contains a technical error, but we might settle the matter by extending permission to make a similar mistake to all those who can write poetry which is the equal of Shelley's. The rest of us, however, would do well to avoid such a use on all occasions where the form of our speech is important.

Some time ago I was appealed to at the close of an oratorical contest to decide the question whether the speaker who won had been correct in using the expression, "Let us, you and me . . ." There were some who contended that it should have been, "Let us, you and I." But the young man was right, as may readily be seen by considering whether one would say "Let me" or "Let I," and it does not take a grammarian to make that decision correctly. And it is well to remember that "Let's" is merely an abbreviation of "Let us," so that "Let's you and I go together" can hardly be justified, though we often hear it. Oddly enough, some people say "Let's us go," apparently regarding "Let's" as a mere adverb of exhortation and not realizing that they are saying "Let us us go."

I am quite willing to agree that one may speak reasonably good English and still go astray on some of these technical points. Indeed many people of culture and education do so. But let us, you and me, remember that these technicalities are the result of rules established by the great mass of intelligent English-speaking people, and let us strive to attain that precision of use which alone is worthy of the possibilities of our language.

SOME MATTERS INVOLVING BRITISH
USAGE AND AMERICAN
COLLEGIATE ENGLISH

VII

"Ain't"

"Why don't they just give up and put 'ain't' in the dictionary?" asked a friend. "Everybody uses it, or nearly everybody," he continued, "including many people of education
and culture. Why not admit that there is such a word?"

He was somewhat surprised to learn that "ain't" is already in the dictionaries, and has been there for a long time,
and also surprised to learn that the inclusion of a word in the
dictionaries is not necessarily a sign that it is fit for use on
the highest level of speech. Modern dictionaries seek to
include every word that a reader would be likely to look
for, regardless of whether it is one that the editors would
recommend. Where the word is not in the best use, however, they usually indicate the fact by marking it "slang,"
"dialectic," "vulgar," "illiterate," or something of the kind.
The new Webster marks "ain't" as "dialectic or illiterate,"
though it does not seem to me that the marking is strictly
accurate.

"Ain't" is used all over the English-speaking world, and
frequently, as my friend said, by people of education and
culture. It is presumed to be a contraction of "are not,"

but it is also often used to stand for "am not," "is not," "has not," and "have not," though these last two uses are chiefly confined to the illiterate. An old Negro who had been told that his son had married addressed him thus:

> "Look here, boy, is you married?"
> "I ain't said I ain't," replied the boy.
> "I ain't asked you is you ain't; I asked you is you is. Is you?"

This is the use of "ain't" on its lowest level, which would certainly justify the dictionary marking of "dialectic or illiterate," for here it is both. But there are circumstances where it is neither, where we might almost say, as we did about "It's me," that it rises to the dignity of a colloquialism. It remains in use among educated and cultured people largely because we lack a suitable conversational abbreviation for "Am I not?" on the same order as "Don't I?" for "Do I not?" or "Didn't I?" for "Did I not?"

In England "ain't" is said to be in somewhat better repute; that is to say, cultured British ladies and gentlemen are more likely to use it without the feeling of guilt that characterizes Americans under the same circumstances. Yet out of England, the story goes, comes the strange expression "Aren't I?" which we see and hear with increasing frequency, and which it is said, was invented to avoid the use of "Ain't I?" as a substitute for "Am I not?" The first spelling seems to have been "A'n't I?" a contraction for "Am I not?" and the pronunciation was "Ahnt I?" But the British are inclined to drop their "r's" like our Southerners and likewise pronounce "Aren't I?" as "Ahnt I?" This fact caused a confusion, and when "A'n't I?" began to appear in print, it was "Aren't I?" and has so remained. I cannot vouch for the truth of this story, but it seems plausible.

I am often asked whether "Aren't I?" is now to be considered in good use. My answer is that it has not yet fully established itself, and that many people are violently opposed to it, so that it is doubtful whether it will ever be generally accepted. The incongruity of using "are" with

"I" is what repels many. If the original spelling "a'n't" had been retained, it would have more chance of acceptance, though most Americans would not naturally pronounce a word spelled in that way as "ahnt"; it would more likely be "ant." As matters stand, we have three expressions to choose from: the rather low "Ain't I?" the weird-sounding "Aren't I?" and the somewhat stilted "Am I not?" It is difficult to make a choice, but mine would be "Am I not?"

Americans are sometimes more careful in their use of English than their British cousins, particularly in the matter of pronunciation. It would be difficult, for instance, to tell by pronunciation alone whether the following sentence was spoken by an illiterate American or a cultured Englishman:

By these figgers I am shore that people et more a hunderd yurs ago than they do now.

Not all Englishmen, of course, say "figger" for "figure," "shore" for "sure," "et" for "ate," "hunderd" for "hundred," and "yurs" for "years," but many of them do who move in the highest social circles. The great Fowler himself says flatly in his admirable book *Modern English Usage* that "ate" is pronounced "et," and does not admit any other pronunciation. There are indeed a few cultured Americans —belonging mostly to that small group on our Eastern seaboard whose speech has many British characteristics—who pronounce the word in this way, but most Americans who say "et" are either children or more or less ignorant adults.

The younger generation of Englishmen are abandoning "figger" and "hunderd," I understand. Both are old pronunciations that were once in general use, and in the case of "hunderd" this was the original spelling as well as the pronunciation. The German "hundert" is essentially the same form. When the pronunciation "hundred" first came into use, it was as much of an error as it now is to turn "modern" into "modren," and was, of course, the result of the same tendency to put the "r" ahead of its proper place. But the new pronunciation spread, finally prevailed, and

brought about the change in the spelling—an excellent example of a fact that many people never seem to understand—namely, that the rules of a language are not eternally
fixed and divinely ordained principles, but vary from time to
time.

"Got"

Another thing that seems odd to most Americans is the
fondness of the British for the use of the word "got," which
they not only use as a past participle where most of us prefer "gotten," but insert in places where it is entirely uncalled
for.   Many Americans, of course, will say colloquially,
"What have you got?" or "I haven't got any," but there is
a general feeling in this country that "What have you?"
and "I haven't any" are decidedly preferable and should be
used on all occasions where dignity of speech is called for.
There seems to be no such feeling among the British, the
obtrusive "got" being actually welcomed rather than looked upon as an interloper.

I think there can be no question of the fact that the overwhelming majority of educated Americans strongly prefer
"gotten" to "got" as the past participle, regardless of the
section in which they happen to reside.   Yet, oddly enough,
a few are violently opposed to its use, and among these few
seem to be practically all the writers of school textbooks on
English, some of whom go so far as to tell their readers that
"gotten" is obsolete.   And this in spite of the fact that the
word is heard on the lips of educated and cultured people
many times daily, may be found on the pages of our newspapers and magazines, and has the sanction of all the dictionaries.

One school text, in its efforts to impress the horrors of
the use of this word, tells a story of a man who bought two
tickets for the opera in New York and wired his wife at
home in a suburb: "Have gotten tickets for the opera.   Meet
me there tonight."   But the telegraph operator split the
word "gotten" into two parts, so that the message as the wife

received it read: "Have got ten tickets for the opera." She immediately gathered together eight of her friends and appeared with them at the opera house, much to her husband's consternation.

The moral of this sad tale, according to the book, is the importance of using correct English. The husband, it says, lost a great deal of money because he did not know that the past participle of "get" is "got," not "gotten." Yet in the back of this very book, where the principal parts of the verbs are given, the past participle of "get" is correctly recorded as *either* "got" *or* "gotten." The fact is that the sad little tale proves only that telegraph operators, like other men, make mistakes, or that men's wives ought to be exceedingly careful to do just as their husbands tell them and no more.

"Gotten" is the original form of the word, and I feel sure that most Americans, at least, find it much more euphonious than "got," particularly after the verb "to be." "Where can it be got?" and "after it was got" produce anything but a pleasing impression on most of us, and seem actually uncouth in comparison with "Where can it be gotten?" and "after it was gotten." But this, of course, is merely a question of taste, and I have no desire to question the right of anybody to prefer "got" to "gotten," strange as it seems to me. Yet I do strongly question the right of our textbooks to make statements not in accordance with the facts of usage and contradicted by the highest authorities.

"One," "one's," and "oneself"

Another point on which American usage differs in general from British is the handling of the indefinite pronoun "one." When once an Englishman has employed it in the beginning of a sentence, he feels duty-bound to continue its use throughout, either in the simple form or as "one's" or "oneself," thus sometimes producing oddities like this:

If one does one's best to improve oneself in one's use of

one's native language, one will soon find one's efforts appreciated by one's friends and acquaintances.

Compare this now with the following, preferred by most cultured Americans:

If one does his best to improve himself in his use of his native language, he will soon find his efforts appreciated by his friends and acquaintances.

The superiority of the American version in simplicity, naturalness, and euphony is self-evident, yet Fowler argues stoutly for the British. His most important reason for preferring it seems to be that one can thereby make a distinction between the indefinite pronoun "one" and the numeral "one." He would interpret the sentence "One hates his enemies" by adding "and another forgives them," thus taking "one" to mean one person, instead of people in general as it does in the sentence, "One hates one's enemies." This distinction is made in speech, however, by placing greater emphasis on the numeral "one," while in writing, the context would, I think, always show which "one" was being used. Surely, if there is any resulting occasional gain in clearness by the British method, it is more than counterbalanced by its extreme awkwardness when the pronoun has to be repeated several times, as in the illustration I have given.

It should be added that there are some British writers who prefer the American handling of "one," while on the other hand there are Americans who think, strangely enough, that the British custom is an absolute rule of English. Even Fowler does not make that contention.

There are several other words that may be substituted for this indefinite "one," if one prefers not to use it or wishes variety. Notice that the following all mean essentially the same thing:

> If one does one's best . . .
> If one does his best . . .

> If a person does his best . . .
> If we do our best . . .
> If you do your best . . . .
> If a man does his best . . .
> If people do their best . . .

This embarrassment of riches sometimes results in confusion. The one who is unskilled in language frequently makes a ridiculous combination of two, or even three—in extreme cases four—of these methods in ways that Ring Lardner has admirably illustrated in his *You Know Me, Al* stories. One of his heroes, if he could be thought of as uttering such a sentiment, would probably have rendered our sentence as follows:

If a person does their best to improve theirself in their use of our native language, we will soon find our efforts appreciated by our friends and acquaintances.

If any reader thinks that such a horrible combination of pronouns is incredible, I invite him to consider the following, taken word for word from an announcement by a well-known master of ceremonies on a national radio broadcast:

Everybody has a place in *their* back that is hard to reach when *you* want to scratch it.

I suppose it is hardly necessary to say that it should have been, "Everybody has a place in *his* back that is hard to reach when *he* wants to scratch it." And here is a similar piece of confusion, which occurred in an invitation sent out by the alumni association of a great university:

Anyone who attended the University, whether *you* graduated or not, is invited to be present.

Collegiate English

Those who have never had the advantage of a college education are likely to attribute at least a part of their

difficulties with the English language to that fact and to
have the quaint notion that college graduates always speak
correctly or at least know how to do so, if they wish. Yet
the truth is that a college course has usually very little
effect on the speech of those who are exposed to it, nor does
it in general give them any real knowledge of the English
language. If you doubt this, read the words of the average
college song, and aside from the poor poetry and general
puerility of sentiment, note the contempt for grammar and
the misuse or coinage of words. The following examples
are taken from an article in the *New Yorker*, by Morris
Bishop.

> Here they come with banners flying,
> In stalwart step they're *nighing*.

> Let Duty be well performed,
> Honor be e'er *untarn'd* . . .

"Untarn'd" is presumably a contraction of "untarnished."

> She treats us *royal*,
> To her be loyal.

"She," of course, is the beloved Alma Mater, who, however,
might have treated her sons still more royally if she had
taught them to discriminate between an adjective and an
adverb.

> Blank College we all praise and *pride* . . .

That is to say, we take pride in her for the skill with which
she has enabled us to turn a noun into a verb.

> Nothing *we* from thee can sever;
> Alma Mater we acclaim.

The thought here is obviously, "Nothing can sever us from
thee," and the writer is not able to claim the necessity of
either rhyme or meter for turning "us" into "we."

One cannot help wondering why the English departments
of our colleges do not feel the responsibility of correcting
such glaring errors as these, instead of permitting the inability

of their students to handle the English language to be advertised to the world. But at least they are not attempting to cover up the situation as it exists. A few years ago a prominent man whose son was ready for college wrote a letter to the head of each of ten universities, inquiring whether he knew of any institution to which he could entrust his son in the confidence that the young man would be taught to speak and write the English language correctly. With one accord they all answered that they knew of no such institution.

There is something to be said in defense of the colleges, of course. No school can *guarantee* to teach a subject successfully to a pupil, for much depends on the ability and application of the pupil himself. And the colleges claim with some justice that the high school and grammar school ought to give pupils the fundamentals of English training before they enter college.

Yet the colleges are to blame more especially in not furnishing to the high school teachers of English who have a real mastery of the language. Specializing in English in college means in the large majority of cases specializing in English literature. Most of our colleges seem not to have realized that English grammar is a subject worthy of graduate study, and that the prospective teacher of English needs to have full and accurate knowledge of it. Such knowledge cannot be obtained in high school or in the usual Freshman composition course in college, yet this is in most cases the extent of the training which English teachers have received in the language.

The simple truth is that many college professors of English have no more than a slight and superficial knowledge of English grammar themselves. Their interest is in literature, and they often apply to it the methods of scholarly research and minute analysis that would be appropriate to grammar, but are not appropriate to literature in most cases, since it is something primarily to be appreciated and enjoyed, rather than to be classified. I have on excellent first-hand authority the almost incredible story of the head of the

English department in one of our largest universities who, when appealed to in a controversy, ruled that the word "high" could not be used as an adverb, "because the dictionary does not record it as one." "High," of course, is frequently used as an adverb in such sentences as, "The bird flew high," and the dictionaries so record it. Why the learned gentleman could not find it in them is beyond my comprehension, but I have unimpeachable assurance that he did make the weird ruling, and have seen a verbatim copy of it.

There was a time when an accurate knowledge and use of his native language was considered the first and most conclusive mark of an educated man. Perhaps the time will come again when we may reasonably expect our college graduates to be educated men and women and to give evidence of that education by the way in which they handle our mother tongue.

THE SPLIT INFINITIVE
AND OTHER MATTERS

VIII

WE FREQUENTLY see humorous reference to the split infinitive, which rather strangely has become, as it were, the
badge or emblem of those who are careless with their grammar. Yet the truth is that many fairly well educated people
do not even know what an infinitive is and much less how
to split one. For their benefit, let me explain.

The infinitive is the noun form of the verb, which in
English usually,—though not necessarily,—has the preposition "to" before it. "To go," "to run," "to see," and "to
think" are all infinitives. So are the simple words "go" and
"think" in the expressions "You need not *go*" and "I cannot but *think* he will be here."

When "to" is a part of the infinitive, it is generally better
not to separate the two words by another. "To go slowly,"
"to see clearly," and "to think deeply" are obviously better
than "to slowly go," "to clearly see," and "to deeply think,"
in which the infinitive is said to be "split," because an adverb
is inserted between the two words which compose it.

It is a mistake to think, however, that it is always an absolute error thus to split the infinitive, for sometimes it is
almost impossible to do otherwise, if the meaning is to be
made clear. Consider, for instance this sentence, given by
the grammarian Curme: "He failed *to* entirely *comprehend*

it." This obviously means that his comprehension was partial, though not complete. If we write, "He failed entirely to comprehend it," the interpretation would naturally be that there was no comprehension at all, and the same thing might be true if we make it, "He failed to comprehend it entirely." There is no way to make the thought clear except by splitting the infinitive or rewording the sentence completely.

What is apparently an excellent example of the mischief that may be done by the notion that splitting an infinitive is to be avoided at any cost, may be seen in the following sentence, taken from a story which appeared recently in a somewhat sophisticated magazine:

> He nearly used to have apoplexy when he heard Pete's fearful phrases reverberating in the composing room.

How can it be said that anyone "nearly used to have apoplexy?" The proper arrangement—the one that brings out the intended sense—is "He used to nearly have apoplexy," and if the author felt that it was an unforgivable literary crime to split an infinitive, he should have expressed the thought in an entirely different way.

Moreover it must be admitted that the split infinitive has been rather abundant in English literature, being used even at times when there is not as much reason for it as in the sentence we have been discussing. Herbert Spencer wrote "to rightly connect" in an essay on style, and here is a line from Burns:

> Who dared *to* nobly *stem* tyrannic pride . . .
> —*The Cotter's Saturday Night*

And it is Browning, with his characteristic liberty of arrangement, who furnishes us with one of the most striking examples:

> *To* quietly next day at crow of cock *cut* my throat . . .
>
> —*The Ring and the Book*

I frequently give my pupils the following safe rule: follow the same policy about splitting the infinitive that you follow about splitting wood; that is, don't split it unless you have to, and don't split it with a "not." Such instruction, of course, will perhaps not appeal very strongly to city-dwelling readers, who have never known the joys of wood-splitting or the difficulty of splitting wood which has a knot, but country-reared pupils have always seemed to catch the point readily. It is, as always, easier to learn the rule than to apply it. Two of my pupils have accomplished the remarkable feat of violating the rule in the act of giving it. Here are quotations from their examination papers:

> It is sometimes permissible to split the infinitive, but it is best *to not split* it with a "not."

> It is better *to never split* the infinitive.

The infinitive without "to"

There are several verbs which are regularly followed by the infinitive without "to," and to illustrate them I have ventured to compose a sentence which involves five at once. Let us suppose that a carpenter is called to a home to build a garage, and that the elder son is delegated to assist him. The younger brother wants to watch the work, but the elder fears he will get in the way, and sends him into the house. Might it not be likely that the boy would appeal to his mother in the following fashion?

> "Mother, have Father *make* Brother *let* me *watch* him *help* the man *build* the garage!"

Here "make," "let," "watch," "help," and "build" are all infinitives just as surely as if the "to" were present. "See," "dare," and "need" may also be followed by the plain infinitive, and the same thing is true of the auxiliary verbs "shall," "will," "can," "may," and "must," in all their forms.

For readers who are interested in grammatical curiosities

like the sentence given above, I have another which makes use of six consecutive infinitives, this time fully equipped with the "to." There are schools which require their pupils to be able to swim a certain distance or to take lessons in the art of swimming. Let us suppose—once more—that a pupil who does not know how to swim and is unwilling to try to learn, enters such a school and communicates to an older pupil his intention of evading the requirement, if possible. "Oh, no," replies the other, "they enforce the rule strictly." And then he adds:

"It is useless for you even to plan to attempt to refuse to try to learn to swim!"

Those who are fond of technical grammar—and I am deeply appreciative of readers of that sort—will be interested in considering that each infinitive, beginning with "to attempt," is the object of the one before it. The whole string beginning with "to plan" may be taken as the subject of "is," "it" being construed as an expletive.

My first example of the use of the infinitive without "to" was the expression "I cannot but think," and I wonder whether some of those readers who are fond of technical grammar are not planning to write to me, questioning the correctness of such an expression. They may save their time and postage, however, for I can assure them that it is correct. Let them recall Wordsworth's lines from *The Daffodils:*

> A poet could not but be gay
> In such a jocund company.

But of course Wordsworth is not the only writer who has used the expression. It is well established both in literature and in common speech.

Its use, however, results in a strange situation. Compare the following sentences:

> I cannot but think you are mistaken.
> I can but think you are mistaken.

Here we have two sentences with the same wording except for the word "not." By all the laws of logic they ought to contradict each other, but their meaning is essentially the same. Yet both are good English sentences. What is the explanation?

The key to the puzzle lies in the fact that the word "but" has different meanings in the two. In the first it means "except," and the words "do anything" are understood after "cannot," so that the thought is:

> I cannot do anything except think that you are mistaken.

In the second "but" means "only":

> I can only think that you are mistaken.

In other words, the omission of "not" in the second sentence is counterbalanced by the shift in meaning of "but," and the sense remains the same. So far as I know, there is no language but English in which such a paradoxical situation is possible.

"But"

The reader may well ask how "but" came to have such varied meanings. We think of the word as primarily a conjunction, as it is, for instance, in the sentence, "Man proposes, but God disposes." Yet "but" was first used in English as an adverb meaning "outside," developed very naturally into a preposition with practically its present prepositional meaning of "except," and acquired its conjunctional use only as a later development. Its meaning of "only" came about in rather peculiar fashion, according to the scholars, who say that it arose from simply omitting "not" in sentences like "There is not but one left." It seems a strange omission, but a little thought will, I believe, make it seem possible that "but" alone might have come to stand for "not . . . but." At any rate our most learned students of language tell us that this is exactly what has happened. Most people now think of a sentence like "There is not but one left" as incorrect. Apparently, however, it is the original form, and certainly not illogical, though it must be admitted that it sounds somewhat better to put it in the newer way, "There is but one left." Children instinctively use the form with "not," and the same thing is true of unlettered persons, which facts, incidentally, are fairly good evidence that it is the original.

"But" in the sense of "except" is in meaning a preposition and should therefore logically take the objective case of pronoun after it, but in English literature up to the present the word in this use ordinarily has been regarded as a conjunction, like "than," requiring the same case—usually the nominative—after it as before. Accordingly, most of our writers would say, "All but I are gone," and, "Death has taken all but me." Mrs. Hemans, in that old favorite *Casabianca*, more generally known as *The Boy Stood on the Burning Deck*, wrote:

Whence all but *he* had fled.

And Thomas Moore in *Oft in the Stilly Night* has these lines:

I feel like one
Who treads alone
Some banquet-hall deserted,
Whose lights are fled,
Whose garlands dead,
And all but *he* departed.

In *My Last Duchess* Browning writes:

. . . since none puts by
The curtain I have drawn for you, but *I*

The comma before "but" in the line just quoted gives an indication of the reason in the writer's mind for the use of "I" rather than "me." He is obviously now considering "but" as a conjunction introducing a shortened clause, which if completed would read, "but I put it by."

These quotations indicate very well the standard literary usage, but in conversation from the earliest times "but" has been treated as a preposition in this use and followed with the objective. There are indications that literary custom is now yielding to the colloquial, which has both reason and history on its side. Since "but" was a preposition before it was a conjunction, and since its meaning in the sense of "except" is clearly prepositional, there is no use in maintaining the literary fiction that it is a conjunction in that sense, even though as able a man as Fowler argues very strongly for it.

School textbooks of the present day usually treat the word as a preposition in this meaning, but are not always careful to explain to the pupils that literary tradition has it differently, with the result that they are frequently confused when they encounter the word in their reading followed by the nominative. In my first year as a teacher I had an embarrassing experience as a consequence of my ignorance of this double usage. I had explained to the class the day before the prepositional status of "but" meaning "except," and behold, here was "All but I" in our literature lesson. "Didn't you tell us that we ought to say, 'All but me'?" asked one of the big boys on the back row. I had to admit that such had been my instruction, and sought in great confusion to reconcile my teaching with the usage of the author whose works we were studying. About this time there arose a whispering of "All but me," accompanied by much laughter on the back row, and I naturally assumed that my pupils were making fun of the ignorance of their young instructor. Later I learned that the real cause of the merriment was the remembrance of the sport they had had at a party held a few evenings before, in the playing of a game of great elegance and refinement, in which an unwitting member of the crowd is instructed to answer "All but me" in reply to every statement that is made to him. When he makes his first reply, all the others lower their heads and butt into him, shouting in answer to his protests that he has commanded them all to butt him and that they are only carrying out his instructions. My unawareness of this innocent pastime, combined with my ignorance of the literary usage with "but," gave me a very unpleasant quarter of an hour.

Great writers and the rules of English

There are those who hold what has always seemed to me the very extreme view that the rules of English are absolutely determined by the usage of our great writers. "Whatever a competent writer writes is good English, let the whole corps of grammarians howl as they will," is the way in which a rather prominent contemporary author has put it. Now it is quite true that grammarians are prone to lay down rules that have no existence except in their own minds, and that in general the literary instinct of a really great writer is superior to the painfully worked-out analysis of the grammarian, but the final judgment rests with the vast body of intelligent and cultured English-speaking people, rather than with either the writers or the grammarians. What makes a writer great except the fact that he appeals to this vast body? And even the greatest of writers is still a fallible human being. Why should it be assumed that he has expressed every thought in a faultless way?

There is to my mind no greater English poet—considered purely as a poet—than Alfred Tennyson. The recent reaction against all things and persons of the Victorian era has unfortunately prejudiced some of the younger generation against him, but his fame is secure. Surely no poet has done more to demonstrate the possibilities of the English language in the production of such various forms of beauty, and few have the mastery of it that is his. Yet even he trips occasionally. In a very familiar poem, *Sir Galahad*, he has the following:

> How sweet are looks that ladies bend
> On whom their favors fall!

As a boy I became very fond of this particular poem, and read these lines over hundreds of times without realizing that there was any exception which might be taken to their wording. Yet the fact is that the poet has made the word "on" do double duty, in a way that is really illegitimate, but is concealed by the beauty and rhythm of the poetry. If we supply "those," which is obviously and legitimately understood before "whom," the sentence would read: "How sweet are looks that ladies bend *on* those *on* whom their favors fall." Or, of course, it might be "on those whom their favors fall on," to end the sentence with a preposition, which I trust my readers have not forgotten is quite permissible. But at any rate there must be two "on's," and we cannot justify the omission of one of them and the throwing of the whole burden on the other. Which one, incidentally, has swallowed the other? Fowler—though he seems not to have noticed this example of it—calls such devouring of a word by another, "cannibalism." Here is a specimen of it which he gives in *Modern English Usage:*

> The facts should be made known in regard *to whom* is actually due the credit of first proving the existence of petroleum in this country.

It should read "in regard *to to* whom, etc.," though this, of course, would be awkward, and it would be better to reword the sentence. Fowler's comment is that a "to" has swallowed a "to."

Ever since Rudyard Kipling wrote his *Recessional*, there has been discussion from time to time about the grammar of the opening line, which reads:

> The shouting and the tumult dies;

The contention of some is that the verb should be "die" instead of "dies," on the ground that "the shouting and the tumult" should be regarded as plural. A recent writer in the *New York Times* takes that view and since a change to "die" would spoil the rhyme, he suggests that the line be amended to read as follows:

> The shoutings cease, the tumult dies;

and then, of course, he would go on with

> The captains and the kings depart;
> Still stands Thine ancient sacrifice,
> An humble and a contrite heart.

Readers, however, leaped to the defense of Kipling. The one who made the best defense, in my opinion, pointed out that "shouting" and "tumult" express essentially the same idea, and that the poet was considering them together as one thing. In such cases in English it is permissible to use a singular verb.

But I wonder how many of my readers know what this particular shouting and tumult was about, and what captains and kings were departing. It is, I think, a tribute to Kipling's poetic genius that nearly everybody admires this poem, though not one in a hundred understands it fully. To do so, we must recall that it appeared the day after the end of the celebration of Queen Victoria's diamond jubilee, marking the sixtieth year of her reign, in 1897. It was the shouting and the tumult of this celebration which had died away, and the departing captains and kings were those who had gathered to do honor to the aged queen. Further on occur the lines:

> Far-called our navies melt away;
> On dune and headland sinks the fire.

The reference here is to the ships which had gathered for the celebration and were now returning to their stations, and to the bonfires which had been lighted all over the British empire in honor of the great event. The poem as a whole is a prayer that the British people might not, in the pride of their world-wide power, forget their duty to humanity and to the Ruler of the universe. It concludes:

> For heathen heart that puts her trust
> In reeking tube and iron shard—

that is, in guns and armor—

> All-valiant dust that builds on dust,
> And guarding calls not Thee to guard—

For frantic boast and foolish word,
Thy mercy on Thy people, Lord. Amen.

It was a timely warning for England, and perhaps for all the English-speaking peoples of the earth. But these, while proud of their achievements in statecraft, government, and war, have been strangely unaware of what is doubtless their greatest contribution to the world—the English language. For I am persuaded that when the British empire has crumbled to pieces and the deeds of its warriors and statesmen live only in books of history, the people of the earth will still pay willing tribute to the glory and splendor of our mother tongue.

THE ENGLISH OF
BUSINESS AND
OF RELIGION

IX

Not long ago I received a very interesting letter from a concern that makes a business of lending—or loaning—money. I insert "or loaning" purposely, for there is a popular belief, fostered by English textbooks, that it is incorrect to use "loan" as a verb. Commercially, however, the verb "to loan" is in good use in America, as our dictionaries will testify. In personal matters, to be sure, it is better to use "lend," to say, for instance, "Will you lend me your pencil?" rather than "Will you loan it to me?"

This does not mean, of course, that it is always permissible to use a noun as a verb. To say, "I suspicioned him all along," is the mark of a careless, if not an ignorant, speaker. "I suspected him" is the proper form, and since we already have the verb "to suspect," there is no need to take the longer noun "suspicion" and turn it into a verb. The same argument might be used against the use of "loan" as a verb, but the fact remains that this use is well established in business circles, which is certainly not true of "to suspicion."

English turns one part of speech into another with great freedom, but this fact does not imply that all experiments of the sort will eventually be accepted. "To contact" in the sense of "to make contact with" is now attempting to edge its way into the best circles, and may succeed, but it will be over the protests of those who cannot hear expressions like, "We contacted him at once," without a shudder. Only this morning I saw in a news dispatch the statement that a small boy had "propositioned" his father to be allowed to play Santa Claus to a group of convicts. It was a touching story of the Christmas spirit, but its effect on readers sensitive to the use of English must have been considerably weakened by this monstrous use of "proposition" as a verb.

Discreditable commercial English

But let us return to the letter from which we have wandered so far afield. Here is an extract from it:

> The fact that you are a person whom we know has a reputation for paying their bills entitles you to secure a loan of any amount up to $50.00 without delay.

Let me hasten to say that I am not giving publicity to this letter to reassure creditors who may perhaps be getting uneasy, but am rather displaying it as a horrible example of how a business letter ought not to be worded. The error of referring to "a person" by the pronoun "their" instead of "his" will at once be evident. But there is another and somewhat more subtle mistake. "Whom," as I have previously said, is the objective case of "who," and here we need the nominative, for it is not the object of "know," but the subject of "has." This will be clear at once, if we arrange it to read, "a person who has a reputation, we know, for paying his bills."

But this is not at all an unusual mistake. Notice this sentence from a popular comic strip:

> Tillie is happy because she has heard from her father, *whom* she thought had passed away.

And the following is from a somewhat higher source, a

very popular weekly news-magazine—a magazine which finds its way into thousands of homes and has had a great influence on present-day thought, both oral and written. From an item concerning the Spanish war we have:

> He shouted the names of personal friends *whom*
> he thought might be in the Alcazar.

It would be easy to multiply examples of this error, and it is not difficult to explain the tendency to make it. We are used to expressions like "the man whom we saw," "my brother whom you know," and so on, and we unconsciously assume that a relative pronoun (such as "who") followed immediately by a subject and verb is going to be the object of that verb. Therefore we say "whom."

Rather strangely, Jespersen (pronounced "Yespersen"), who, though a Dane, is one of the world's leading authorities on English grammar, has argued seriously that this use of *whom* is correct, which, he says, is put in the objective "because the nexus is dependent." It is difficult to follow this reasoning, and to the best of my knowledge no other grammarian of standing agrees with him. I cannot help feeling that this is a point on which the usually keen-minded Jespersen has gone astray.

My readers might be led astray, however, if we stopped the discussion at this point. Under certain circumstances "whom" is undoubtedly correct in expressions of this general nature. Consider, for instance, the following sentences:

> I spoke to the man whom I thought to be you.
> I selected a driver whom I judged to be dependable.

Readers who have forgotten their grammar, or who never knew a great deal of it, will wonder somewhat at this correct wording, though I am sure that the sound of it will not offend them. But they will be puzzled to know why it is correct to say, "the man whom I thought to be you" and incorrect in a previous sentence to say, "friends whom he thought might be in the Alcazar." The answer is that "to be" is an infinitive, and it is a generally accepted rule in English, as in Latin, that the subject of the infinitive goes in the *objective* case—not the nominative. (This rule is not the whole story, and is a matter of some dispute, but as a practical guide, it is sufficient.)

It likewise follows as a consequence that the pronoun which stands in the predicate after the infinitive "to be" must be in the objective case, to agree with the subject of the infinitive. This explains why we say correctly:

> I knew it to be him,

and likewise correctly:

> I knew that it was he.

In these sentences both "he" and "him" are predicate pronouns, each agreeing with "it." But "it" in the first sentence is objective because it is the subject of an infinitive, while in the second it is nominative, because it is the subject of the ordinary (finite) verb "was."

I have spoken of the King James version of the Bible as having had a profound influence on English speech. It is a remarkable translation, filled with evidences of a literary skill apparently not possessed by those who have attempted to put the book into English of the present day. But there are errors in it, notwithstanding, and one of them occurs in the book of Matthew where Christ asks the disciples, "But whom say ye that I am?" It should be, "*Who* say ye that I am?" or, putting it in statement form, in order to show the construction more clearly, "Ye say that I am who." I trust, however, that no devout reader will feel that I am taking undue liberty in criticizing the language of Jesus, since the mistake was, of course, not his, but that of the translators. Jesus spoke in Aramaic, which, incidentally, is not a member of the great Indo-European family of languages, to which English belongs, but joins with Hebrew, Assyrian, Arabic, and others to form the Semitic group. The New

Testament, however, has been handed down to us in Greek, the Old Testament in Hebrew.

Biblical speech

The King James version was issued in 1611, and shows us quite well what the English of that time was like, though successive generations of editors have gradually modernized the spelling. It is true, too, that the King James is based on still earlier versions and that its translators deliberately clung to usages that had perhaps already begun to sound a little old-fashioned, as befitting the dignity of the sacred volume. In it "thou" is always used in addressing one person, "ye" and "you" for more than one, whereas in the plays of Shakespeare, written at about the same time, "you" is used in the singular as well as the plural, just as in present-day English. "Ye" in the Bible, incidentally, is always the form of the nominative, "you" being used only in the objective, and, of course, "thee" is the objective of "thou."

In the grammars of a generation or two ago the verb "to love" was conjugated in this fashion in the present tense:

I love	we love
thou lovest	you love
he loves	they love

But in present-day texts "thou lovest" in the second person singlar has been replaced by "you love." This change will impress the average person as highly commendable, as indeed it is—up to a certain point. In ordinary speech "you" has long been the pronoun of address in the singular, and our grammars ought not to misrepresent the living language. But, unfortunately, the "thou" forms have disappeared from the grammars almost altogether, though they still abound in the language of the Bible, prayer, and poetry. The result is that most people who attempt to use them, either in jest or earnest, make ridiculous errors, such, for instance, as saying "thou loveth." This "-eth" ending, of course, belongs to the third person singular, not the second. This Biblical verse illustrates the usage:

> The wind *bloweth* where it *listeth*, and thou *hearest* the sound thereof, but *canst* not tell whence it *cometh*, and whither it *goeth*.

The verb which follows "thou" ends in "-st" or "-est," except for a few common ones like "shalt," "wilt," "art," and "wert." It would seem that of all persons ministers of the gospel ought to be familiar with this usage, but some of them are not. Here, for instance, is the beginning of a prayer recently delivered by a minister at the opening of the session of one of our state legislatures:

> We pray that Thou *will* blest the members of this House, its officers and employees . . .

"Will" should, of course, be "wilt."

It sounds like only common sense that our school grammars should concern themselves primarily with the ordinary forms of speech rather than the unusual. But surely they ought not to neglect the unusual entirely. After all, it is the latter that especially need to be *taught*, for the ordinary forms are already familiar to the student. English-speaking persons don't need special instruction in order to be able to say "you love," but many of them will never master "thou lovest" and "he loveth," unless they have it. And the proper use of "thee" is another mystery that needs to be inculcated.

"Thou" and "thee" are both singular, the plural being "ye" and "you," as has been stated. But there are a great many who do not know this comparatively simple fact, among whom, I regret to say, is Mickey Mouse. In a recent fantastic episode of the comic strips, in which he becomes lost in the pages of an old book and adopts for a time the costume and language of the middle ages, he valiantly waves a big stick and cries out to his ruffianly opponents, "Bow down, *thou* scurvy knaves!" instead of addressing them correctly as "*Ye* scurvy knaves."

Just what Mickey's educational opportunities have been I

am not certain. It is quite possible that the exigencies of the thrilling life he leads have not allowed him the leisure to become acquainted with the niceties of English usage of a bygone day. But what are we to think of the use of "thee" in the poem given below, which appeared recently in a magazine published by a scholarship fraternity to which only the best students are eligible—a scientific fraternity, to be sure, but why should not scientists use the English language correctly? The poem is addressed to the founders of the fraternity, and its Latin title means "With Eternal Praise":

CUM LAUDE ETERNA

Men of consecrated will,
. . . .
Men of vision, . . .
. . . .
Men of purpose, .
. . . .
We salute *thee*.

Bear in mind that this poem was written by a college graduate of intelligence enough to have unusual scientific attainments, that he had enough familiarity with Latin to give it a Latin title—though this would have been better if it had read "*Aeterna cum Laude*"—and that the poem had to pass the scrutiny of an editor, likewise a college graduate of unusual scientific attainments, not to mention that of a proof-reader. Is something wrong with our teaching of English when such a slip can get through?

Perhaps the author of the poem felt that the old-fashioned form was necessary for the sake of dignity, and did not realize that for plural use "you" would be correct here in the archaic style as well as in modern language. It is, however, a great mistake to use "thou" and "thee" and "thy" indiscriminately with "you" and "your" when the reference is singular. Amateur poets are quite likely to do this, as will be seen from the following stanza of a college song:

Dear Alma Mater,
Ev'ry son and daughter
With one accord to *thee*
Turns with pride, old Varsity.
Blank College, great and grand
Loyalty and helping hand
We pledge anew
To *you*.

We hear occasionally in public prayer the use of "you" instead of "thou" in addressing the Deity. This is, of course, a matter of taste, and, no doubt, the prayers of the one who says "you" are just as sincere and just as likely to be heard and answered as those of the one who says "thou." It is fortunate for most of us that the manner of our address to the Lord is not all-important. Nevertheless I think that for a long time to come the taste of most cultured English-speaking people will lead them to employ "thou" for such a purpose.

There are ministers of the type of which Billy Sunday is perhaps the best-known example who discard all formality in the pulpit, are careless in their grammar, and sprinkle their discourse liberally with slang. Billy's defense for his method was that he had a message of the greatest importance to give to the people and that therefore he wanted to give it to them in the language with which they were most familiar. That he made a great temporary impression on the mass of the people and that he did some permanent good, I have no doubt. Possibly the method in which he spoke was the only one natural to him, and in that case he was wise not to affect any other. But over against Billy Sunday let us place John Wesley, the founder of Methodism, who produced a much greater effect on his own generation and whose influence has lasted over many succeeding ones, with prospects for an indefinite continuance. Wesley used to address almost incredibly large outdoor audiences, drawn in some instances from the lowest classes of the people, such, for example, as illiterate coal-miners, with the most amazing results. Yet

Wesley was Oxford-bred, used excellent English, and never dreamed of lowering the tone of his speech to suit the nature of his audience.

Some years ago, when I was living in a small Tennessee town, a minister from a distance came to conduct a series of meetings. He was a man of education and genuine religion, who preached well and pleased the people who heard him. An illiterate neighbor of mine was especially enthusiastic about his preaching. One day, when praising him highly, he reached the climax of his encomium with the following rather surprising statement: "And the best of all is I ain't never heerd him use nary slang yit!" I have always treasured the remark as concrete evidence that the man who cannot use good English himself may yet prefer to hear it from others.

It is true, however, that some ministers are guilty of talking over the heads of their congregation, as the saying goes. They use needlessly technical expressions and clothe simple thoughts in unfamiliar, high-sounding words. The minister of whom I have just spoken did this once in a rather surprising fashion—and, I must add, in a way not at all characteristic of him. Here was the sentence: "I am glad that Jesus Christ spoke in terms of monosyllabic simplicity." What a contrast between the thought and its expression! One could not help feeling that he might better have imitated the simplicity that he was rejoicing over and have said, "I am glad that Jesus Christ used short and simple words."

Another minister of my acquaintance had a notice inserted in the newspapers to the effect that he was planning to preach a special series of sermons on a certain topic. The final sentences of the notice ran like this:

> These sermons will be designed to appeal to the average listener. The thoughts will be expressed in simple language, and all theological terminology will be carefully eschewed.

I never heard whether the eschewing was as carefully

carried out as he had planned, but from the language of the notice I have my doubts.

And finally there is the story of the young minister just out of the theological seminary, who got up to make a talk to the Sunday School. This is how he began:

> My dear children, I should like to present to you this morning an epitome of the life of St. Paul. And for fear, dear children, that you are not familiar with the meaning of the word, I will say that "epitome" is in its signification synonymous with "synopsis."

No doubt the reader has noticed in these examples of obscure ministerial language that the obscurity is brought about by the use of nine large words, all of which come, not from the Anglo-Saxon core of English, but from Latin, French, or Greek: "monosyllabic simplicity," "theological terminology," "eschewed," "epitome," "signification," "synonymous," and "synopsis." Let us now contrast their elegant ineffectiveness with the natural expression of deep religious feeling found in one of our fine old hymns:

> Abide with me; fast falls the even-tide;
> The darkness deepens; Lord, with me abide.
> When other helpers fail and comforts flee,
> Help of the helpless, O abide with me.
>
> I fear no foe with Thee at hand to bless;
> Ills have no weight, and tears no bitterness;
> Where is death's sting? where, grave, thy victory?
> I triumph still, if Thou abide with me.

Every word in the two stanzas is familiar, and all but three—"comfort," "victory," and "triumph"—are Anglo-Saxon. The abstractions of theology can find indeed their suitable vocabulary in English, but it is such simple yet sublime utterances of the deep religious longings of the human heart that constitute one of the chief glories of our language.

SOME RATHER SUBTLE
MISTAKES AND SOME
VERY OBVIOUS ONES

X

ON THE day before the first fight between Schmeling and Joe Louis, a dispatch containing the following sentence was sent out over the country by a news-gathering agency:

> One of the few persons who *thinks* Schmeling has a chance is the stubborn, stolid, steel-nerved German himself.

"Thinks" in this sentence should have been "think," for its subject is "who," which refers to "persons," and consequently takes the same form of the verb that "persons" would take. We say, "persons think," and therefore, "persons who think."

And the day before the Pastor battle with the same Joe Louis the same mistake occurred in a dispatch sent out by another news-gathering agency:

> Pastor is one of the few who *argues* that he has a chance of whipping the dark destroyer from Detroit.

"Argues" should be "argue" for the same reason that "thinks" should be "think" in the preceding.

But lest my readers think this sort of language is peculiar to those who write about the prize-fighters, I ask them to look at this sentence taken from a book-review:

> On the basis of this remarkably promising situation Doreen Wallace has constructed one of the queerest novels that *has* recently come out of England.

"Has" should, of course, be "have."

The truth is that this type of error is perhaps the most common one to be found on the lips and from the pens of educated persons. Some time ago the president of one of our very largest universities was discussing the sad situation of college athletics with regard to subsidization of football players, which he said was not the policy of his institution, a fact which put it under an unfair handicap in competition with most others. Here is the conclusion of his statement as reported in the press:

> Until this situation is corrected, however, Blank University must remain one of those institutions that *pays* the penalty.

To make sure that the distinguished gentleman was not misquoted and that there was no typographical error, I took the trouble of writing to the publication in which the statement appeared and found that the quotation was accurate. In their reply the editors expressed considerable surprise at his mistake, but it was not surprising to me, for I was already familiar with the prevalence of the type, and, as an Irishman might put it, had come to expect it from unexpected sources. It is so common that most people do not notice it at all, and it is not surprising even when it occurs in the speech of those who are more careful than usual with their English.

Indeed, it requires some argument to convince certain persons that it is a mistake at all. They contend that the pronoun may refer to "one" rather than to the plural noun, making the verb in the relative clause correctly singular.

This is, to be sure, the feeling that leads the writer astray. To take the college president's sentence as an example, if he had phrased it, "Blank University must remain *one institution* that pays the penalty," his grammar would have been unimpeachable. But the sentence does not say this; it says that Blank University must remain "one of *those* institutions," and explains what institutions are designated by "those" by adding "that pay the penalty." At least, that is what it should add.

Such errors are very common after superlatives, as in the passage from the review. Another instance might be this: "It was one of the most beautiful sights that *has* ever been seen," to put it incorrectly. "Has" should be "have," for "that" must refer to "sights." Here we cannot even make the change, as in the other, which would render the singular verb correct. It would be nonsense to say, "It was one most beautiful sight that has ever been seen." To be sure, we could make it, "It was *the* most beautiful sight that has ever been seen," but our original sentence does not say or imply that; it merely states that it was *one* of the most beautiful. If the reader has trouble in making such a sentence sound right when correctly worded, let him try beginning with "of": "Of the most beautiful sights that have ever been seen, it was one." This straightens things out neatly and makes it crystal-clear that "have" is the only correct verb here.

A rule and some applications

The technical rule that governs the form of the verb "to be" employed in such sentences as we have been discussing is that the relative pronoun agrees with its antecedent in person and number. The relative pronouns are ordinarily "who" and "which"—though not when they are used to ask questions—and "that" in the sense of "who" or "which." It would be much better to call them conjunctive pronouns than relative, for they act not only as pronouns, but also as conjunctions, connecting the clause that they introduce with the word that the pronoun refers to.

This rule has some other interesting applications. It explains, for instance, the verbs in the following sentence:

> I, who *am* speaking to you who *are* listening
> in defense of him who *is* absent, tell you the facts
> in the case.

Here "who" is followed once by "am," once by "are," and once by "is," because it refers to "I" the first time, to "you" the second, and to "him" the third. Do you think that "I, who *am*" sounds strange? But what else would you substitute? Try "I, who *is*" and "I, who *are*," and you will find them stranger still. The strangeness of "I, who am" is not due to its correctness, but to the fact that we so seldom have occasion to use such an expression.

A rather troublesome point in English is found in the expression, "It is not I who am to blame." This is the accepted way of expressing the thought, though the rule I have just given is not strictly followed in it. Technically, "it" rather than "I" is the antecedent of "who," yet I am sure that no one with a feeling for English would ever write, "It is not I who *is* to blame." We should, of course, say, "I am not the one who is to blame," and even, "The one who is to blame is not I," but when "I" stands immediately before "who," it seems somehow to attract the relative into the first person.

But the rule does explain a poetical usage which may have troubled some of my readers, particularly those who are religiously inclined, for illustrations of it may be found in some of our hymns. The one that occurs to me just now is the line that runs as follows:

> O Love that wilt not let me go!

Why "wilt" rather than "will"? Because "thou" is understood in this dignified form of address, "O Love, thou that wilt not let me go!"

But let us leave these subtleties which are of interest largely to the scholar, and turn to matters of more concern in the everyday speech of the average person. After all, there are few of us who will ever write or speak a sentence in which "thou" is understood, and we are all much more likely to say, "I am not to blame," than "It is not I who am to blame." To strike a good average by descending to the other end of the scale, let us consider for a while some very obvious and simple errors, which a few of our readers will perhaps feel are beneath their dignity. Let them be careful, however, for even highly cultured and educated people sometimes make mistakes that are the same in principle as those which cause them much amusement in the speech of the illiterate.

Many years ago when a train on which I was a passenger stopped at a small station, a gaunt, whiskered man, with an obviously swollen jaw, approached the conductor, and in evident distress asked: "Can you tell me is there ary tooth-dentist in this town?" Poor fellow! I could not help feeling sorry for him, and not wholly because of his aching tooth. That would doubtless be all right in a few days, but his use of English would probably continue to stamp him as an ignorant man for the remainder of his life.

Tautological expressions like "tooth-dentist," "pneumonia-fever," (or rather "pneumony-fever"), and "side-pleurisy" are rather common among uneducated people in the Southern mountains and more or less so with the same class in the lowlands. I specify "uneducated people," for, contrary to popular belief, not all mountaineers belong in that class. Some mountain families have had a considerable degree of culture and education for several generations, and properly resent being classed with the ignorant, who, they rightly point out, may be found everywhere. But, of course, the average in the most remote mountain districts has been rather low, and the speech of these people, as we have often heard, is different in some respects from that of any other group in the United States.

But before the reader makes too much fun of needless repetitions like "tooth-dentist," let me ask him what he calls an omelet which is not a Spanish omelet or a cheese omelet or any other particular kind of omelet? Does he refer to it as an "egg omelet"? I have heard some rather cultured people use that term, but they were wrong. It is a "plain omelet," as a reference to cook-books will show. All omelets contain eggs. They would not be omelets otherwise. And a similar thing is true of custards. You may have chocolate custard, coconut custard, caramel custard, sweet-potato-custard, but if you have a custard that contains only eggs, milk, sugar, and perhaps flavoring, it is not an "egg custard," but a "plain custard." Like omelets, all custards contain eggs.

Since we have wandered to this subject of foods, perhaps it is as good a time as any to mention some differences in nomenclature of the subject between the North and the South. All over the South, in the mountains and the lowlands, among the cultured and the uncultured, the terms "sweet milk," "Irish potatoes," and "light bread" are used to designate those articles of food which elsewhere are usually known simply as milk, potatoes, and bread. There are reasons for all these, I think, aside from the fact that time-saving in speech has never been considered as important in the South as in the North. "Sweet milk" is so designated to distinguish it from buttermilk, which usually holds an honored place on Southern tables, the "Irish potato" must be kept from confusion with the sweet potato, which is likewise greatly enjoyed in the South, and, of course, "light bread" is not the usual Southern bread, for that is biscuits. The Southern biscuit, incidentally, is not a cracker, as a biscuit is in Canada and England, and not a roll, as it frequently is in the North. It is much thicker than a cracker, but not nearly so thick as a roll. It may be lightened by beating in air—the so-called "beaten biscuit," which is now seldom seen —or by buttermilk and soda, or by baking powder, and while it may vary in thickness according to individual desire, it is almost never so light and puffy as those illustrations of biscuits appear with which the advertisements of Northern flour-makers seek vainly to beguile Southern people into buying their flour. They may buy it, to be sure, but never because they want to make biscuits with it that look like those in the picture.

I was surprised recently to learn that the dessert known in the South as "ambrosia" seems to be unfamiliar to most people of other sections. Ambrosia, of course, was the mythical food of the gods, but Southerners have for a long time regularly applied that name to a dish made by cutting the pulp of oranges into small sections, mixing it with grated or shredded coconut and sweetening with sugar. When properly made it deserves the name.

"Ary" and "nary"

But let us return to the language of the poor fellow with the toothache. He used the word "ary," which, with its negative "nary," is frequently heard in the mountains and elsewhere among very ignorant people. The words, however, are not at all of ignorant origin. They are merely contractions for "ever a" and "never a," which are now largely poetical expressions. The transformation is simple and natural. Take the sentence:

> Never a one did I see.

It is good English, and might indeed be a line of poetry. Now contract it to:

> Ne'er a one did I see.

and the same things are true. But change the order of words and the spelling of "ne'er a," add an extra negative, and behold the degeneration:

> I didn't see nary one.

How thin is the line sometimes between the best English and the worst!

There are other expressions and many words in use among the mountain people, which like "ary" and "nary" are merely the remnants of what once was irreproachable English. Few things sound worse than the use of "hit," for

"it," for instance, but originally the word was "hit," and at
first the omission of the "h" was a grave mistake itself.
Why was the "h" lost in standard speech, the reader may
ask. The answer is that "it" is so often unimportant and
closely attached to a verb or preposition that the "h" was
sounded with difficulty or not at all. We frequently now
omit the "h" from "him" in rapid speech for the same
reason. We write, "Could you get him?" but we say,
"Could you GETim?" We write "Look at him," but we
say, as likely as not, "Look ATim." If it were not for the
fact that "him" is more frequently emphatic than "it," and
hence sounded fully and clearly, it might have lost its "h"
also.

The *Century Dictionary* says that the present-day use of
"hit" should be taken as an ignorant corruption of "it,"
rather than as a survival of the original spelling and pronunciation. I cannot help feeling that this must be a mistaken view. Is there any other instance where "h" has been
added to a word by Americans? "Hain't" is not a formation
of this kind, for it is a corruption of "haven't," not a form
of "ain't."

It is a mistake to think, however, that the speech of the
remote Southern mountains is merely old-fashioned English
that has been preserved intact from Elizabethan days. As is
true elsewhere, many mountain expressions never were good
English, but are simply the corruptions that ignorant people
are likely to make anywhere. One may hear "I seed" or
"I seen" for "I saw," and "I taken" for "I took," expressions
unfortunately not limited to the mountains, but more or less
common among the uneducated classes of other sections,
though "I taken" is said to be limited to the South.

I have often wondered why it is that errors having to do
with the parts of irregular verbs are so common in the
speech of ignorant or careless people and yet so repulsive.
Surely the worst possible error in the use of our language
is to say "I taken" for "I took." At the same time it is perhaps the most tenacious. I wonder sometimes whether
anybody was every really cured of it. Teaching seems to

produce no permanent effect. It is easy, of course, to get the afflicted one to recite "I took" very glibly; it is not even very difficult to get him to understand that "taken" is the past participle, while "took" is the past indicative, and that therefore "taken" is not to be used as a verb by itself; but it is a herculean (pronounced "herCUlean," by the way) task to get him to adopt "I took" as an instinctive habit of speech, for even when surrounded entirely by people who say "I took," he will go on placidly through life saying "I taken" in apparent utter unawareness that his speech is different from that of anybody else.

Next to "I taken" comes "I seen," and closely following that is "I done." And then come a host of others. "He come up and give it to me," may be heard always with certain speakers for "He came up and gave it to me." "Throwed" is used for "threw," and is often pronounced "thowed." "Drawed" is also used for "drew." There is no tendency to substitute "gone" for "went," but it is not so very uncommon to hear "I would have went." Bear in mind that I am now speaking of English on a very low level, which H. L. Mencken would probably call the speech of the proletariat, though there never has been in America any sharp line separating the proletariat from the rest of us, and it is to be hoped that there never will be.

In his book *The American Language* Mr. Mencken seems to feel that this proletariat has developed a sort of language of its own, from which no amount of instruction on the part of teachers of English will ever separate it. I am willing to agree that the task of changing the speech habits of an individual or a class is one not to be taken lightly and one in which it would be unreasonable to hope for early and complete success. But I by no means entertain so hopeless a view of the situation as Mr. Mencken. The desire to speak his native language correctly lies in the heart of each of us, often hidden, often dormant, but responsive, if only feebly, when the proper chord is struck. I have spoken of the "I taken" group as almost hopeless. Yet I know a man who says "I taken," who spoke with scorn once of the bad English he had observed in certain others.

Nor can I sympathize with the notion more or less prevalent that, after all, this so-called proletarian speech is merely another way of expressing thought, as good, or almost as good, as standard English, and nothing to be seriously concerned over. Those who hold this view point out that English was originally a despised dialect spoken by a comparatively small number of rude and uncultivated people and that French is merely a corruption of Latin by those who could not learn it correctly.

It is quite true that English and French had these humble origins, but both languages, as they now stand, are the product of intelligence and culture, and the same thing is true of other languages, ancient and modern, that have played a prominent part in the world's history. A language is the reflection of the people who speak it. As they grow in understanding and taste, it becomes more capable of expressing thought and more beautiful. But always there are some speakers who lag behind this general advance. Those Americans who have done so, and who have the good sense to recognize their position, could do nothing better for themselves than to bend every effort to obtain a genuine mastery of those rules which the great body of intelligent and cultured English-speaking people have already made for the use of our mother tongue.

DISPUTED POINTS
AND
INDISPUTABLE ERRORS

XI

MANY bitter battles have been waged over points of English, and among them is the controversy over the pronunciation of "tomato." Shall it be "tomahto" or "tomayto?" Dictionaries commonly give both pronunciations, the new *Webster* giving the preference to "tomayto," but the *Century* and the *Standard*, rather strangely, putting "tomahto" in first place. I say rather strangely, for there is surely no question that the overwhelming majority of Americans say "tomayto," most of whom would rather die than change to "tomahto." The latter, however, prevails in a portion of Virginia,—the only part of the South where this is true—is rather common throughout the East, and is the accepted pronunciation in England. A few Americans to whom "tomayto" is natural have adopted "tomahto" with the idea that somehow it is a more "cultured" pronunciation.

It is amazing how eager some persons are to adopt a new pronunciation that is different from the one ordinarily used in their section of the country, with the idea that it will mark them as possessing breeding and cultivation. As a matter of fact, too great an eagerness in this direction proclaims the opposite to the world. The true aristocrat is tolerant of other people's pronunciations, and perfectly willing to admit even that they may be just as good as those to which he is accustomed, but he does not adopt them except for serious reason, such as the desire not to make himself unpleasantly conspicuous by his speech in a region where his mode of utterance is so unusual as to attract an immoderate amount of attention. This feeling has caused some Virginians who have made their homes in other sections to discard some of their characteristic speech-habits, such as the turning of "garden" into "gyarden," "car" into "cyar," and so on, and their peculiar pronunciation of words like "house" and "about," which I do not know how to put into print. Not all do this, of course. Some take pride in maintaining these marks of difference, and in others they are so ingrained that they could not drop them if they would. Fortunately for them—and for all of us—people are tolerant, and the speech of another section which sounds disgustingly affected when heard from the lips of those to whom it is unnatural, is quaintly pleasing in one to whom it is native.

"Either" and "neither"

The situation with regard to the pronunciation of the words "either" and "neither" is much the same as that of "tomato." In England "eyether" and "neyether" prevail—though not exclusively—in cultivated speech. It is noteworthy that one of the bishops who took part in the coronation of George VI used the pronunciation "neether." In America the majority is overwhelmingly in favor of "eether" and "neether," which are given first place in our dictionaries. But along the Eastern seaboard—not, however, in Virginia or anywhere else in the South—"eyether" and "neyether" may be heard with moderate frequency, particularly from people of the higher social classes and those who like to imitate them.

The use of "eyether" and "neyether" seems to be growing somewhat, but whether it is only a fad which will shortly die away, remains to be seen. It is still true that these pronunciations have an odd sound to the average American, who is likely to think that they are affected. An Irish-born friend, who himself says "eyether" and "neyether" told me once with considerable relish the following story:

> In the early days of the Far West a citizen of a small town encountered a crowd of cowboys who were dragging a man behind them, with the evident intention of lynching him.
>
> "Wait a minute, boys," he said. "What's he done?"
>
> "Stole a horse," was the answer.
>
> "Well, that's pretty bad, boys," said the citizen, "but we need more law in this town. Why not turn him over to the sheriff and give him a fair trial?"
>
> "Yes, pardner, but he shot the man that the horse belonged to, besides," replied the cowboys.
>
> "That's terrible, boys, but it's not your place to settle with him. Let the law do it."
>
> "Yes, but besides all that, he says 'eyether' and 'neyether!'"
>
> "Oh, well, take him on out, boys."

Then there is also the story of the Irishman who was asked whether he preferred "eether" or "eyether," and answered "ayther will do." This might well be true, for "ayther" was at one time an accepted pronunciation, though whether it survives in Ireland, I am unable to say. And a third story current about the words is that the pronunciations of "eyether" and "neyether" originated in the effort of courtiers to imitate King George I, who was a German, in his German pronunciation of the "ei," but the story, I believe, is without foundation.

President Roosevelt's use of "eyether" and "neyether" has probably done a great deal to bring this pronunciation to the attention of many to whom it has been quite unfamiliar. This is one of the few ways in which the speech of the president differs notably from that of the great mass of his fellow-countrymen, except, of course, that his language is much more careful and much more nearly free from errors than that of most of us. On the whole it sets an excellent example for the American people. When King George V, father of the present king of England, was on the throne, during Mr. Roosevelt's first administration, the two great English-speaking nations could congratulate themselves and each other on having as their rulers men whose manner of speech might well serve as a model to their respective peoples. King George had little or none of what Americans commonly call a British accent, and except for his British pronunciations—quite a different thing from "accent"—it would have been difficult to tell in what part of the English-speaking world he was reared.

A similar thing is true of Mr. Roosevelt. He has one or two pronunciations, such as the already mentioned "either" and "neither," and those of "again" and "against," which are out of line with the general tenor of American speech, but otherwise there is little to strike the listener as distinctly sectional or individualistic. There is no absolute, universally accepted standard for the use of the English language, and consequently no means of deciding just how closely the speech of a given man approaches perfection, but Mr. Roosevelt's speech would surely be considered as highly pleasing, even by the bitterest opponent of his policies. Its effectiveness in his "fireside talks" has been abundantly demonstrated.

Some adverse criticism has been made of the president's use of "like" as a conjunction in the expression "like I do." "As" is undoubtedly preferable here, but if Mr. Roosevelt wishes to argue the matter, he can point to Shakespeare, Darwin, Southey, Newman, Morris, and Hazlitt—all writers of good standing—who have used "like" as he did. Yet I would not urge my readers to imitate him in this respect—certainly not in writing, though "like" as a conjunction is considered by many to be reasonably good colloquial English.

I have listened with care to nearly all of Mr. Roosevelt's

radio addresses—though I am glad I live in a country where you can shut off the chief executive when you feel like it—and have read the published text of many of his speeches with an attention to grammatical details that has become almost automatic through years of studying, teaching, talking, and writing about the use of English, and I find little to criticize adversely. One rather delicate point to which exception might be taken is found in the following from one of his early speeches:

It has increased instead of diminished.

Or it may have been, "It has diminished instead of increased," but in either case the point is the same. I suspect that many of my readers will feel vaguely that something is wrong here, but will be at some loss to know what it is. The trouble is that "instead of" is a preposition and must have a noun, pronoun, or substantive of some kind as its object—not the word "diminished," which is a participle, or verbal adjective. The sentence should read, "It has increased instead of diminishing." And don't imagine that "diminishing" is a participle also, for it is not—not here at least. It is a gerund, or verbal noun. To be sure, it looks exactly like the present participle "diminishing," but its use is different.

The sentence might have been corrected in another way, however, that would have enabled us to retain the word "diminished." We might have said, "It has increased *rather than* diminished," and since "than" is a conjunction, not a preposition, the grammatical construction would have been correct. The clause which is introduced by "than" is regularly contracted. If we write it out in full here, the sentence would read, "It has increased rather than it has diminished."

Oddly enough, there appeared in a popular magazine not long ago an error which is the exact opposite of the one we have been discussing. Here is the passage:

Unsuitable for war in Ethiopia is the Fascist

black shirt, which absorbs heat rather than reflecting it.

This should be either, "which absorbs heat rather than
reflects it," or "which absorbs heat *instead of* reflecting it,"
and I trust the reasons for the changes are obvious. These
are fine points, I will readily admit, but I should like to ask
the reader whether he does not think that the sound of both
sentences is improved by the corrections, even though the
errors might have been previously unnoticed.

A word about the use of "than"

I said a moment ago that "than" is a conjunction. This
is an important point to bear in mind, for it is often incorrectly treated as a preposition. This explains why we say,
"He is taller than I," rather than "He is taller than me."
The full sentence would be, "He is taller than I am tall,"
though nobody ever completes it except for illustrations
like this. "Me" may correctly follow "than," however.
For instance, "He likes you better than me,"—that is to say,
"He likes you better than he likes me."

But regardless of the fact that "than" is a conjunction, we
never say "than who" in English. The established form is
"than whom," even though it is not logically correct. "He
is a man than whom there is none more fitted to receive the
honor," is the accepted, though inconsistent, way of putting it. "Than who" is reasonable, but simply not in use.

The most careful speakers and writers are inclined to
avoid the use of "than" after the words "different" and
"differently," though it is quite correct after "other,"
"otherwise," and "else," as well as after comparatives. "It
was no other than he," "I cannot do otherwise than trust
him," "What else than this could I do?" are all examples of
the proper use of the word. After "else" we probably hear
more frequently "but," as in "What else but this?" which is
illogical, but in good use.

The one word accepted unquestionably for use after

"different" and "differently" is "from," though "than" has its supporters and "different to" is fairly popular in England and has Fowler's approval as a natural idiom. "Things are different now than they used to be," is one way of putting what many people would prefer to see expressed as, "Things are different now *from what* they used to be." But "He acts differently than he used to act," is not so easily changed. We may make it: "He acts differently *from the way in which* he used to act," but this is quite a circumlocution— one which some will prefer to make, however, rather than use the obnoxious "than." There are many other ways of expressing the thought, of course; among them, "He does not act as he once did." When one is hesitating between a wording which, though unimpeachably correct, is cumbersome and one which is simpler, though doubtful, it is sometimes best to change the form of expression altogether.

A rather difficult situation arises concerning the use of "than" after the verb "prefer." Ordinarily we prefer something *to* something else. But suppose that the thing which we prefer and the thing to which we prefer it are both designated by infinitives, each of which begins with the word "to." Let us say, for instance, "I prefer to go at once to to wait till tomorrow." That will never do, of course, for, though it is perfectly logical, the combination of those two "to's" is horrible, and we instinctively and properly seek to avoid it. That is to say, our seeking is proper, but the manner of avoiding it is often highly improper. Some make it, "I prefer to go at once *than* to wait till tomorrow," but is unacceptable. "Than" alone just doesn't fit, though it would be possible to use "rather than," as I have done in the preceding paragraph, where I said, "which some will prefer to make, however, rather than use the obnoxious 'than.' "

One way of expressing the thought is, "I prefer to go at once to waiting till tomorrow." That sounds better than the version with the two "to's" but if we are to use the gerund "waiting" after the preposition, then it would be a much more symmetrical arrangement to express our preference with a gerund also, in which case the sentence would read:

"I prefer going at once to waiting," which is a very good way to put it. Another possibility would be simply to say, "I would rather go at once than wait till tomorrow."

The rather strange case of "like"

Considerable stress is usually laid in our schools on the fact that "than," being a conjunction, is in most instances followed by the nominative case of a pronoun. Pupils who say, "He is taller than me," are sharply corrected and told that it is properly "than I." Many of them unfortunately get the notion that the same thing is true after "like," and so proceed to say "like I," or—more often—"like John and I." I have even heard of an argument between college graduates over whether "like me" or "like I" is correct. Of course it is "like me," and also "like him," "like her," "like them," "like us," and "like whom." The word "like" is a preposition—or may be regarded as one—and hence must be followed by the objective case. To be strictly correct "like" is either a combination of adjective and preposition or one of adverb and preposition. We cannot say it is a pure preposition, for we are able to compare it, saying "liker" and "likest" or "more like" and "most like," which would be impossible with a pure preposition such as "of," for instance.

A childhood game will illustrate this double nature of "like." Perhaps children are too sophisticated for it now, but in my day it was considered great sport and a wonderful trick to play on the uninitiated. We rejoiced at finding some one who had never played it and inducing him to agree to respond "Just like me" to everything that was said to him, whereupon the following colloquy ensued:

"I went up one pair of stairs," says the initiated one.

"Just like me," agrees the uninitiated.

"I went up two pairs of stairs," continues the first.

"Just like me," repeats the second, and it goes on:

"I went into a room."

"Just like me."

"And looked out the window."

"Just like me."

"And saw a monkey." Now for the big moment——

"Just like me," innocently replies the other, and then what an outburst of unholy glee—unless indeed the second player is only pretending to be unfamiliar with the game and disappoints his interlocutor by cleverly replying, "Just like *you*," as sometimes used to happen.

The children don't know it, of course, but the trick depends on the grammatical fact that "like" is sometimes an adjective and sometimes an adverb, both in addition, of course, to being a preposition. In the first "Just like me" it is an adverb, modifying "went" understood, and a similar thing is true for all the others—in the mind of the speaker, at least. But in the last, it is possible to interpret "like" as an adjective modifying the noun "monkey"—indeed, that is the more reasonable interpretation, for "monkey" is the last word the interlocutor has used, and he seizes on it at once.

In passing, let me remark that "near" is likewise a combination of adjective or adverb with a preposition. And to avoid any possible confusion it is doubtless best to mention that "like" may also be a verb, as in "I like to swim," or a noun, as in "I shall not look upon his like again." Noun, verb, adjective, adverb, preposition, and even sometimes a conjunction, as we saw in the discussion of our president's speech,—a very good record for one little word and an extreme illustration of the way in which English turns one part of speech into another without making any change in the appearance of the word.

The pronunciation of "often"

The mention of the president brings to mind the fact that he has been criticized also for sounding the "t" in the word "often." The testimony of the new *Webster* on this point is very interesting. After giving the pronunciation without the "t," it adds a note: "The pronunciation 'of-ten,' until recently considered more or less illiterate, is not uncommon among the educated in some sections, and is often used in singing." This is, I think, a true representation of the situation. Nevertheless, it seems to me much better not to sound the "t" in "often." Does anyone sound it in "soften" or in "listen"? Let me venture a little rhyme in this regard:

> If your speech you would soften,
> Be sure to say "of'n,"
> For in this particular word,
> As in "castle" and "listen,"
> And others, like "glisten,"
> The "t" should be seen, but not heard.

Southerners are inclined to make a similar omission for a similar reason in words like "candle," "bundle," "handle," and "fondle," which they are likely to render as "can'le," "bun'le," "han'le," and "fon'le." This method of pronunciation has no support in the dictionaries, and is considered very slovenly by many people of other sections, especially New Englanders.

The combination "sc"

The letter "c" is nearly always silent in English in the combination "sci." Familiar words in which this is true are "scissors" and "science," and one not so familiar, but still not uncommon, is "rescind," pronounced, of course, "resind." In view of these words and others, I cannot help wondering why so many want to pronounce "scintillate" as "skintillate," when naturally it is "sintillate." And likewise the old Roman name "Scipio" is in English called "Sipio," not "Skipio," as some would make it. Similarly "scion" is called "sion." In the word "schism," neither the "c" nor the "h" is sounded, the pronunciation being "sism," though "sch" is usually pronounced as "sk" in English. For some peculiar reason, however,—at least it seems peculiar to Americans— the British insist on pronouncing the word "schedule" as if it were spelled "shedule." Possibly it is just a "sheme" on their part to confuse our "sholars." But we, as well as they, pronounce the word "schist," meaning a kind of rock, "shist."

Logically the words "Fascist" and "Fascism" ought to be pronounced in English "Fasist," and "Fasism," in accordance with the usual pronunciation of the combination "sci," and they are in fact pronounced in that way by some. But most people now say "Fashist" and "Fashism," which is more in accord with the Italian pronunciation, and is given first place in the new *Webster*.

If the reader will take a dime from his pocket—or from her handbag, as the case may be—he will find on one side a design which close inspection will reveal as a bundle of rods with the head of an old-fashioned axe (or "ax," if you prefer) protruding. In the days of ancient Rome such a bundle of rods was carried before magistrates on their walks through the streets, as a symbol of their power. The Roman name for it was *fasces*, the plural of the Latin word for "bundle," and it stood for the authority which the magistrates possessed to punish evil-doers—the rods for flogging and the axe for beheading. Just why this old Roman symbol of authority should have been put on an American coin is not quite clear to me, but it has for many years appeared on our dimes.

From the Latin *fasces* comes the Italian word *fascio*, meaning "club" or "organization," that is to say, a "bundle" of men. In the year 1919, when Mussolini's followers were organizing clubs all over Italy, they seized upon this word *fascio* to designate their local organizations, partly because of its Italian meaning and partly because it suggested the power and authority of those who once were preceded on their walks by the *fasces*. With these two ideas in mind they called themselves *Fascisti*—pronounced "fasheesti"—and from this word come the English "Fascist" and "Fascism."

Though Fascism, with its spirit of blind obedience to authority and relentless suppression of contrary opinion, has spread to other countries than Italy, it is noteworthy that it has as yet made little impression on the people of any English-speaking nation. Nor is it likely to do so if the temper of a nation may be judged by the character of its language. For English has stubbornly resisted all attempts to set up a dictatorship over it. Its speakers are widely scattered over the globe, and no group of them is willing to accept the authority of any other group to regulate its speech. The result is that in some instances it is difficult to say whether a given rule actually exists in English or not, and very frequently absurd to insist that a certain pronunciation is exclusively correct.

Under these circumstances the task of one who attempts to give advice upon the use of English is more than ordinarily difficulty. I propose to simplify mine, however, by frankly recognizing the differences of usage in the various parts of the English-speaking world, and am content frequently to point out these variations, without insisting that one of them is necessarily to take precedence over all the others. Uniformity is desirable, but it is false to assert it where it does not exist, and futile to attempt to force it on the people who speak English.

SOME MORE
MISTAKEN TEACHINGS

XII

ONE of the false rules with which some well-meaning people seek to restrain the freedom of the English language is the one that forbids the use of the word "whose" in the sense of "of which." "Whose," they say, like its nominative "who," should always apply to persons, never to inanimate objects. They insist that a sentence such as, "We gazed at the house, whose windows were lighted by the setting sun," should be revised to read, "We gazed at the house, the windows *of which* were lighted by the setting sun."

Yet the facts of the matter are that historically "whose" may apply to things as well as persons, that it is at present in good use in the sense of "of which," and that there are many cases in which for smoothness of wording it is decidedly preferable. Take the sentence just given, for instance. While the difference is not great, is not the effect of the use of "whose" more pleasing than that of "of which"? In sentences of a slightly different type, the improvement when "whose" is substituted is quite striking. Fowler, who argues strongly against the burdensome restrictions of this so-called rule, gives the following example:

It is a game of the rules of which I am quite ignorant.

Notice how much more smoothly it reads when we substitute "whose."

It is a game of whose rules I am quite ignorant.

Brevity, ease, and clearness are all on the side of the second version. Supported as it is by historic usage and the opinions of the dictionaries, why should anyone hesitate to use it? What valid reason supports the use of "of which" in such a case?

"Not so . . . as" vs. "not as . . . as"

But surely one of the strangest notions that ever existed about the use of English is one that is found frequently in the minds of those who consider themselves specialists on the subject—namely, that it is incorrect to say, "John is not as tall as Henry." They will accept such a statement in the affirmative. To "John is as tall as Henry" they offer no objection. But for no reason at all that I have ever been able to fathom, they assert that when the sentence is made negative, we must use "so" in place of "as" and make it read, "John is not *so* tall as Henry." I saw such a statement just the other day in—of all places—a magazine devoted to the correct use of English. No reason was given for it and no authority quoted except that of a book issued by the magazine.

There is, of course, no rule of this kind in English. If there are writers who wish to limit themselves in this way, we cannot prevent them, but there is certainly no general agreement among writers of reputation to that effect, nor has such a limitation the support of the dictionaries. The *Standard* says correctly, I think, that the use of "so" implies that the second member of the comparison has more than an ordinary amount of the quality in question. To put that in a simpler way, when we say, "John is not *so* tall as Henry," we imply that Henry is more than ordinarily tall, but when we say, "John is not *as* tall as Henry," we do not imply anything—Henry may be either very tall or unusually short.

I believe these are the interpretations that most English-speaking people would put on such statements. "The temperature is not so high as it was yesterday," implies that it was unusually high yesterday, but "not as high as yesterday" makes no implication.

"Imply" and "infer"

May I digress a moment to call attention to a remarkable thing about this word "imply," which I have just used? It is not used nearly as often as it ought to be, because "infer" is frequently—and erroneously—put in its place. The speaker or writer implies. The listener or reader infers. But how often do we hear or see a statement like, "Do you mean to infer that I am not telling the truth?" It should be, "Do you mean to imply . . ." or, if "infer" just must be used, "Do you mean *me* to infer that you think I am not telling the truth?" This use of "infer" has occurred so frequently that it is actually now listed in the new *Webster* in the sense of "imply," but I am happy to say that the editors mark it as "loose and erroneous."

The case of "literally"

Another word that has been misused so often as to gain dictionary recognition of its misuse is "literally," which really means "actually," "with close adherence to the meaning of the word," "*not figuratively*." Yet I suspect that most people now use it in the sense of "figuratively," the exact opposite of its true meaning. "I was literally scared to death," some one says, but if he had been literally scared to death, he would be dead and unable to tell us about it. What he means is, "I was scared so badly that I can best express it by saying that I was scared to death, though of course I do not expect you to believe that I am really dead." "He literally burned up the course," said a news dispatch of Lawson Little's golfing triumph in England a few years ago, but of course Mr. Little did nothing of the kind. He merely played such excellent golf that the reporter thought he could best convey the idea by saying that he burned up the course— that is to say, by using a metaphor, a figure of speech, in other words speaking *figuratively*. Yet, although he knows well he *is* speaking figuratively and knows that the reader knows it, he deliberately tells us that he is not speaking figuratively, but literally. It is an amazing situation. Of course most people who now use "literally" in this way never think of its true meaning, but regard it simply as a convenient intensive word to make what they say more vivid. But how did the misuse originate? The new *Webster* says that it is used "hyperbolically" in this way. "Hyperbolically" means in the manner of a hyperbole, and the hyperbole is a figure of speech in which one consciously exaggerates for the sake of effect—not to deceive. But to assure the reader that one is not exaggerating is a strange way of exaggerating.

"Crazy" and "fond"

Yet exaggeration in speech is more or less common in all languages and all ages. Women are particularly given to it, for they are more concerned than men that what they say shall be interesting. But exaggeration eventually ruins itself. Listeners make allowances for it, and realize that when some one is said to have been "perfectly furious," the chances are that he was merely slightly displeased. "I'm crazy about it," means "I am slightly fond of it." But the remarkable thing is that "fond" itself originally meant "foolish." We still use it in that sense in the phrase "a fond delusion," which does not mean a delusion that one is fond of, but a foolish delusion. So "I'm fond of it" meant originally "I'm foolish about it," in other words, "I like it so well that reason is upset," which is exactly the thought in "I'm crazy about it." "Fond" is now interpreted, however, as merely implying a mild liking, but it is in good use, while "crazy" in the sense we are speaking of is highly undignified, to say the least.

"Either" in the sense of "both"

A great many people are disturbed by the fact that the word "either" is more or less frequently used in the sense of "both," whereas they feel that it properly means "the one *or* the other," rather than "the one and the other." Yet the fact is that the meaning to which they offer objection is very old, well established in literature, and supported by the dictionaries. Stevenson wrote:

> Dark brown is the river, golden is the sand;
> It flows along forever, with trees on *either* hand.

And Tennyson in *The Lady of Shalott:*

> On *either* side the river lie
> Long fields of barley and of rye.

It is true, of course, that the meaning "the one or the other" is now more common, and it would probably be better if we should let the other die, substituting "each" or "both," when we wish to express the thought. But it will certainly survive in poetry for a long time, for the poet sometimes needs a word of two syllables for the sake of his meter. After all, no great harm is ordinarily done by using the word in this sense, for the meaning will, I believe, always be clear except in certain situations. As long as we admit both senses, it will be doubtful what we mean when we ask, "Are there trees on either side of the river?" On the whole, we should doubtless do well to leave the meaning of "both" or "each" to the poets, though it is a mistake to assert that the use of "either" in this sense is incorrect.

"I don't think so"

Another very common English expression to which objection is sometimes offered is "I don't think so," or the same idea in a slightly different form as found in sentences like, "I don't think I shall go." The really correct expressions, according to the objectors, are "I think not," and "I think I shall not go." Logically they are right. The one who says, "I don't think I shall go," really means "I think I shall not go." While his statement is actually true, it does not accurately express his thought. Nevertheless it is the established conversational habit of millions of cultured English-speaking people to put the matter in this way, and I do not see how anybody could possibly be misled by it. Those who teach that such expressions are not good English are laboring under the delusion that good English must be strictly logical. But neither English nor any other language has ever been so, and surely their time would be much better employed if it were devoted to the uprooting of the numerous expressions that, while strictly logical, are nevertheless actual errors in speech, since they do not accord with cultivated usage.

"*The reason why*"

Another expression which is often condemned as incorrect because it is slightly illogical is "the reason why." Yet the dictionaries list it as reputable English, and it is no more illogical than "the place where" or "the time when." Let us consider for a moment the sentence:

There is no reason why you should be afraid.

"Why" so used means "on account of which reason," and there is hence some repetition in the sentence, since it is the same as saying, "There is no reason on account of which reason you should be afraid." If we want to express the thought without any repetition, we shall say, "There is no reason on account of which you should be afraid," but this is somewhat stilted. Those who object to "the reason why" generally prefer to put it, "There is no reason *that* you should be afraid," which I think is permissible, but not any improvement over the use of "why." Notice that it throws quite a burden on "that," making it equivalent to "on account of which." It is true that we burden "that" in this way in other expressions, but on logical grounds it is as objectionable—though in the opposite way—as is the expression "the reason why."

I have said that this expression is no more illogical than "the time when" and "the place where." When analyzed, these mean respectively "the time at which time" and "the place at which place," giving the same repetition which we found in "the reason why." Yet nobody, to the best of my knowledge, has ever objected to either of them. The truth is that all three expressions are well established in English and there seems to be no really vital *reason why* they should not be used in any *place where* they are appropriate at any *time when* the speaker or writer sees fit.

"Sturdy indefensibles"

There are, however, a number of expressions frequently heard among English-speaking people in which the illogicality is so glaring that those who have any regard at all for the claims of logic should certainly try to avoid them. How often do we hear people say things like this:

> Don't spend any more than you can help.

Yet what they really mean is, "Don't spend any more than you *can't* help," and their hearers so interpret it. Now by what mental process do they succeed in saying the exact opposite of what they mean? I think it must arise from a confusion of two ways of putting the same thought. One is, "Don't spend any money that you can help (that is, "keep from") spending," and the other, "Don't spend any more than you have to." To such contradictions of the thought by the words Fowler has applied the name "sturdy indefensibles"—"sturdy" in that they have persisted for generations even in the speech of the cultured, and obviously entirely "indefensible" from the standpoint of logic.

Another "indefensible" is:

> He is the ablest of any man I know.

"Of any man" obviously means "of all the men," and is probably used because the speaker is thinking of, "He is abler than any man I know," which would be another way of saying the same thing.

And a somewhat similar one is:

> He is the man of all others for the place.

Here I think the confusion is between, "He is the man of all men for the place," and "He is the man better fitted than all others." Milton uses a similar expression when he calls Eve "the fairest of her daughters," and other good authority may be found for it, but it is nevertheless better to avoid it and let it die, if it will.

Phrases with "but"

There are several phrases containing the word "but" which are rather well established in either literary or colloquial usage but are open to question from the standpoint of logic, and hence are frequently condemned—like others discussed in this chapter—by teachers and textbook writers who are unaware of their real standing. "But" may correctly be used to mean "that . . . not" in questions and negative statements, as in the following quotation from Swinburne:

> Who knows *but* on their sleep may rise
> Such light as never Heaven let through?

And "but that" is likewise used with the same meaning, though it is evident that the "that" is superfluous. Yet we find it in regular literary use, as a line from one of Tennyson's most touching passages will show. It is spoken by Arthur in his farewell to Guinevere:

> . 　　　Let no man dream *but that* I love thee still.

And "but what" is used colloquially with the same meaning, as in "Who knows but what he might come tomorrow?" This is surely complicating the matter enough, but as I feel that it would be unfair not to give my readers full information on these rather confused matters, I must add that often after verbs of doubting and fearing that are used with a negative, "but" and "but that" are used to mean simply "that" —not "that not" as in the preceding. Here is a quotation from Ruskin that will show what I mean:

I do not doubt *but that* you are surprised.

It seems to me, however, that in such expressions it would be much better to eliminate the word "but" and simply say, "I do not doubt that you are surprised," which is equally idiomatic and much more reasonable.

And still another phrase of this kind is "cannot help but," as in the sentence, "I cannot help but think you are mistaken." I judge that this must arise from a confusion of "I cannot but think you are mistaken," and "I cannot help thinking you are mistaken." This latter is, in the opinion of most authorities, the better way to put it.

"That long nose of yours"

Expressions like "a friend of mine," "that brother of his," "that long nose of yours," and so on, have given much trouble to many people. On the surface they are double possessives, since they combine a possessive pronoun with "of," and the one who analyzes them for the first time is likely to consider therefore that they are incorrect. But they have long existed in English, and are so thoroughly reputable that grammarians approve them and exert considerable effort to explain how they came about. One explanation frequently given is that "a friend of mine" means "a friend in the number of mine," that is to say, "one of my friends," or "a friend among my friends." This is plausible for this particular expression and some others, but breaks down completely with "that long nose of yours," for surely that does not mean, "that long nose among your noses."

It is very sad to see that the usually keen-minded Fowler has branded "that long nose of yours" and similar expressions as "sturdy indefensibles," because they cannot be explained on the basis of "a friend of mine," just given. But

Fowler has failed entirely to grasp the rationale (pronounced "rashuNAYlee") of the idiom. So have most English grammarians, for that matter, and it has remained for a Dane, Jespersen, whom I have previously referred to, to give the true explanation. He points out very keenly that the "of" in expressions of this kind does not denote possession, but is the appositional "of," such as is used in the expression, "the city of New York," which really means "the city New York." Let it be noted that all the phrases of which we are speaking are brought about by the need of modifying a noun by a word like "a," "the," "this," "that," "these," or "those" and by a possessive like "my," "your," "his," "her," "our," or "their." We want to say, for instance, both "a friend" and "my friend," but we cannot very well make it "a my friend," so we say "a friend" and then join "mine" to it by this appositional "of." We choose "mine" rather than "my," because "mine" is the pronoun form which does not need a following noun, as does "my." Similarly, we wish to say "that long nose" and "your long nose," and not being able to say "that your long nose," we make it "that long nose of yours."

Logic and language

The reader who is unfamiliar with other languages—and there are proportionately many more readers of this sort in America than in Europe—may conclude from what has been said in this chapter that English is alone in the use of idioms that are illogical. Yet such things are found in all languages. In ancient Greek, for example, double and triple negatives were common, the idea being that the more negatives one used, the more strongly negative was his sentence. This, to be sure, was once true in English. Chaucer, who lived about five hundred years ago has these two lines in description of the knight in *The Canterbury Tales:*

> He nevere yet no vileinye ne sayde
> In al his lyf unto no manner wight.

Put into modern speech this would be, "He never yet did not say no unbecoming word in all his life to no sort of person," in which four negatives are used with the meaning of one, the present-day version being, "He never yet said an unbecoming word in all his life to any sort of person."

As English has sloughed off this illogicality, so we may expect that, in the course of time, it will rid itself of others. Meanwhile we may well do what we can to hasten the process, without getting unduly excited or mistakenly insisting that a given expression is a piece of bad English merely because it does not strictly conform to the rules of logic. And let us by all means examine a suspected expression with care before we condemn it, for if we do so, we shall frequently find that beneath a surface of apparent whimsicality there is a deeper, finer logic in our English idioms.

SOME TROUBLESOME VERBS,
AND A FEW WORDS
ON SLANG

XIII

THE variety of English speech is strikingly exemplified by the fact that a certain very simple act that ordinarily marks the beginning of the life of the day for each of us may be told of in the following ways:

> I woke
> I woke up
> I waked
> I waked up
> I awoke
> I awaked
> I wakened
> I awakened

All eight of these mean exactly the same thing, all are approved by the dictionaries, all are in good modern use. The forms with "up" are conversational rather than literary, and "woke" is rather more common than "waked." The forms "awoke," "awaked," "wakened," and "awakened" are more likely to be reserved for writing or formal speech, but by no means confined to them. All eight may be heard in conversation—if you listen for them—and all eight may be found in literature.

This amazing embarrassment of riches calls for a more systematic treatment than is usually accorded to it in English textbooks. Many educated people find themselves in some perplexity as to the proper or best form to use in the various tenses of these verbs, and the only way to relieve it, as far as I can see, is to take each of the four verbs and set down its principal parts, with discussion where it is called for. The principal parts of a verb in English are often considered to be the present tense (indicative), the past tense (indicative), and the past participle—as for instance, *sing, sang, sung*. It would be somewhat more accurate to say that the first part is the infinitive (without "to"), though the difference is of little practical importance, for in all verbs but one the present tense is exactly the same as the infinitive except, of course, that in the third person singular of the present "s" or "es" is added, as in "sings" and "goes." The one verb whose infinitive differs from its present is "to be," the present of which is "I am," "you are," and so on.

Here then are the principal parts of the four verbs that mean "wake":

Present	Past	Past Participle
wake	*woke* or *waked*	*waked*, preferably *woke*, possibly *woken*, not good in America, but has some vogue in England.
awake	*awoke* or *awaked*	*awaked*, preferably *awoke*, possibly *awoken*, said by the new *Webster* to be obsolete, but possibly still in use in England.
waken	*wakened*	*wakened*
awaken	*awakened*	*awakened*

The reader who remembers his grammar will note that "waken" and "awaken" are "regular" verbs, since they form both the past tense and the past participle by adding "ed," while "wake" and "awake" have a strange confusion of regular and irregular forms. Why don't the grammarians clear up this mess, do away with needless forms and reduce it all to regularity? This is no doubt what many readers will ask. But let them remember that, speaking generally, *grammarians do not make grammar*. The people make it, and the grammarians' task is to record it. Now and then the grammarians do exert some influence and bring about some slight changes in the language, but in the long run the language is under the control of the people who speak it— and no people are more jealous of their prerogatives and less inclined to follow the mandates of the grammarians than we who speak English.

"Sit" and "set"

With regard to the verbs meaning "wake" it should be noticed also that any one of the four may be used either with or without an object. You may wake, awake, waken, or awaken all by yourself, and after you have done so, you may wake, awake, waken, or awaken somebody else. In the language of the grammarians, the four verbs are both transitive and intransitive. But there is a pair of verbs which are often confused with each other, when they should be distinguished by the fact that one of them takes an object while the other does not. They are "sit" and "set," and here are their parts:

Present	Past	Past Participle
sit	sat	sat
set	set	set

It is "set," of course, that takes the object. When you set, you always set something, though there is an apparent exception to this rule when we say that the sun, moon, and stars set, and supply no object. The explanation is that when we say, "The sun sets," we mean "The sun sets itself," and in characteristic English fashion we discard the word "itself" and merely understand it. Those who have studied German and French have doubtless noticed how often these languages use the word "self" where it would be omitted in English. A Frenchman or a German says that he shaves himself and bathes himself, whereas an English-speaking person merely shaves and bathes.

There is considerable discussion in English over the question whether hens sit or set. The answer is that grammarians' hens sit, while those of farmers set. Unfortunately grammarians have very few hens compared with those owned by farmers, so that the large majority of hens set—in the opinion of their owners, at least. But, though the grammarians are handicapped in the matter from a practical standpoint, a careful consideration will show that they have the better of the argument technically. The farmers cannot even claim that the hen sets herself, like the sun, for when they speak of a "setting" hen, they do not refer to the act of setting herself on the nest, but to her continued sitting there for the period of three weeks necessary to hatch the eggs. She is, therefore, not really a setting hen, but a sitting hen, though I very greatly fear that she will never be so referred to on the farm.

"Lay" and "lie"

But the confusion between "sit" and "set" is nothing compared to that of "lay" and "lie." The ignorance concerning these two verbs seems to me to be little short of a national scandal. In a recent issue of one of our most prominent magazines this sentence appeared in the midst of an article describing the author's childhood in—of all places—Boston:

Gravely and kindly he *lay* the case before me.

"Lay" should of course be "laid," and the difference between the two words is so great as to preclude, I think, the possibility of a typographical slip. But it seems incredible that such a glaring error could have been made by the writer, passed by the editor, and overlooked by the proof-reader. To write or say "lay" for "laid" is not, of course, the usual error, for it is more frequently the other way, a great many people saying, "He laid there," for "He lay there." Perhaps it was an effort to avoid this mistake that caused its opposite. But it is surprising how many Americans say they are laying when they are really lying.

There is some excuse for the confusion between these verbs, however, for we have the peculiar situation that "lay" is at the same time the present tense of the verb "lay" and the past tense of "lie." Let us present the principal parts of the two:

LIE (never takes an object)

Present	Past	Past Participle
lie	lay	lain

LAY (always takes an object)

Present	Past	Past Participle
lay	laid	laid

The statement that "lay" is the past tense of "lie" needs a little discussion. The past tense in English—like the present, indeed—has three forms, known respectively as the regular past, the progressive past, and the emphatic past. "I lay" is the regular past of "to lie," "I was lying" is the progressive past, and "I did lie" is the emphatic past. "I lay" is also the regular *present* tense of "to lay," "I am laying" is the progressive present, and "I do lay" the emphatic present. Perhaps a series of sentences in which the various forms of these verbs are correctly used will be the best means of meeting questions that are forming in the minds of readers. Those who are satisfied with their knowledge on these troublesome points may omit them, but others would do well to read them over carefully several times:

He lies down, he is lying down, he was just lying down as I entered. The book lay there on the floor, where it had been lying for two days, or where it had lain for two days. Has it lain so long? Will it be lying there tomorrow? Did you lay it there? Who laid it there, if you did not? When was it laid there? Why have you laid it there? It was not lying there a while ago when I entered, and I saw you laying it there. Will you lay it there again?

It would be quite possible for one to use "lay" and "lie" correctly who had no knowledge whatever of technical grammar, but not, I think, if he had once become confused on them. In that case there is nothing better than to go as deeply as possible into the grammar of the situation to learn exactly why a certain form is the proper one in the circumstances. And this applies in general to all types of mistakes. No one ever learned to speak correctly by the study of grammar alone. But to deny that it is of any aid to correct speech—as some do—is a patent absurdity. A large part of the trouble in the present situation, however, is due to the fact that our students in general get just a smattering of grammar—just enough to make them an easy prey to the multitude of superstitions that are gravely taught in the name of good English. I believe we are going to find that we had better give up grammar entirely or go into it more thoroughly. But since its most bitter opponents admit that a certain amount of it is desirable, there seems nothing left except for our schools to attempt to give their pupils a really adequate knowledge of it.

Before we leave the subject of "lay" and "lie" completely, it ought to be remarked that there is, of course, another verb "to lie," meaning "to tell a lie," which has no connection with the one we have been discussing, and is perfectly regular, its principal parts being *lie, lied, lied.* And since I have mentioned it, it occurs to me to present to my readers a very remarkable puzzle involving the use of words that has come down to us from ancient times. Suppose a man makes the rather unusual statement, "I am lying," meaning "I am telling a lie." Now, if he is lying, he is telling the truth, for he *says* he is lying. But if he is telling the truth, he is lying. Obviously, however, he cannot do both in the same statement. Is he, then, lying or telling the truth? This is not really a point of English, for the dilemma would be the same in any language. The difficulty arises from the fact that the man who says "I am lying" is attempting to make a statement and to give a judgment as to its truth or falsity in the very words of the statement itself. Such a double feat is an impossibility. We cannot pass judgment on the truth or falsity of a statement till *after* the statement is made, so that the declaration "I am lying" is merely a piece of non-sense. It has no meaning, though it seems to have one, and consequently cannot be said either to be true or to be false.

And then the question arises whether we shall say "the lay of the land" or "the lie of the land." According to the new *Webster* both expressions are in good use, though "the lie of the land" would seem more reasonable, since the meaning is apparently "the way in which the land lies." And another expression that needs some comment is "to lay waste." "Waste" is here an adjective, not a noun, as many seem to think. "The enemy laid waste the country," is the way to put it, not "laid waste *to* the country." Then there is the expression "to lay for" someone, meaning to watch for an opportunity to trap him, to injure him, or to take revenge on him. Since there is no object, it would seem that the verb should be "lie," but that is never used, and the new *Webster* records "to lay for" as a colloquialism, which means, as I have indicated before, a term considered good or reasonably good in ordinary conversation, but not best for use in formal, dignified speech or writing.

Language and clothing

It is sometimes a little hard to distinguish between col-loquialisms and slang. The difference is that colloquialisms are in general used by all classes and last for generations, while slang is found mostly in the speech of the young or the sport-loving and is likely to be of short life. Slang might, indeed, be called the sport-clothes of speech, and colloquialisms would then correspond to the informal garments which we wear when lounging around home. Evening dress is literary English, the language of poetry and of the most dignified prose, speech at its best. Nothing else is equal to it, but it would be inappropriate for the ordinary life of the workaday world. For this we need good English, to be sure, but of the type found in the best newspapers and in magazines not distinctly literary. But to what shall we compare illiterate speech, which abounds in glaring errors of grammar and pronunciation? It resembles nothing so much as those dirty, ragged, buttonless garments which no self-respecting person will wear under any conditions, even if there is no one else to see him. There is never a time or place when it is appropriate.

There is one point in which this parallelism between clothes and the use of English is very striking. We have in America many people who suddenly acquire wealth—*nouveaux riches* (pronounced "noovo reesh") is the French term for them. Some of them know instinctively or rapidly acquire the art of dressing well, while others seem to think that it is the duty of people with money to make as big a display as possible, and that those costumes are the best which attract the most attention. Their counterparts in the field of speech are those who without any cultural background acquire a knowledge—or a pseudo-knowledge—of some of the rules of English, take perhaps a course in expression, adopt a few entirely unnatural pronunciations along with an artificial manner of speech, sedulously avoid a few natural English idioms which they believe to be "incorrect," and ignorantly imagine that they are among the leading exponents of the use of good English. They might be quietly ignored if it were not that many people who properly and sincerely wish to improve their own use of the language take them at their own valuation on the assumption that surely no one would speak so strangely without adequate reason, and either mistakenly try to imitate them or being repelled by their artificiality, decide resignedly that "good

English" is not for them, and cease their efforts toward improvement.

But the art of wearing clothes correctly is far easier to acquire than a cultured speech. A great many Americans who dress with excellent taste and build themselves beautiful and beautifully furnished homes use English that is shamefully out of keeping with their general mode of living. If language could be ordered like a suit of clothes, or built once and for all like a house, instead of having to be made and remade momentarily as it is used, their speech would no doubt show a similar amazing improvement.

Slang

The use of slang is looked upon by some people as typically American, but slang is found in all countries and in all languages. It—the British variety, of course—is in rather better standing in England than in America, and the French have a great abundance of it.

I have heard that some years ago one of the Chicago newspapers took a vote of its readers to find whether they preferred to have the sporting news written in slang or standard English, and a very strange thing happened. The majority of the professors of the University of Chicago who voted on the question were in favor of slang, while most of the baseball players and others directly connected with sports preferred standard English. The reason for these seemingly contradictory preferences will, I believe, explain why slang exists at all—and that reason is in short the human desire for something new. To the college professors, whose daily life and work brought them in contact with serious and dignified English in books, magazines, and conversation, the slang of the sporting pages was something new and fresh; it had a kick in it, as the slang phrase goes. But the baseball players heard and talked slang all day long; to them it was standard English that had the kick.

A similar, but apocryphal, incident concerns a father who became distressed over the amount of slang used by his young son and engaged a tutor whose speech was particularly choice to take the boy out into the woods for a camping trip, in the hope that when he was away from his slang-using associates, he would pick up the good English of his companion. When at the end of a month the two campers returned, they were greeted with fond expectation by the father, who said:

"Well, I trust you had a good time and accomplished your purpose." To this the tutor replied:
"You said a jawful; *I'll* say we did."

Sometimes the difference in form between slang and good English is very slight. It may be a mere matter of accent. "POSitively" is good English; "posiTIVEly" is slang. "Believe me" is good English; "believe ME" is slang. Take the first line of Thomas Moore's beautiful song, "Believe me, if all those endearing young charms . . ." and read it "Believe ME," and so on. You will remember that the stanza ends, "thou wouldst still be adored as this moment thou art, let thy loveliness fade as it will . . ." but when we start with "Believe ME," we should naturally expect the conclusion to be something like: "Well, all I gotta say is, 'You would still look good to me, kid.' "

In introducing a pianist on the radio, the versatile Mr. Deems Taylor stated that because of the peculiarities of the English language he might say either that the gentleman was no mean piano player or that he was a mean piano player, both expressions having the same significance. This is true, but it is well to remember that the second use is slang of recent origin, while the first is well-established English. In the King James Version of the Bible, the words of the Apostle Paul are given to the effect that he was a citizen of Tarsus, "no mean city." This was the language of three hundred years ago, 1611 being the date of the issuance of the King James Version. Do you suppose that three hundred years from now the expression "a mean piano player" will be understood as it is at present? It is hardly likely. The chances are that even thirty years from now it will be so out of date as to excite the laughter of those who will at that time constitute the younger generation and who will think it quaint that their staid fathers and mothers ever used such a ridiculous expression and one so far inferior to the bright bits of slang that they will be using at that time.

How many readers can remember when it was the latest thing to say, "Twenty-three for you—Skidoo!" About thirty years ago this was the expression used by the cleverest and most brilliant of the younger generation to indicate that they desired the speedy departure of the one addressed. It was the acme of cleverness and brought forth loud and prolonged laughter whenever it was uttered, which was about once in every half-hour. It almost seemed, to paraphrase the language of Shakespeare, that age could not wither it, nor custom stale its infinite variety. Yet now it is only a memory and a legend.

And so it is with all slang—or nearly all. One expression in a thousand survives, becomes really an addition to the language. The other nine hundred and ninety-nine pass and are forgotten. The only real danger from slang comes from the inability of some of us to distinguish it from good English. It is permissible to use it when the occasion is fitting and when one knows he is using it, just as it is sometimes permissible to violate the conventions of polite society for a definite purpose. But the one who ignorantly breaks the rules either of society or of English is likely to be secretly pitied, even if not openly laughed at.

We need not be alarmed if our young people seem to be unduly fond of that style of speech whose chief charm is its freshness and novelty, for, with the passage of time, constant repetition will dull this freshness, and their beloved phrases will, to quote again from Shakespeare, come to seem "weary, flat, stale, and unprofitable." Then they will turn in relief to that form of English whose richness and power have survived all the changing fashions of the years.

MORE ABOUT FALSE TEACHINGS
AND NEEDLESS HAIR-SPLITTING

XIV

THE expression "to enjoy oneself" is fairly common in English, though sometimes adversely criticized by those who mistakenly expect idioms to be logical. "Did you enjoy yourself at the party last night?" asks the mother of the daughter, and these critics say that she should ask, "Did you enjoy the party?" Nevertheless the expression has the support of good usage and is duly recorded in the dictionaries. Similar expressions are very common in French, German, and Spanish, as those who have attempted to master the use of these so-called "reflexive" verbs in those languages can testify. And perhaps, after all, we do generally enjoy ourselves, whatever may be the apparent source of the enjoyment, so that the idiom is not as illogical as it sounds.

Another usage that is frowned upon—and by persons with more knowledge of English than those who object to the one we have been discussing—is the employment of the word "anxious" in the sense of "eager," as, for instance, in the sentence, "I am anxious to see him," uttered under circumstances in which the speaker feels no special anxiety or fear of not seeing the one of whom he is speaking. "I am eager to see him," is the way in which English textbooks usually say that the thought should be expressed. "Eager" does seem a better word in this connection, but the dictionaries give one meaning of "anxious" as "earnestly desirous," and their definitions of both words indicate that there is little room for choice between them in such a sentence. Surely the average person is not greatly to blame if he fails to make such a nice discrimination in ordinary conversation.

"Nice" and "fine"

English texts likewise usually make a great to-do over the common habit of applying the words "nice" and "fine" to any and every person or thing that pleases us, as when we speak of a nice day, a fine man, a nice time, a fine book, nice weather, a fine shot, and so on and so on. They would have us speak of a pleasant day, an honorable man, an enjoyable time, an interesting or inspiring book, bright weather, a skillful shot—and when it is a question of the careful wording of some important piece of writing or dignified spoken matter, they are eminently right. But I fear that they leave the impression on our pupils that there is something wholly incorrect about the employment of the words "nice" and "fine," as the average person uses them. If so, they are wrong, for the dictionaries support these uses, and common sense tells us that it is too much to expect of the ordinary person with no particular literary gift that he pause in his conversation to select the one word that would most accurately express his thought. Many people will be doing exceedingly well if they can be induced to refrain from designating as "swell" everything that strikes their fancy.

Writers on English and teachers of the subject frequently do great harm to the cause that they are trying to serve by seeming to expect more than is reasonable. It is well to hold up high ideals, but not well to make people feel that their situation is hopeless if they are not able to express themselves in the manner of trained and gifted writers, not well to urge upon them the niceties of language before they are ready for them. In that word "nicety," incidentally, we have the earlier meaning of "nice," the sense for which the English books usually plead, and the one in which I was employing it in a previous paragraph, when I spoke of a "nice discrimination." Here the word is obviously used in the sense of "exact" or "accurate." Yet this is by no means its original meaning, for that, strange to say, is "ignorant," the word being ultimately derived from the Latin *nescius*. The process by which it changed its significance from "ignorant" to "accurate" and finally to "pleasing" is a remarkable study in the shifting of meanings and will be a revelation to those who have imagined that a certain meaning is inherent and permanent in a certain word. From "ignorant" it came to mean "unwise," then "imprudent," then "foolish," then "fastidious," then "particular," then "exact," then "delicate," then "fine," then "agreeable," then "pleasing." Notice that while the jump from "ignorant" to "pleasing" is almost incredible, the change in meaning in the various steps is comparatively slight. An ignorant person is, of course, usually also unwise, imprudent, and foolish. His foolishness may show itself by his being fastidious or particular in an unwarranted way. But one may sometimes wisely and rightly be particular and pay attention to detail, and we speak of him in praise as exact and say perhaps that he has a delicate taste or touch. Delicate things are likely to be fine and valuable, therefore agreeable and pleasing. Notice, too, that the meaning of "nice" runs into that of "fine" on the way, though "fine" meant originally "finished," and the two go on together to become "pleasing" in popular speech. Surely we could never have imagined that such a transformation would be possible, but our scholars assure us it is true.

"Slow" and "loud"

Many people who are careful in their speech are offended by our numerous highway signs that read "Drive slow," and insist that they should be altered to read "Drive slowly." I wonder why it never occurs to them to look into the dictionaries with regard to this point. If they ever do so, they will find that "slow" is in excellent standing as an adverb. It cannot, indeed, take the place of "slowly" in every connection, but in some circumstances it is just as good or possibly better. Fowler says that it is appropriate wherever slowness is the main idea to be expressed—and this is exactly the situation in the warning, "Drive SLOW!" On the other hand it would never do to say, "As we were slow driving down the street," for here the main idea is in the word "driving," and since the slowness is merely incidental, it should be, "As we were *slowly* driving down the street."

A similar thing is true of "loud," which is often an adjective, but may be used as an adverb as well as "loudly." We may say, "Speak loud," or "Speak loudly," but "Speak loud," it seems to me is more common and more forceful. Yet in, "He went around loudly proclaiming his own virtues," only "loudly" would do.

Adjectives that end in "ly"

It is true, of course, that "ly" is often added to an adjective to turn it into an adverb, as in the case of "rapid" and "rapidly," for instance. From this undoubted fact, many people have acquired two false notions: first, that every adverb ends in "ly," and second, that every word that ends in "ly" is an adverb. It was the first of these that must have caused a teacher to say once in my hearing, "The ice cream is melting *fastly*," which is absurd. "Fast" is both the adjective and the adverb, and there is no such word as "fastly" in present-day use. "First" is also both adjective and adverb, and as the latter is better than "firstly."

A great many of the "ly" words are adjectives, as may be seen from the following list, which I am not attempting to make complete: lovely, friendly, ugly, surly, curly, burly, sisterly, brotherly, fatherly, motherly, masterly, kingly, queenly, weekly, monthly, quarterly, yearly, early, timely, courtly, manly, womanly.

All these that pertain to time—those from "weekly" to "early"—may be used both as adjectives and as adverbs, but another "ly" must be added to the others to make them into adverbs. "Friendly," for instance, becomes "friendlily," the first "y" changing to "i" when the suffix is added. In some instances, however, the addition of this "ly" would make an awkward word, and then our recourse is to a phrase. We can hardly say, for example, "She spoke to him sister-lily," so we make it, "in a sisterly manner."

"Kindly" is another word that may be either adjective or adverb. In the well-known hymn, "Lead, kindly light," it is an adjective, as the punctuation shows. A shift in the position of the comma, however, turning it into "Lead kindly, light," would make it an adverb.

"Did you hear from him today?"

In an advertisement for a course in English, appearing in the magazines not long ago, the sentence "Did you hear from him today?" was given as an example of the errors that uninstructed people make. According to the advertisement, it should have been, "Have you heard from him to-day?" It seems to me that this is the misapplication of a sound principle to a particular instance. "Did you hear from him today?" probably means "Did you hear from him in today's mail?" that is, at a particular time, since there usually is a particular time, or certain particular times, at which we expect to hear from our friends. If this is true, "Did you hear from him today?" is no more incorrect than "Did you hear from him last month?" Surely there are enough real errors to correct without thinking up these false ones.

The sound principle misapplied in this instance is that when a verb refers to no particular time in the past, but includes the whole of the past to the very moment of speech, "have" is the auxiliary to be used, not "did." In other words, the perfect tense, rather than the past, is the one needed. This is particularly true when the word "yet" is used, for this word very definitely indicates that the time referred to extends up to the present. Pupils sometimes ask their teachers, "Did you grade the papers yet?" when it should of course be, "Have you graded the papers yet?" Similarly, "Did he leave yet?" should be "Has he left yet?" though it is quite correct to ask "Did he leave yesterday?" for there a definite time is indicated.

There are those who insist that the perfect is likewise necessary with "ever," but it does not seem to me that this word brings the time so clearly up to the present as "yet" does. "Did you ever see such a sight?" is really more common than "Have you ever seen such a sight?" and I do not believe that its sound is offensive to anyone except those who have been taught that the perfect must always be used with "ever." In like manner we say very naturally, "I never saw him before," meaning "never at any time in my past life," and while "I have never seen him before," would be also correct, it seems to me to be needless hair-splitting to insist that it is the only suitable way of expressing the thought. In his wonderful poem on death, *Prospice*, Browning says, "I was ever a fighter, so one fight more, the best and the last." Notice that he uses the past "was" instead of the perfect, "have been," even though it is evident that he is still a fighter, since he wants to fight again. Certainly in ordinary speech it is no mark of lack of culture or lack of feeling for the English idiom to use the past tense, rather than the perfect, with "ever."

"Donchu?" "Canchu?" "Diju?" "Wouju?" and so on

Whenever in rapid speech a "t" sound stands just before a "y" sound, it is the almost universal custom of English-speaking people, cultured and uncultured, to combine the two into a "ch" sound. This takes place in words like "culture," "nature," and "future"—where the long "u" (pronounced "yoo") furnishes the "y" sound—and also between two words in expressions like "Don't you think" (pronounced "Donchu think") "Can't you see it?" (pronounced "Canchu see it?") and a great many others. It does not usually take place when the word "you" is emphatic, as in "*I* think so; don't *you?*" for here there is normally a slight pause before "you." And for a similar reason it does not in the speech of most people take place in a word like "mature," in which the emphasis falls on the syllable containing the "y" (or long "u") sound.

When under the same conditions a "d" sound stands just before the "y" sound, the resulting combination is a "j" sound. Examples of single words are "education" (pronounced "ejucation") and "individual" (pronounced "indivijual"); combinations are "Did you see him?" (pronounced "Diju see"), "Would you care" (pronounced "Wouju care") and many others of the same sort.

The technical name for this combining process is palatalization, though when it occurs between two words it is frequently called "telescoping." It is, as I have said, almost universal with English-speaking people, and has excellent dictionary support. The new *Webster* gives a full discussion of it in its introduction, and approves it both for individual words and for combinations of two. Strange to say, nevertheless, many English textbooks and many teachers of English and expression condemn it as slovenly, especially in the combinations. Under their influence a number of people, scattered over various parts of the country, have by a great effort of will succeeded in training themselves to avoid these natural palatalizations or "telescopings" and imagine that they have taken a great stride toward the acquisition of a cultured speech, when in fact they have done just the opposite. Cultured English-speaking people, both in England and America, normally say "Canchu," "didju," "wouju," and so on, when the "you" is unemphatic. The spellings look odd, but so does all phonetic spelling. If the reader has any doubts on the subject, let him listen, as I have done for years, particularly to speakers and actors of high rank on the stage or over the radio. President Roosevelt, for instance, makes these condemned telescopings; so do John Barrymore, Elsie Ferguson, Alois Havrila, (who won a medal for diction), Clark Gable, Lawrence Tibbett (another medal-winner), Charles Laughton, Helen Hayes,

Tallulah Bankhead, George Arliss, and Walter Hampden. If there is a speaker or actor of standing who does not do so, I have never heard him. Anything else would sound odd and foreign. Is it possible that the English-speaking people do not know how to speak English? That is apparently what those who oppose this practice would have us believe.

"Can" and "may"

If there is one point of English that teachers are insistent upon, it is that "may" must always be used in asking permission. It starts in the early years. "Can I sharpen my pencil, Miss Smith?" asks the child, and the answer often is something like this: "Certainly you *can*. Surely you have the physical ability to do so, but I am sure you mean 'May I' since it is permission you are asking for. Yes, you *may*."

Now in asking for permission the most appropriate word is unquestionably "may." Yet the child, if he had sufficient knowledge, could certainly make out a very strong defense for the use of "can" in such circumstances. There is no law of English that says that the use of "can" must be restricted to cases of physical ability. Most of the time, indeed, it is not used in that sense, but indicates a limited possibility—that is, a possibility under the circumstances. What the child means is, "Can I with your permission," or "Can I without disturbing the room unduly," or perhaps even "Can I without incurring punishment." It may actually be a tribute to the teacher and a sign of a well-trained child that he regards it as impossible, so to speak, to do anything without the teacher's permission.

The testimony of the new *Webster* on this point is interesting and partly self-contradictory. Under "can" it says: "Loosely, to have permission, to be allowed—equivalent to 'may.'" But in the discussion of the two words under "may," it says: "The use of 'can' for 'may' in asking permission is incorrect, but in denying permission 'cannot' is common." In other words, it is wrong for the child to say, "Can I sharpen my pencil?" but right for the teacher to

answer, "No, you cannot." It would be somewhat difficult, I think, to explain to the child why "can" is right in the
answer, but wrong in the question.

A physician of my acquaintance told me a story of how,
as he put it, he was quietly rebuked by a Negro for what he
termed his incorrect use of words. His car had broken down
on a city street, and wishing to call a mechanic, he rang the
bell of the nearest house, which happened to belong to the
Negro, and when the owner came to the door, asked: "Could
I use your telephone?" The Negro's reply was, "Yes, you
may," which the physician was modest enough to feel gave
him a lesson in English. He was particularly humiliated
that he had used "could" in his question, his idea apparently
being that "can" would have been bad enough, but "could"
was much worse. I could not help admiring the willingness
of my friend to learn from any source, but the fact is that
he was a little too quick to confess himself in error. It
seems to me that under the circumstances "could" was
quite appropriate. "Could I use your telephone?" meant
"Would it be possible for me to use your telephone without undue inconvenience to you or your family?" In such a
sentence "could" is not the past indicative of "can," but the
past subjunctive, and its use in this instance is to soften the
request, to make it more polite. When we come to treat
the vexing question of the subjunctive, more will be said of
it.

Our Episcopalian friends have a passage in the prayer-
book which reads: "We have left undone those things we
ought to have done, and we have done those things which
we ought not to have done." I hope it will not be considered
sacrilegious (Notice the spelling; the best pronunciation is
"sacriLEEjus") if I say that many people are in a somewhat similar situation with regard to English—they have
learned things about it that they ought not to have learned
and have left unlearned the things they ought to have
learned.

The superlative with two

Another point on which teachers and school texts usually lay great emphasis is the absolute necessity, for correctness, of using the comparative degree, rather than the superlative, when only two objects or persons are under consideration. Here again it seems to me that they are in error. What logical reason is there for limiting the use of the superlative to more than two? Suppose that there are three boys in a room, and that one of them is taller than either of the other two. He is then unquestionably the tallest boy in the room. Now suppose that one of the others goes out. Is not the same boy still the tallest boy in the room? If not, why not? When the law requires a piece of property to be sold to the highest bidder and there are only two bids, is the higher not legally and rightfully considered to be also the highest one? In fact, if there is only one bid, is it not the highest? I fear our textbook writers have been led astray by the fact that there are three degrees of comparison. It is so easy to say that the positive applies to one, the comparative to two, and the superlative to three or more. But the truth is that when we say that a certain thing is the largest of a group, we mean that it is larger than any other in that group, whether there are a million others or only one. Indeed, as in the case of the single bid, there may be no others.

So much for the logic of the matter. Now the question arises, what is the actual usage of the English-speaking people? In answer consider the old proverb, "Put your best foot forward." The normal number of feet to each person is only two, but does anybody think of saying, "Put your better foot forward?" When two teams meet in an athletic contest, it is customary to say, "May the best team win." But, of course, we can't let a point of English rest wholly on old sayings or proverbs, valuable as they may be for showing our instinctive usage. Let us turn to our writers.

Do you recall the lines from Lowell's *Vision of Sir Launfal:*

He sings to the wide world, and she to her nest;
In the nice ear of nature which song is the best?

But, to be sure, Lowell needed a rhyme for "nest," and could hardly have used "better." It might be poetic license. But Joseph Addison, long held up as a model of style, was not a poet, and he spoke of "the most ancient" of two chairs. Coming to the present day, we find a very striking example of the use of the superlative with two in Fowler's *Modern English Usage*. On page 43, where he gives two spellings for "barytone" (the other is "baritone"), he says, "The first is the *best*." (In America usage favors "baritone.") A few pages later, in the identical situation with regard to the word "behove" (usually "behoove" with us) he says, "The first is the *better*." Obviously with him one of two things may be either the better or the best. His usage means much to me, for I doubt whether we have ever had a writer on English who was keener in detecting the errors of others or more careful of his own use of words than Fowler.

"*A more perfect union*"

The first line of the Constitution of the United States contains the words, "In order to form a more perfect union," and the expression is frequently held up by sticklers for what they consider good English as an example of a grammatical error. "Perfect," they say, cannot be compared, since it means "complete" or "finished." If a thing is perfect, they ask, how can it or anything else be more perfect? And similar objection is offered to the comparison of words like "round," "white," and "pure." Such objections are not, in general, upheld by the dictionaries, which record usage rather than logic. And to be strictly accurate—as the sticklers apparently wish us to be—it should be called to their attention that if it is an error to say "more perfect," it is not an error of grammar, but of logic. But if our speech is to be strictly logical, can we apply terms like "perfect," "round," or "pure" to any physical thing? We shall have to eliminate them from our vocabulary, except for idealistic use, or replace them by "nearly perfect," "almost round," "approximately pure," and so on. I shudder to think of what will happen to our language and our literature if this principle is carried to its logical extreme. It was a stickler for accuracy who is said—no doubt apocryphally—to have written Tennyson:

> Dear sir—I notice that you say in one of your poems:
> "Every moment dies a man,
> Every moment one is born."
> May I call your attention to the fact that if this were true, the population of the earth would remain stationary, whereas by the best estimates it is constantly increasing. May I suggest that it would be nearer the truth if you would make the lines read:
> "Every moment dies a man,
> Every moment one and one-sixteenth is born."

Such hair-splitting seems to me unworthy of the common sense that is an outstanding characteristic of the English-speaking people, even though the lack of it is conspicuous in so many of those who set themselves up as authorities on the English language. Yet I realize that the line between pedantry and reasonable accuracy is difficult to draw, and that what the average person needs is more accuracy of speech rather than less. If hair-splitting is a necessity of nature to some, let them indulge in it, but let them by all means confine their attentions to the hairs that will really bear splitting. Too often their fancied accuracy is actually the grossest inaccuracy, brought about by their ignorance of the real rules and their failure to catch the spirit of our mother tongue.

MORE ABOUT
PRONUNCIATION

XV

THE vagaries of English pronunciation are admirably illustrated by the fact that in the first edition of *Webster's New International Dictionary* (issued in 1908, and now superseded by the one referred to in these pages as "the new *Webster*") there were recorded no fewer than six pronunciations for the word "quinine." The ones approved were "QUINE-ine" for America and "quinEEN" for England, and these rightly maintain their place in the new edition, but there were given also "QUIN-ine," "quin-INE," "QUINin" and "kinEEN," the last being approximately the French pronunciation, though the word is not originally from that language.

French pronunciations

We have so many French words in English that we are likely to give the French pronunciation to one which is not entitled to it, as in the case of "rationale," mentioned previously. Another of this sort is "robot," which should be pronounced with the "t" sounded, either "ROW-bot" or "ROBot." This very useful word is Czech in origin, coming into English not many years ago through Capek's play

R. U. R. (Rossum's Universal Robots). It is difficult to see how we made out so long without it.

But genuine French words present their own difficulties, as we have seen in the former chapter devoted to pronunciation. "Valet" is particularly interesting. The overwhelming majority of Americans say "vaLAY," which they think is the French pronunciation, but which finds, somewhat strangely, no support in any dictionary. Our lexicographers apparently argue that people who have no dealings with valets are not entitled to be consulted about the pronunciation of the word. Those who have them—mostly Englishmen—say "VALett," sounding the "t" in good English fashion, and this is the pronunciation favored by the dictionaries, though it was almost unknown to the great mass of the American people before the advent of the talking pictures. The true French pronunciation is more like that of the English word "valley," than anything else I know how to compare it to.

But the difficulty of pleasing everybody in the matter of pronunciation is shown by my experience with this word in a hotel in New York. Wishing to have some pressing done, in accordance with printed instructions on the wall I took down the telephone receiver and said to the operator:

"Give me the VALett's office, please."

"Do you mean the vaLAY?" came the reply, and feeling properly rebuked, I was forced to admit that I did.

The word "debut" presents a pretty puzzle. The new *Webster* gives as the preferred pronunciation the French method, in which the "u" has a sound unknown in English, though common in German as the "u" with umlaut. It is usually described as a long "e" with the lips rounded as if to pronounce long "o." But "debut" is certainly now an English word and it seems absurd to me to maintain that its correct pronunciation involves a sound which few English-speaking people ever learn to make properly. The second pronunciation of the new Webster—"deBEW"—would seem much better, and I prophesy that the struggle is going to lie between that and the common American utterance

"DAYbew," which has scarcely any dictionary support. In England "DAYboo" seems to be favored, though Jones, the accepted authority on cultured Southern British speech, gives no fewer than seven pronunciations for the word.

It seems a sound principle that when a French word becomes thoroughly Anglicized, it should be uttered in the English method, provided of course that there is an English method of pronouncing it that has any currency among cultured people. For that reason, I prefer to hear "promenade" given as "promenaid," rather than "promenahd," which dictionaries generally prefer. Why should we say "lemonade," "cascade," "cavalcade," "arcade," "serenade," and "cannonade," but "promenahd"?

It is a pleasure to notice that the dictionaries do not give any support to the pronunciation of the word "restaurant" current in New York and Eastern cities in which the last syllable is prominently brought out—"REStauRAHNT." "REStaurant" it is according to the new *Webster*, with the "a" of the last syllable sounded obscurely, so that for practical purposes it might be "u." And it should be remarked also that the dictionaries pronounce "nonchalance" and "nonchalant" likewise without this emphasis on the last syllable which a great many people give. Not "NONshaLAHNT," but "NONshalant."

"Caprice," which comes from the French, has retained its original pronunciation—"caPREES," but in "capricious" the principles of English prevail, and it is "caPRISHus." "Parisian" is often incorrectly turned into "PaREEzhun," but should be "PaRIZHun." And North and South Carolinians are "CaroLINians," not "CaroLEENians," though some of them do not know it.

The case of "vase"

The word "vase" has four possible pronunciations. The one favored by all American dictionaries and used by the great majority of Americans is that which rhymes with "case" and "base." Some Americans say "vaze." In England "vahz," approximately the French pronunciation, is most popular, and even "vawz" may be heard. Not many Americans use these pronunciations, but the few who do are said to feel that they are more "cultured." This feeling was amusingly satirized many years ago in a clever and highly popular poem by James Jeffrey Roche. It represents four young ladies in an art museum, lost in admiration of a beautiful vase. One is from Kalamazoo, one from New York, one from Philadelphia, and one from Boston. It continues:

> Long they worshipped, but no one broke
> The sacred stillness, until up spoke
> The Western one from the nameless place,
> Who blushing said, "What a lovely vase!"
> Over three faces a sad smile flew,
> And they edged away from Kalamazoo.
> But Gotham's haughty soul was stirred
> To crush the stranger with one small word.
> Deftly hiding reproof in praise,
> She cries, "'Tis indeed a lovely vaze!"
> But brief her unworthy triumph when
> The lofty one from the home of Penn,
> With the consciousness of two grandpapas,
> Exclaims, "It is quite a lovely vahz!"
> And glances around with an anxious thrill,
> Awaiting the word of Beacon Hill.
> But the Boston maiden smiles courteously,
> And gently murmurs, "Oh, pardon me.
> I did not catch your remark, because
> I was so entranced with that charming vawz!"

Nevertheless, Americans who wish their speech to be as pleasing as possible to the greatest number of their fellows will imitate the despised young lady from Kalamazoo.

More troublesome pronunciations

The word "suite" is of course French, and is to be pronounced "sweet" in all its meanings, according to the dictionaries. But in the furniture trade, dealers often prefer to pronounce it as "suit." It seems to me that they would do well in that case to spell it "suit" also. The two words are the same in origin, but the furniture of a room dresses it up, as it were, serving much the same purpose as a suit of clothes on a person, and it would save trouble and confusion if we could all agree to write and speak of a "suit" of furniture. But in a suite of rooms, the rooms do follow one another, so to speak, so that the original French significance (it comes from *suivre*, to follow) is preserved, and the French pronunciation seems appropriate.

"Envelope" comes from the French, though it is now spelled "enveloppe" in that language. Its English pronunciation may be "ENvelope" or "ONvelope," or even "en-VELop," when it is spelled without the final "e." Of these three "ENvelope" is undoubtedly the most reasonable and the most widely used. If those who use the other pronunciations could just agree to drop them and center on "ENvelope," the cause of uniformity would be greatly aided and a needless source of possible irritation removed.

Some English words have the accent on what seems a strange syllable to those who have seen them in print, but are not familiar with their sound. "Quintuplet" has been in such prominence since a famous event in Canada that it seems as if everyone would surely be familiar with its pronunciation, but there are apparently still a great many who do not know that the accent is on the first syllable— "QUINTuplet." "Pyramidal" and "maniacal," are not accented on the first syllable, like the words "pyramid" and "maniac," of which they are derivatives, but are pronounced "pyRAMidal" and "maNIGHacal," believe it or not. The dictionaries used to hold out for such a pronunciation in "gladiolus," recording it as "glaDIGHolus," but both the *Standard* and the new *Webster* now give the flower as preferably "gladi-O-lus," though they stick to the other for the name of the genus to which it belongs. "Gladiolus," incidentally, is a Latin word meaning "little sword," the name being given on account of the obviously sword-shaped leaves. There is at present a tendency in many quarters to make the name "gladiola." There is a dictionary authority for this in the new *Webster*, and it would have at least two advantages. It seems somewhat more reasonable for the name of a flower to have a feminine form, and it gives us the easily pronounced plural, "gladiolas." Otherwise we have to take a choice in the plural between the Latin "gladioli" and the awkward English "gladioluses." If the Romans had only thought of swords as feminine, rather than masculine, we should be rid of the difficulty.

The dictionaries have long contended that the word "harass" should be accented on the first syllable—"HARass" —but so many have insisted on saying "haRASS" that the new *Webster* has finally yielded and recorded that pronunciation also. A shift has likewise been made in "acclimate," which had formerly always been put down as "acCLIME-ate," to the great distress of many who felt that "ACclimate" sounded better. "AcCLIME-ate" is still given the preference, but "ACclimate" has been added.

Without exception the dictionaries pronounce the word "traverse" with the accent on the first syllable—"TRAVerse." It seems a little odd that their editors have never discovered that many millions of educated Americans pronounce it "traVERSE." So common is this in the South that many Southerners have never heard any other pronunciation and will be greatly surprised to learn that there is another. It would be interesting to see statistics on the use of the two pronunciations over the country as a whole, if they could be gathered with any approach to accuracy.

One cannot help wondering sometimes whether the editors of dictionaries have ears of the same type as those of other people. By far the most common pronunciation of "your," for instance, is with a long "o," exactly as if it were spelled "yore," but uttered perhaps a little more rapidly than that word. Yet no dictionaries record it, to the best of my knowledge, their usual pronunciation being "yoor," with the "oo" as in "good." Why they should persist in ignoring the usual pronunciation, which is not a sectional matter, is more than I have been able to fathom. Not only do the large majority of people say "yore" for the possessive, but I notice that on the stage it seems quite the thing to turn the contraction "you're" into "yore."

The word "err" is both actually and officially pronounced as if it were spelled "urr." It is a mistake to give the "e" its natural sound in it. "Erring" and "unerring" may likewise be called "urring" and "unurring," but the new *Webster* sanctions their pronunciation also with the "e" sound as in "error." This latter seems particularly appropriate for "unerring."

When the words "aye" and "ay" mean "yes," they should be pronounced like the pronoun "I," but when they mean "forever," the sound should be that of "a" (as in "take"). Either spelling may be used for either meaning, but it is not common to see the spelling "ay" used to mean "forever." "Ay" occasionally means "alas," as it does in a line from Milton's *Lycidas:*

> Ay me! I fondly dream.

and in such cases it should be pronounced "a." Notice, incidentally, that in this line "fondly" is used in its original meaning of "foolishly," which we mentioned in a previous chapter.

A difference in pronunciation is sometimes helpful in distinguishing words of similar spelling. "Precedents" and "precedence" are two of this sort. "Precedents," meaning "foregoing instances," is "PRESSedents," while "precedence," meaning "higher position or rank," is "preSEEDence." The two are often given the same pronunciation, "PRESSedents," but there would seem to be an advantage in following the guidance of the dictionaries and keeping them separate, though, to give the reader full information, it should be added that Fowler dissents from this.

Some words require an effort if their consonants are to be sounded, and this is why many people turn "recognize" into "reckernize." Of course it indicates carelessness not to sound the "g." "Length" and "strength" are likewise turned into "lenth" and "strenth" without any justification. In these the "g" should have a "k" sound before the "th"—"lenkth" and "strenkth." Filling-station people seem to be often of the opinion that they sell automobile "assessories," when of course the proper pronunciation of the word is "acksessories." I have even heard "assept" instead of "ack-cept" as the pronunciation of "accept."

Pronunciations like "reckernize," "lenth," and "assessories" will seem very amusing to many readers of culture and education, who will no doubt condemn them as incredibly slovenly. Nevertheless, some of these same readers will undoubtedly omit the first "g" in "suggest," making it "sujest" instead of "sugjest," and what is more, they have good dictionary authority for doing so. The new *Webster* is the only dictionary that gives the preference to "sugjest." The *Oxford* and *Standard* give only "sujest," a fact which is still incredible to me and will be to most of us who say "sugjest," and feel that it is as slovenly to omit the "g" in this word as the one in "length." But it must be admitted that English pronunciation does not always go by reason, though I think it is undoubtedly true that the editors of *Webster* are right in feeling that "sugjest" prevails in this country. May it long continue to do so!

Long before the radio was ever dreamed of the word "aerial" was in use in English in literary connections in the sense of "airy" or "lofty." Its pronunciation was in four syllables, "a-EE-ri-al," the derivation being from "aer," Latin for "air," in which the "a" and the "e" were separately pronounced, just as they were in Greek, where the word originated. But when the radio came in, millions of people who had been entirely unfamiliar with "aerial" began to use it as part of their daily speech and very naturally called it something like "AIRial," the sound of the first syllable varying slightly. The dictionaries still put "a-EE-ri-al" in first place, but I notice that the new *Webster* now records also the new pronunciation, which many of us will never be able to use, but which will no doubt eventually become universal.

It will surprise a great many people who are familiar with a certain patent medicine to know that the word "draught" is pronounced "draft," not "drawt." Indeed "draught" is only another spelling for "draft," but is usually now employed only in reference to a drink of one kind or another. "Culinary" is likewise often mispronounced. It should be "kewlinary," not "cull-inary." But though this sound of long "u" is appropriate to "culinary," it is entirely out of place in "percolator," as the spelling shows. Why do so many want to call it a "perkewlator"? And "column" is another word in which the long "u" is a mistake. It is not "colyum," but "collum" ("lum" as in "Lum and Abner").

It seems a little odd that there should be any difference of opinion about the pronunciation of a simple word like "wash," and there is none with the dictionaries. They all give only "wahsh," yet are many people—mostly in the Middle West, I think—who prefer to say "wawsh" or "warsh." One cannot help wondering why the "r" should intrude, but it does and the people who put it into "wash" usually do the same thing with "Washington," turning it into "Warshington." "Wawsh" seems strange also, but those who use it may call attention to the fact that the pronunciation preferred in the dictionaries for "water" is "wawter." The new *Webster* is, I think, the first one to record the pronunciation "wahter" at all, though it is undeniably used by many.

"Wash" and "water" both suggest "creek," which by the dictionaries and the great majority of Americans is pronounced as it is spelled, but in localities scattered over various parts of the country is regularly uttered as "crick." "Crick" for "creek" causes much amusement to those not familiar with it, but it is not a sign of illiteracy. According to the new *Webster*, it goes back to Middle English. We have the same phenomenon in our colloquial word "slick," which is really only a corruption of "sleek," but has now attained to the dignity of a dictionary entry for itself, since its meaning has become different from that of "sleek."

It is very surprising to note how much trouble the word

"malefactor" gives to educated people, who, of course, are the only ones who use it. It is really "MALLey-factor," in four syllables, but some want to turn it into "male-factor"—as if there were no female malefactors—and others make it "mal-factor," neither of which pronunciations has any justification or authority. Why they persist is a mystery. "Malefactor" is the opposite of "benefactor," and the rhythm of the two pronunciations is the same.

There is a group of five words, all adopted bodily from the Latin, whose pronunciation seems to be changing, though no dictionary has yet admitted it. They are "data," "status," "stratum," "gratis," and "apparatus," which are all pronounced with a long "a" in the dictionaries—"dayta," "staytus," "straytum," "graytis," and "apparaytus." But the mass of the people seem bent on using the short "a" in them, and the usual pronunciations actually heard are "dat-a," "stat-us," "strat-um," "grat-is," and "apparat-us." In a situation, like this, it is sometimes difficult for one to make a decision as to his own pronunciation, but two circumstances would seem to make it better to abide by the older and official method. First, it is still used by a sufficient number of careful speakers to prevent its sounding extremely odd; second, the words concerned are all a little unusual—not a part of ordinary daily speech—and hence it may be possible to prevent the change from going further or even to win back some to "dayta," "staytus," and so on. Educated people ought always to be conservative in these matters, though there is no use in clinging to a pronunciation when practically everybody else has abandoned it.

The pronunciation of the word "usage" itself presents an interesting example of the power of usage. All the dictionaries except *Webster's* give it as as "uzage," although for a great many years, in America at least, that pronunciation has been rather rare, being confined mostly to a few conscientious teachers of English. The first dictionary recognition of the usual pronunciation, in which the "s" has the ordinary "s" sound, not that of "z" was in the first edition of the *New International* in 1908, where that mode of utterance was put in second place. The new *Webster*, issued in 1934, boldly advanced it to first place, so that the pronunciation with the "s" sound now has the complete sanction of the latest American dictionary, and no one need hesitate to use it for fear that it is not "correct." But the question now arises, when did it become "correct?" Was it in 1908, when it was put into second place, in 1934, when it was put into first place, or at some other time? Do pronunciations become correct by being put into a dictionary, or are they put into the dictionaries because they are correct? Very obviously, the latter is the truth. The new pronunciation must be correct *before* the dictionary editors will record it. Just as obviously, then, there is a possibility, and indeed it is very often true, that the really preferable pronunciation is not the one in the dictionaries. Dictionaries are style-books, and styles may change considerably in the space of from fifteen to twenty-five years that usually elapses between two editions of a given dictionary.

Some words seem to be very troublesome to the tongue. A great many people find it difficult not to turn "cavalry" into "Calvary." "Statistics" has three "t's" with an "s" before two of them, and some want to put the "s" before all three. But it is "sta-tis-tics." In "bronchial" the "i" is sometimes put before the "ch," instead of after it, where it belongs. Not "bron-i-chal," but "bron-chi-al." "February" is very commonly pronounced as if spelled "Febuwary," but careful speakers say "Feb-ru-ary."

Proper names

Some geographical names call for comment. People who live in Alabama never call it "AlaBAHma," as geographies and dictionaries sometimes insist they should, but always "AlaBAMa." "Massachusetts" is "MassaCHUsetts," not "MassaTUsetts." And my information is that the pronunciation "LouEEZiana" is almost never heard in the state itself. It is, formally, "LOUeyziana," and frequently simply

"LOOZiana." "New Orleans" is not "New Or-LEENZ," but "New OR-le-ans."

"Helena," whether located in Arkansas (pronounced Arkansaw) or Montana, is accented on the syllable that makes it sound most profane, but St. Helena, the scene of Napoleon's captivity is "St. HeLEENa."

"Newfoundland" is not "NewFOUNDland," though the name of the dog may be pronounced in that way. The people of the island itself do not agree on the pronunciation, but it is either "NewfundLAND," "NEWfundland," or "NewfoundLAND."

It always puzzles children to learn that the names "Leicester," "Worcester," and "Gloucester" are pronounced as if they were spelled "Lester," "Wooster" ("oo" as in "good") and "Gloster." These pronunciations originated, of course, in England where anything is likely to happen to a proper name—such as pronouncing "Cholmondeley" as if it were spelled "Chumly," for instance,—and are the result merely of a very rapid utterance. "Leicester," for example, was once pronounced "LESSester," and if the reader will say "LESSester" rapidly several times in succession, he will find that it dwindles down practically to "Lester."

The "cester" with which these words end is one of the few linguistic relics of the Roman occupation of England, which lasted more than four hundred years, yet had almost no effect on the English language, for the very good reason that English had not at that time arrived in England, but was still being spoken in Germany, where it originated. "Cester" is a corruption of the Latin "castra," meaning "camp," and places of that name in England originated as Roman camps. The same thing is true of those ending in "chester," such as "Winchester," and in "caster," such as "Lancaster."

A curious example of how over-precision leads to incorrectness is seen in the pronunciation of the name "Marguerite." The name is originally French, and the only purpose of the "u" is to keep the "g" hard, that is, with the sound of "g" in "gate." The "u" itself is not sounded at all, but the "e" has about the sound of "u" in "but." Nevertheless many people, especially singers, render the name as "Mar-gyu-reet," feeling as they do so, no doubt, that they are enunciating very carefully. But it is another instance of taking great pains to be wrong. The true pronunciation might best be represented by the spelling "Mar-guh-reet." Of course, any young lady who is named "Marguerite" has the right to pronounce it "Margyuerite" if she wishes, for each of us has full authority over the pronunciation of his own name, but since that pronunciation originates in a misunderstanding, it is certainly not advisable. Without the "u" the word would be pronounced "Marzhereet." The same difference may be seen in the words "rogue" and "rouge" (correctly pronounced "roozh," not "rooge").

It probably makes no difference to Anne Boleyn, and possibly not a great deal to anybody else, but some of my readers may be interested to know that reference books usually give the pronunciation of her surname as "BULLin," not "BoLIN," as we frequently hear it.

Two ancient names often mispronounced are "Ulysses" and "Darius." Both should be accented on the second syllable, not the first. Not "YULE-isees," but "uLISSeez"; not "DARius," but "daRIGHus."

"Semi-" and "anti-"

The prefixes "semi-" (half) and "anti-" (against) should both be pronounced with a short "i"—not "semigh" and "antigh," but "semy" and "anty." This is a little unfortunate in the case of "anti-" at least, for it makes its pronunciation so close to that of the Latin prefix "ante," meaning "before," that the two are practically indistinguishable by sound. It might be better if we should all agree to pronounce "anti" with a long "i"—but no such agreement has as yet been reached.

"Impious," "infamous," and "impotent"

The accepted pronunciation of "impious" is not "im-PIous," but "IMPious"; of "infamous," not "inFAmous," but "INfamous"; of "impotent," not "imPOtent," but "IMPotent." These facts cause great distress to many people and arouse a spirit of rebellion in some of them. Why this shifting of accent, they ask. "If "PIous" is the positive, why is not "imPIous" the negative?

A little consideration will make it evident, however, that the pronunciations are not as unreasonable as they seem. "Impious" is not, after all, the mere negative of "pious." To say that a man is not pious is quite a different thing from saying that he is impious, for today the word "pious" carries usually the implication that the one to whom it is applied is excessively religious, or if that is impossible, that he is exceedingly devoted to the outward forms of religion, whereas "impious" means "blasphemous" or "actively opposed to religion." Likewise "infamous" does not mean merely "non-famous," but "famous for wickedness," and "impotent" is not simply "non-potent," but "helpless." Whether or not it has been deliberately adopted for the purpose, the shift in the accent of the three words is a useful recognition of these differences of meaning.

It must be admitted that English pronunciation is a perplexing thing. There are more than a thousand words on which the dictionaries differ with one another, often only slightly, sometimes radically. Such a situation would be impossible in languages like French, German, and Spanish. They have their dialects, to be sure, which vary rather widely, but the literary language used by the educated and taught in the schools is in general well standardized, and disputes over pronunciation are somewhat rare, at least in comparison with those which arise in English.

The stubbornly individualistic nature of the English-speaking people and their wide distribution over the globe, with their numerous centers of culture, seem to be the two chief reasons for the condition of English pronunciation.

But let no English-speaking person imagine that because of this condition he is free to adopt whatever pronunciation he pleases for any word, or that pronunciation is a matter of no importance.   On the contrary, one's pronunciation of a word or two may be sufficient to stamp him definitely in the minds of those who hear him as uncultured and ignorant. The man who asks, "Whur'd you git it?" for instance, may be a very admirable character, honest, hard-working, kind, unselfish, even highly intelligent, perhaps.   But his speech betrays him.   His pronunciation of the words "where" and "get" has put a great gulf between him and others who in all the major virtues may be his inferior, but who will nevertheless look down upon him.

On the other hand, the question of just what is the most desirable pronunciation for a given word is not to be settled nearly so easily as some people think.   It is surprising to learn how many there are of intelligence and education who feel that the verdict of the dictionaries settles the thing without room for further discussion.   Soon after I began to talk about these matters on the radio, a lady of obvious education wrote me: "It is as wrong to question the correctness of the dictionary as it is to question the axioms in mathematics."   Such a statement reveals an entire misunderstanding of the rules of good English and how they are made.

For common words the safe and wise rule is to consult the usage of the cultured people of your section of the English-speaking world, rather than the dictionaries.   Of what advantage is it to you to pronounce a word in accordance with the dictionaries if that pronunciation sounds odd or affected to those who hear you?   Of course you have the consciousness that the authorities are on your side—which leaves you about in the situation of the driver who has the right of way, but gets his car smashed up nevertheless.   Yet he is really better off than you, for he can sue and recover damages—if the other man has anything—while your hearers have put you down as either ignorant of the cultured usage of your section or affected, and there is nothing you can do about it.

On the other hand, in the case of words that are not a part

of everyday conversation, the judgment of the dictionaries is indispensable. The enormous vocabulary of English and the wide variety of the sources from which it is drawn make it necessary for us all to draw heavily upon the scholarly researches of their editors, if we are to become masters of its pronunciation.

PLURALS AND POSSESSIVES—
WITH A FEW DIGRESSIONS

XVI

As most people know, a tailor's large smoothing-iron is called a "goose," on account of the resemblance of its handle to the neck of that fowl. There is an old story of a tailor who wanted to send in an order for two of these articles, but was unable to decide whether he should write "two gooses" or "two geese." He finally solved the difficulty by ordering one goose, and adding a postscript reading, "Please send me another one also."

The fact is that according to the dictionaries the correct plural in such a case is "gooses." The idea seems to be that since the iron is not really a goose and its resemblance to one is only accidental, it is not entitled to the irregular plural "geese," but should have the regular one in "s." A similar question was laid before me by a little girl regarding a paper cup of ice cream known in her locality as a "Mickey Mouse." If she wished two of them, should she ask for two "Mickey Mice" or "Mickey Mouses"? Of course, the same principle that makes "gooses" correct in referring to the irons calls for "Mickey Mouses" here.

Another somewhat troublesome question concerns a singular rather than a plural. What do you call one of a pair of dice? If the question were left to those most familiar with the articles themselves, the answer would probably be that it is a "dice" also. But grammarians and lexicographers say it is a "die." This makes clear the meaning of the saying "The die is cast," which is the English translation of the Latin words attributed to Caesar when he led his army across the Rubicon: *"Alea jacta est."* "The dice have been thrown" would be the modern way of putting it—that is to say a step has been taken from which there is no retreat, and we must accept the outcome.

"The exception proves the rule"

May I digress for a little to speak of other proverbs that are often not clearly understood or are misinterpreted? Chief of these is, "The exception proves the rule." As generally used, it is an absurdity. Someone says, "It never rains at night during July." (There are people who really believe that.) You answer, "Oh, but it rained frequently at night last July." "Well," replies the other, "that is just the exception that proves the rule." The fact is, of course, that such an exception actually *disproves* such a rule, and it is ridiculous to contend otherwise.

The proverb in question originated as a legal maxim and its true meaning is that the admission that a certain thing is exceptional proves the rule to be otherwise. When a Californian tells a visitor that the rainy weather he is experiencing is "unusual," he is trying to prove the rule by establishing the exceptional *as* exceptional. If a visitor at a boys' boarding school hears the headmaster announce that on Saturday night bedroom lights may be kept on till eleven o'clock, he is justified in inferring that the rule is that they are ordinarily turned off earlier than eleven.

Another interpretation of this proverb which is sometimes given is that the word "proves" is used in its original sense of "tests." Though I doubt that it is the true explanation, this interpretation will do no harm. There are exceptions to most rules, and if they are excessively great or numerous, they are likely to destroy the value of the rule, and hence their existence may be said to test it.

When a law or rule is more often broken than kept, someone is likely to remark of it that it is "more honored in the breach than the observance." He may or may not realize that he is quoting from Shakespeare's *Hamlet*, which has provided us with an amazing number of highly quotable lines, far more than any other single piece of literature of anything like comparable length. But a careful reading of Scene I of Act IV, in which the line occurs, will show that Shakespeare was expressing quite a different thought. Hamlet himself speaks the line and says that to his mind the Danish custom of firing cannon and striking up a jazz band—or the equivalent of it in those times—whenever the King took a drink was one that would be "more honored in the breach than the observance," meaning obviously that it would be better to break the custom than to keep it. The common misinterpretation probably does not do any particular harm, but English-speaking people of education ought really to be more familiar with the greatest work of their greatest writer.

"*And a little child shall lead them*"

When a child does something out of the ordinary or exercises some strong influence over grown people, such as reuniting his divorced parents, for instance, the Biblical verse "And a little child shall lead them" comes to the minds of most of us. A reference to the eleventh chapter of Isaiah, in which it occurs, however, shows no such thought. The picture is one of a time of universal peace: "The wolf also shall dwell with the lamb, and the leopard shall lie down with the kid; and the calf and the young lion and the fatling together; and a little child shall lead them." The emphasis is clearly not on the power of the child, but his weakness. The animals are to forget their natural enmities and become so gentle that even a little child can lead them. But again the misapplication does no particular harm, and it is time to cease this digression, which may seem a little hypercritical (not "hypocritical"; "hyper" is the Greek for "over") to some, and return to our plurals.

"Data," "insignia," "strata," and "phenomena"

People often say "This data shows us . . ." when it should be "These data show us . . ." for "data" is a plural. The singular is "datum," though this is seldom used, and the peculiar formation of the plural is accounted for by the fact that "datum" is a Latin neuter, and neuters, as some of my readers will recall from their schooldays, form plurals ending in "-a." The use of "data" in the singular, however, has gone so far as to be mentioned in the new *Webster*. It may some day be accepted, but at present it is more or less a mark of ignorance.

"Insignia" is another Latin neuter plural that is often mistaken for a singular. "An insignia" is an incongruous combination. The singular in Latin is *insigne*, but as this is not used in English, when there is only one, we must say, "a badge," "an emblem of office," or something of the kind.

"Strata" is the plural of "stratum," but it also is often used as the singular by those who are not aware of the fact.

"Phenomena" is another plural, though not from the Latin. Its singular is "phenomenon," from the Greek. These words have one meaning to the ordinary man and another to the scientist. As commonly used, a phenomenon is something very unusual, almost incredible, but any change in which the scientist is interested is called by him a phenomenon. And yet the uses are hardly as far apart as they seem, for the truth is that the ordinary processes of plant and animal life, the simplest workings of nature, are beyond our comprehension. We live in a world of miracles, of the most wondrous phenomena, but seldom realize it.

Singulars that seem to be plurals

In contrast with the words we have been discussing there are some singulars that end in "s" and therefore have the appearance and sound of plurals. It is strange how easily some intelligent people can be misled by them. Why should anybody say "these molasses"? "These water" would be just as appropriate, for molasses is a substance like water. And "these cheese" is still worse, but not at all uncommon in grocery stores. The plural, by the way, is "cheeses," when the meaning is "heads of cheese," or perhaps "varieties of cheese." But "grits," a favorite Southern dish, is plural. This molasses, this cheese, but these grits.

Some physicans bring discredit on the name of "doctor," which signifies "learned man," by using "pulse" as a plural. "His pulse are weak" may sometimes be heard instead of the correct "His pulse *is* weak," which seems so natural that I have often wondered why anybody would want to use "are" in such a sentence. "Mumps" and "measles" are really plural formations, but since each is the name of a disease, it is best to treat them as singulars, and they are so construed by careful speakers. "Mumps *is* a children's disease, and so *is* measles," is the proper way to express it.

I have known at least one very intelligent and reasonably well educated person who used "lens" both as a singular and a plural, and insisted that he couldn't make "lenses" sound right to him. There is a strong tendency among sign-painters to treat the word "tourist" as if it were a plural, as those who live in regions frequented by tourists can testify. It is not at all uncommon to see a sign in front of a private home reading "Tourist," when it should, of course, be "Tourists"—unless indeed the word is used as an adjective, as it sometimes is in combinations like "Tourist rooms" or "Tourist accommodations."

The strange belief that "tourist" may be treated as a plural arises no doubt from the fact that many people cannot—or do not—sound the "s" on the end of the true plural "tourists." It must be admitted that it takes some effort to pronounce the word correctly. This is true of similar plurals, such as "desks," "tests," "texts," and "nests," and also of certain verb-forms such as "asks" and "costs." In older English an "e" was present before the "s" in words like these, and this pronunciation is still retained in the speech of many people in the remote mountain or rural sections of the South, where "desk-es" and "nest-es" may frequently be heard.

The most remarkable transformation of a singular into a plural that I have ever heard came from the lips of a shopgirl to whom a companion had remarked after witnessing her experience with some trying customers:

"I should think people like that would make you lose your patience!"

"Well," came the reply, "I do almost lose 'em sometimes."

It was a while before I could realize that " 'em" referred to "patience," which the girl probably thought of as being spelled "patients" and vaguely plural, like "feelings" in the expression "My feelings are hurt."

"Species," "series," "sheep," "deer," "bear," and so on

For a number of words in English the plural is exactly like the singular. "Species" and "series" are two of these, the reason in their case being that they are merely Latin words brought over bodily, and retain their Latin plurals, which in words of their sort did not differ from the singular. In a magazine of wide circulation there appeared recently a reference to a new "specie" of germ. It should, of course, have been "species," for "specie" is an entirely separate word, meaning in present use metallic money as opposed to paper currency. It is true that the new *Webster* gives one meaning of "specie" as the equivalent of "species," but it adds "now rare," and this listing should not be taken as authorizing its use, which was never really justified.

Everybody knows that "sheep" never becomes "sheeps," regardless of the number concerned, and that we speak with equal correctness of one deer or two deer. The plural is likewise always the same as the singular in the case of these names of animals or fishes: bison, chamois, grouse, moose, muskellunge, menhaden, pickerel, swine. The word "fish" itself is now usually "fish" in the plural also except in reference to different kinds, as when I spoke a moment ago of "names of animals or fishes." In older English, however, "fishes" was common, as in the Biblical passage concerning "five loaves and two fishes." Many names of fishes follow the rule for "fish" also. We ordinarily say, for instance, "I caught ten trout," but we might speak of the *trouts* of the Rocky Mountains, meaning the various kinds of trout that are to be found in that region. "Bream," "cod," "halibut," "mackerel," and "perch" are of this type.

For some reason there is a strong tendency on the part of sportsmen—hunters and fishers—to use the singular as a plural. They speak regularly of hunting bear, beaver, elephant, fox, rabbit, quail, and so on, where other people under other circumstances would say "bears," "beavers," "elephants," "foxes," "rabbits," "quails." The dictionaries recognize this sportsmen's usage for these and many other names of game, but of course approve of the ordinary plurals also.

Many people still speak of "two pair of gloves," but the present tendency is to say "two pairs." And while it is correct to speak of a "ten-year-old child," it is a sign of ignorance to say, as the uneducated frequently do, "I have lived here ten year." In like manner, it is right to speak of "a six-foot pole," but hardly acceptable to say, "He is six foot tall." The same difference is seen in the expression "a ten-mile walk," and the statement "He walked ten miles."

"Mother-in-law," "court martial," "Knight Templar," and so on

On a national radio program listened to by millions, a man who was attempting to do honor to the mothers-in-law of the country referred to them repeatedly as the "mother-in-laws," his kindness of heart being obviously superior to his knowledge of English. Naturally the plural is "mothers-in-law," and a similar thing is true of all the words that end in this way. The plural sign goes on the main noun of a compound like these, though the apostrophe and "s" that denote possession are always applied to the last word. "My two *brothers-in-law* live in my *mother-in-law's* house," is the correct way to put it.

Following the general rule just given, these plurals are

the correct ones: Aides-de-camp, attorneys at law, attorneys general, battles royal, commanders in chief, courts martial, poets laureate, postmasters general, sergeants at arms, sergeants major.

In "attorneys general," and "postmasters general" the word "general" is an adjective. But when it is a noun, as in "major general," the plural sign is added to it, and we say "major generals." Likewise the correct plurals are "advocate generals," "brigadier generals," "lieutenant generals," and "judge advocates."

Grammars used to teach that in "Knight Templar" both words are nouns and hence both pluralized: "Knights Templars." The new *Webster* confines this plural, however, to the ancient military and religious order of which the villainous Brian de Bois-Guilbert of Scott's *Ivanhoe* was a member, and for the modern branch of the Masons it gives the plural "Knights Templar."

"*Acoustics*" *and other words in* "*-ics*"

The word "acoustics" is regarded as a singular when it refers to the science, but as a plural when it means acoustic qualities. We say, "Acoustics *is* an interesting study," but "The acoustics of the room *are* good." A similar rule applies to the other nouns in "-ics," which are always singular when they denote a science, but may be plural, in other uses. "Athletics" is particularly likely to be used as a plural in the meaning of the various forms of sport. "Politics" is sometimes singular, sometimes plural. One may hear from careful speakers, "What are his politics?" or "What is his politics?" though I believe the present tendency is toward the use of "is" in such a sentence.

"*How is your family?*" *or* "*How are your family?*"

I am frequently asked whether it is correct to use a plural verb, such as "are," with an apparently singular noun like "family." This is a point covered in every school grammar, but many reasonably well educated people seem somehow not to have grasped it. The word "family" denotes a group, composed, like all groups, of two or more members. Such nouns are called collective nouns and may take verbs in either the singular or the plural, according to a rule that is the essence of common sense. When we think of the group as one thing and not of its parts, we use a singular verb, but when the individuals that compose it are uppermost in our minds, the verb is very naturally plural. Consequently it is correct to ask either "How is your family?" or "How are your family?" The idea in the first is "How is your family as a whole?" and in the second "How are the various members of your family?"

A woman once told me of a dispute she had had with two college graduates, who insisted that she was wrong in saying, "This couple have seen better days," and that the correct wording would be "This couple *has* seen . . ." Both "have" and "has" are correct here, but since seeing is something that each of us must do for himself (Yes, "himself," not "ourselves"), "have" seems more appropriate. Some other collective nouns are: crowd, committee, jury, company, army, series, flock, herd, bevy, majority, school. Of course there are many others. Any one of them may be considered either as a singular or as a plural.

The Joneses, the Williamses, and the Rogerses

Of all plurals I believe that the most difficult for the average person to form correctly are those of a proper name that already ends in "s," especially if it has more than one syllable. If you meet Mr. and Mrs. Jones down town, how do you report the fact to your family? Do you say, "I saw the Jones today," or, "I saw the Joneses"? A little thought will show that only "the Joneses" is correct. Mr. Jones is one Jones, Mrs. Jones is another, and the two together are the Joneses, just as surely as one house and another house make two houses. And, equally of course, if it is Mr. and Mrs. Williams, the correct expression is "the Williamses."

Likewise the Rogers family should be referred to as "the Rogerses." What surprises me is that so many people seem to think there is something wrong about such plurals. Some even go so far as to say that they sound incorrect.

The possessives of names ending in "s" are also very troublesome to most people. If a word ending in "s" is *plural*, we form the possessive by simply adding an apostrophe. "The ladies' hats," for instance, means "the hats of the ladies." But when the word ending in "s" is a proper name—not a plural—the grammars all recommend that in most instances an apostrophe and another "s" be added. "Mr. Jones's (pronounced "Joneses") house" is considered to be the best form, though in the case of a word such as "Jesus" in which there are already two "s" sounds the simple apostrophe is recommended. "For Jesus' sake" sounds better than "for Jesus's sake." And in a long name like "Demosthenes" it is also better not to add another syllable, but to say, for instance, "Demosthenes' orations."

Yet many people will have none of "Mr. Jones's house." They tell me that it sounds ignorant, and their idea of elegant speech is "Mr. Jones' house," which the grammarians grudgingly tolerate, but that is all. If one wishes to speak of the novels of Dickens, the form recommended by most authorities is "Dickens's novels" (pronounced "Dickenses"); "Dickens' novels" is conceded to be a possibility; but the form actually written by an immense number of people is "Dicken's novels," which is entirely without reason or authority. The writer's name was "Dickens," not "Dicken." If it had been "Dicken," it would have been correct to write "Dicken's novels," but since it was really "Dickens," if the task of adding an apostrophe and an "s" is too much for us, surely we can at least add the apostrophe *after* the "s" that is already a part of the name.

But there is one more thing to be considered—the possessive *plural* of these names that end in "s." Suppose the house belongs to both Mr. and Mrs. Jones, as houses generally do, both actually and technically. In that case we should speak of it as "the Joneses' house," or if we omit the word "house," as is frequently done, we may say, "I was over at the Joneses' today." Note that this gives us three spellings for the word that is pronounced "Joneses." Here are all three used in the same sentence: "I was over at the Joneses' today, and saw Mr. Jones's brother and all the other Joneses." The reader who sees clearly the reasons for these various spellings has the essence of what I have been trying to say.

"An attractive feature is the shady walks"

When we say, "John is a good boy," the grammarians tell us that "boy" is a predicate noun, indicating the same person as the subject "John." In "What a good boy am I" the predicate noun is put first and the subject "I" comes after the verb, a reversal of the usual order. Since the subject and the predicate noun denote the same person or thing, a peculiar and apparently contradictory situation arises when one of them is singular and the other plural. Yet this is quite possible. Consider, for instance, the sentence, "An attractive feature of the resort is the shady walks." This wording is correct, for the verb naturally agrees with the subject, which is "feature." If we reverse the order, however, and make "walks" the subject, we must change "is" to "are": "The shady walks are an attractive feature of the resort."

There is much confusion on this point in the minds of some otherwise good writers, and a little, I am sorry to say, with one or two grammarians. It is only reasonable, of course, that the verb should take its number from the subject, but when the subject is far removed and the predicate noun close at hand, there is a tendency to make it agree with the latter. Here, for example, is a sentence from a newspaper writer of national reputation, some of whose sentences are quoted in the new *Webster* as illustrations of the correct use of certain words. In speaking of a plan proposed by a political demagogue, according to which the government would take over the wealth of the country and use it to furnish a homestead to every family, he wrote: "The only part of the Ford wealth that could be used for homesteads *are* the profits."

"Are" should be "is," and if it had been closer to "part," he probably would have written "is." Some readers may be inclined to argue that "profits" could be taken as the subject here. The answer is that in normal prose the subject stands before the verb and the predicate noun after it, and there is no reason to think that the writer was using a poetical inversion.

A similar sentence occurred in a newspaper that is more than ordinarily careful in its use of English. In describing a little girl's visit to a session of a state legislature and her disappointment with it, the writer said: "The only thing that came up to expectations *were* the newspaper reporters." "Were" should be "was," of course, for the subject is "thing," not "reporters."

"Awaits alike th' inevitable hour"

It is not unusual for the subject to follow the verb in poetry. "A merry old soul was he," is an example from Mother Goose, and from Dickens, who in addition to his novels wrote a little poetry, we have: "A dainty plant is the ivy green." The reader recognizes instantly that these are merely poetical variations of the normal statements, "He was a merry old soul," and "The ivy green is a dainty plant." But there is one poetical inversion that usually escapes notice, though it occurs in perhaps the most famous stanza of a poem that is one of the glories of the English language—Gray's *Elegy*. As the poet wrote it the stanza reads:

> The boast of heraldry, the pomp of power,
> And all that beauty, all that wealth e'er gave,
> *Awaits* alike th' inevitable hour.
> The paths of glory lead but to the grave.

Most people read and quote the first word in the third line as "await," but Gray's reading, "awaits," shows that he intended "hour" to be the subject. In his view, the boast of heraldry, the pomp of power, and so on, are not waiting for the hour of death, but it is waiting for them. As far as the general sense is concerned, the difference is trifling, but the poet's view seems more accurate than the usual interpretation—or rather, misinterpretation.

These are the lines that Wolfe is said to have quoted to his officers on the night before he captured Quebec, adding the comment that he would rather have been the author of them than take the city. His death in the hour of victory was a striking illustration of the truth of the poet's words.

A subtle error

It would seem a comparatively simple thing to keep the verb in agreement with its subject, but now and then the wording of a sentence is so unusual that even an able writer is likely to slip. One of the last places one would look for a grammatical error is in the opening sentence of a book on English literature, but that is where one occurred, according to the late C. Alphonso Smith, that rare combination of accurate scholar, gifted writer, and inspiring teacher, who quotes it in one of his works. The author of the textbook began with this definition:

> By the term literature *is* meant those written
> or printed compositions which preserve the thought
> and experience of a race recorded in artistic form.

"Is" should be "are," for the subject is not "literature," but "compositions," yet I venture to say that many excellent students of grammar would read such a sentence without being aware that anything was wrong with it. It is one of the few instances in which the incorrect thing sounds correct. But that it is incorrect will be more clearly shown if we rearrange the words so that the verb comes after the subject. Let us begin, "By the term literature those written or printed compositions—" and now it is impossible to continue with "is meant"; it must be "those written or printed compositions *are* meant."

This chapter has dealt with many things that doubtless to

some readers seem of slight importance. The study of our language shows many little traps for unwary feet, and sometimes the multiplicity of them and their comparative triflingness make us all feel rebellious. People often argue that it makes no great difference, after all, *how* we say a thing— what matters is *what* we say, and as long as we express our thoughts so others can understand them, why should we worry over whether our language is in accord with the technical rules of English or not?

There is much truth in such an argument. The important thing *is* what we say, rather than how we say it, and he who does not see this is not fit to teach English. The vigor and directness that sometimes go with crude and incorrect speech are better than the elegant insipidity of that whose only virtue is correctness. But I have noticed that those who protest loudest against the restrictions of rules nevertheless observe many rules themselves with the utmost care and look down upon those who do not observe them. "I taken the car" expresses exactly the same thought as "I took the car," and expresses it just as clearly and forcefully. There can be no mistaking its meaning, but how many of these protesters would be willing to say it? How many would not be deeply humiliated if they heard any member of their family say it?

No, we all observe rules. It is impossible otherwise to speak and be understood. It is merely a question of which rules we shall observe and whether we shall make the effort to learn and observe them all. It is fortunate for us that most people are not highly critical, and our speech may be quite pleasing to others even when it is far short of perfection. But there is something in the human mind that urges it persistently, though haltingly, toward the ideal. We may never reach it, but there is a pleasure in making progress toward it— a pleasure sometimes even in imagining that we are making progress toward it. The way is not easy, and the journey seems slow at times, but we would not willingly give up even the most trifling bit of real knowledge that we have gained about our mother tongue.

ERRORS OF VARIOUS
TYPES AND GRADES

XVII

IT IS quite easy to see how some errors of speech come about,
but more difficult to fathom the causes of others. When
the illiterate Negro uses "is" indiscriminately after "I,"
"you," "he," "we," or "they," it is obviously because "is" is
more frequently used than "am" or "are," and since he lacks
the discrimination to vary the form of the verb according
to its subject, he seizes on the most familiar form and makes
it do duty for all. Incidentally, it may be remarked that
those anecdotes in which the Negro is represented as saying,
"He am," or, "Dat am a fact," are hardly true to life. "Am"
is scarcely in the uneducated Negro's vocabulary.

We had a Negro maid once who had a very curious way
of speaking of a pint as a "point." It was very odd to hear
her talk of a "point of milk," and as there was no reason to
suspect Irish ancestry, I was quite puzzled by the pronunciation, till finally what I believe is the true explanation dawned
upon me. She was a schoolteacher, and had no doubt been
trained not to allow her pupils to turn the verb "to point"
into "pint," as is more or less common among the colored
people. Hence the conclusion that "pint'" was always
wrong, and "point" always right. I have known white
schoolteachers whose precepts and practices on matters of
English were equally absurd. We have far too many

178

teachers of English in this country who have no home background of cultured speech, and whose knowledge of the language has been gained entirely in the schools. With them the whole thing is a matter of rules, and they fail to realize that there is much of importance concerning the use of English that cannot be reduced to rule, but must be absorbed through contact with people of culture and books. And even when a rule can be given, it is frequently difficult to state it in such a way that it will not be misinterpreted and misapplied by the unintelligent.

Strange uses of "ever"

While there is no doubt a reason for every error, some seem to be the product of a mere perversity. In some rural or mountain sections of the South—perhaps also in other sections—it is not uncommon to hear "whoever," "whatever," and "whichever" reversed into "ever who," "ever what," and "ever which." For example: "Ever who finds it must give it back." "That was So-and-so, or ever what his name is." "Ever which way you looked you could see the people a-runnin'." The reason for such an inversion is entirely beyond me, and if any reader has an explanation to offer, it will be received with gratitude.

Another strange misuse of "ever" current among people in much the same localities is the substitution of "whenever" for "when." There are, of course, sentences in which either word may be used with substantially the same meaning. "Tell him that when you see him," and "Tell him that whenever you see him," are not materially different in thought, though the use of "whenever" seems to make it more doubtful that you will see him soon. But the misuse I am speaking of occurs in a sentence like, "I was glad whenever he told me that," where it is obvious that the telling took place only once, and that "whenever" means simply "when." Those who have the habit use "whenever" regularly for "when" in adverb clauses, though not in questions. Possibly the "ever" is simply added for a sort of emphasis.

It is of course common with uneducated people to confuse "ever" with "every," but here the similarity of the words makes the reason obvious.

"They's" for "there is" or "there are"

Another almost incredible error that may be heard among people of the regions where the misuse of "ever" is prevalent, is the substitution of "they's" for "there is" and "there are." "They's a man at the door," and "They's a good many who think so," are typical specimens of this usage, which, rather oddly, may be heard from those who would never dream of saying "they is" under ordinary circumstances. Indeed they probably do not think of "they's" as I have spelled it, but more likely as a rapid utterance of "there is," which it may be, though in that case, of course, they are equally reprehensible in using it for "there are." It is really remarkable how sometimes people of considerable culture and education will habitually be guilty of a gross mistake like this, continuing to make it in utter unconsciousness, unless something happens to call it sharply to their attention. Writers on English and teachers of the subject are rather too prone to assume that there is no need of mentioning the glaring errors, and so they concentrate their efforts on such doubtful and delicate points as inculcating the use of "may" instead of "can" in asking for permission, while they neglect to correct these things that seem almost too simple to need correction, but are after all the most important.

"Attackted"

If anybody thinks that these simple things do not need attention, let him ponder over the fact that one of our national political figures, a college graduate, who has held high office and sought still higher, in an address over the radio that was listened to by millions, pronounced the word "attacked" as if it were spelled "attackted," turned "malefactors" into "mal-factors," "believe" into "blieve," and "tremendous" into "tremenjous." I have often wondered over that pronunciation "attackted." People seem to have no difficulty in pronouncing correctly such words as "tact" and "tacked," in which the sound is exactly the same as the last syllable of "attacked." Whence, then, comes the trouble with the latter?

But people do strange things with their tongues. I know a lady of culture who says "mee-yuns" for "millions," and I wonder whether she realizes that her pronunciation of the word differs from that of practically everybody she associates with. And I recall another who turned "different" into "diffunt" in apparent unconsciousness that her utterance of the word was in any way "diffunt" from anyone else's. A young college student, I noticed, habitually said "bofe" for "both." After some hesitation I asked him about it and learned that it was an unconscious habit, probably persisting from early childhood. He could say "both" as easily as anybody, and immediately set out to introduce it into his speech in place of the childish utterance he had been using, though, as the reader may imagine, it proved to be a matter of some difficulty to make the change.

A very peculiar mispronunciation is that of "overhauls" for "overalls." It is fairly common among uneducated people, and I have often wondered whether a false etymology is not responsible for it. Might it be that those who use it think that the garment is so named because it is "hauled" on "over" the other clothing? If so, why does not the true and obvious explanation occur to them—that overalls are called overalls because they are put on "over all" the other clothing?

"Drug" for "dragged"

Mistakes in the formation of the past tense of irregular verbs have already been discussed, but not mentioned at that time was the fairly common use of "drug" for "dragged," for which I can find no shadow of authority even in those dictionaries that record "dove" as a colloquial possibility for the past tense of "dive." Yet I recall hearing a young man

who had been an instructor in English in a small college
narrate his experiences in the World War and tell how he
"drug" a wounded foot for a mile to the dressing-station.
The foot, I am glad to say, had made an excellent recovery,
but his English seemed to be still suffering.

"Irregardless"

Another young college instructor—in the fine arts this time
—was so careful of his speech that he had affected a slightly
trilled "r" in words like "great" and "grime," which amused
me considerably since I happened to know that it was
entirely unnatural. My amusement was heightened when
one day I heard him use the word "irregardless," which is
usually associated with ignorance or ineptitude in matters of
the use of language. Incidentally, a strong argument against
affectation in speech is that it throws one's errors into such
bold relief. We usually and rightly attribute most of the
mistakes of our friends to mere carelessness. But when they
occur in the speech of persons who are obviously taking great
pains to speak in a manner which they consider to be "correct," we can attribute them only to ignorance. And in
matters of dress, manners, and language, carelessness is somehow considered much more excusable than ignorance.

"Irregardless" seems to be a sort of absurd combination
of "irrespective" and "regardless," but irrespective of its
origin and regardless of its occasional use by some who ought
to know better, it is a word entirely without standing in the
speech of cultured people.

Another common error that it seems appropriate to mention at this point is the adding of the "s" to the word
"regard" in the expressions "in regard to" and "with regard
to." It is amazing how one little letter can affect our judgment of the culture and education of a speaker. As soon as
"in regards to" pops out, we feel instinctively that the one
who uses it is—well, let us say unfortunate in early associa-
tions, or extremely careless. But this, like so many mistakes,
seems to be the result of mixing two forms of expression,

"in regard to" and "as regards." Possibly also the common use of the word "regards" in expressions like "Give him my regards" has something to do with it.

"As" used for "that" or "than"

It is not now considered good to use "as" for "that" in sentences like "I don't know as I do," but I have been told that it may be still heard colloquially in the speech of some cultured New Englanders. And there was a time when it was quite correct to use "as" for "than" after comparatives, but that time is past, though it may still be heard in the rural South—and doubtless elsewhere—particularly after "rather," as in "I would rather go as to stay." How frequently good speech is a matter of being in accord with the present style! Today it is almost a mark of illiteracy to say, "I'd rather hit would be this 'un as that 'un," but at one time "it" was spelled and pronounced "hit," "as" was used for "than," and "one" was pronounced about as it is spelled, without the "w" sound that we now so curiously put before it. The words "alone" and "atone" were originally "all one" and "at one," and their present pronunciation shows how the word "one" was pronounced when they were first formed. The "w" sound seems to have been brought about by emphasizing the vowel and letting it trail off into an "uh" sound, as a long "o" in English frequently does. If the reader will pronounce "oh-un" rapidly several times in succession, he will see that it turns practically into "wun."

"Idear," "sawr," and "lawr"

It is very interesting to speculate as to the reasons for changes in pronunciation, both those which come to be considered a part of standard speech and those which remain the peculiarity of a certain section or small locality. One of the strangest of the latter is the habit common to many people who live in or near New York City—particularly in Brooklyn, I believe—of adding an "r" to the words that end in "aw," thus making "sawr" out of "saw," "lawr," out of "law," "droring" out of "drawing," and so on. It sounds almost incredible to one who hears it for the first time, and is apparently utterly without reason or excuse. But I have noticed that some people who do not add the "r" to these words do give a slight "uh" sound at the end of them, saying "law-uh," "saw-uh," and so on. Now an "uh" sound on the end of a word is by some speakers regularly turned into "ur," the reason being that they are unconsciously imitating the sound of the multitude of words in English which do properly end in this way, such as "runner," "reader," "baker," and a host of others. That is why many people—few of them in the South, of course—say "idear," "Emmar," and so forth, pronunciations that are common among those who say "lawr," but not restricted to them. The explanation of "lawr" is, then, that the speaker—or one of his ancestors—sets out to say "law-uh," and in accord with his usual habit adds the "r" sound.

Yet this does not explain why such a habit should be restricted to a small locality or why it originated in the East, where the people, as a rule, do not sound their "r's" very strongly. It would seem much more reasonable to find it in the Middle West, where the "r" is usually very prominent. Yet to the best of my knowledge, while many of our Middle Western friends hold their "r's" and sound them very vigorously, they do not add them improperly.

"Foist" for "first" and "erl" for "oil"

Another peculiar pronunciation, apparently originating on the East Side of New York is that represented by the spelling "foist" for "first" or "joinal" for "journal." These spellings do not, however, accurately represent the sound, and I know of no way of doing so in type. Rather strangely, some people in the South pronounce such words in much the same way, though there is a perceptible difference, and certainly no connection between the two, for it would be hard to find two sets of Americans of more widely differing habits, general outlook on life, and ancestry than these Southerners and the East Siders. About the only thing they agree on is voting the Democratic ticket, but this is merely another proof that politics makes strange bedfellows.

The East Siders who say "foist" and "joinal" are frequently accused of doing exactly the opposite with words in which the "oi" sound legitimately occurs by turning it into "er." It seems, for instance, as if they said "erl" for "oil." But the explanation for this remarkable contradiction is said to be that they really use the same sound for "oi" and "er," a sound midway between the two, but identical with neither. When used in "first" it seems nearer "oi," but when used in "oil," it seems nearer "er." This ingenious and plausible explanation I have taken from Mr. H. L. Mencken's *The American Language*, though Mr. Mencken does not claim the credit for it.

"Leave out" for "leave"

Some uneducated people—and some educated ones whose use of English has not been noticeably improved by the process of education—habitually use "leave out" for "leave." "When does the train leave out?" they ask. This, of course, has nothing to do with the "leave out" that means "omit," but is probably merely a failure to realize that the verb "leave" alone usually means "to go out from." Possibly their confusion is increased by the fact that it is correct to say, "The train leaves from the Pennsylvania Station," meaning, of course, that the train leaves *the city* from the Pennsylvania Station, not that it leaves "out of" the station.

"In back of" for "behind"

It is becoming more and more common to see the awkward phrase "in back of" used for "behind." It may seem strange to those who like it that "in front of" is in excellent standing with careful speakers, while "in back of," formed in exactly the same way, is not. I think the reason for this is that "in front of" has developed as a substitute for "before," since "before" has so many other uses, which pertain to time. But "behind" is used chiefly only in reference to place, and needs no substitute. Be that as it may, the fact remains that "in back of" is frowned upon at present, though it may some day have a better standing. Yet, rather oddly, "back of" is in very good colloquial use in America.

It would not be fair, however, to conceal from my readers the fact that the new *Webster* lists "in back of" as meaning "behind" without indicating that it is not in the best of use. Nevertheless, those who use it will find that there are many whom they would like to please who object strongly to it.

"Could of"

In rapid speech the word "have" is frequently cut so short that it is represented merely by "'ve" in print and sounds very much like "of." As far as sound goes, "You could've seen him," and "She would've gone," might well be "You could *of* seen him," and "She would *of* gone." There are people who think the word is "of" and actually write it in that way. This is ordinarily a sign of rather gross ignorance, but I recall among my pupils a young man with a decided literary gift who amazed me by writing "could of" in one of his themes. Another young man similarly gifted began the story of his life with the words, "I was *borned* . . ." though it is hard to see how any literate person could fail to know that "I was born" is the correct expression. Experiences like this have made me realize that it is not safe to assume that even the simplest points of English usage will be familiar to all those to whom we might reasonably expect them to be familiar.

"If I had have seen him"

There is a decided tendency among English-speaking people everywhere to add a syllable to the word "had" in expressions like "If I had seen him," making it "If I hada seen him." This extra syllable is sometimes expanded into the word "have" and so spoken and written, though, of course, it is entirely unreasonable and incorrect to say "If I *had have* seen him." Nevertheless, the Danish authority on English, Otto Jespersen, has made a list of a number of the appearances of this improper "had have" in English literature, most of them representing the speech of the illiterate, but a few representing a higher level of usage. It is probable that this unwarranted addition of "have" comes about from the fact that it is so often used to express past time with "would," "could," "should," and "might" in phrases like "could have," and so on, that it seems right to add it also to "had," though, as I have indicated, when the phrase is spoken, "had have" is more likely to be simply "hada." Similarly "could have" may be "coulda," as in "I wish you coulda been there." And, of course, the incorrect "had have" may turn into "had of," just as the correct "could have" turns into "could of."

The correct use of "had" . . . "have"

But the reader must not assume that there is never a time when the combination "had have" is in order, for there are certain sentences in which it is correct and the simple "had" incorrect. In the review of a book on Napoleon, appearing recently in a prominent news-magazine, the statement is made that at a birthday dinner on the island of St. Helena Napoleon wonders "if he had not better died after one of his victories." It should be, "if he had not better *have* died . . ." The expression "had better," like "had rather" and others of the same sort, is always followed by the infinitive without "to," as in "You had better go, stay, come, run," and so on. "Had" is here not the indicative and not an auxiliary, but the subjunctive of a main verb, meaning "would have, hold, consider, or find" and the infinitive is its object. A teacher may say to a pupil, "You had better study your lesson," but if the studying is something that should have taken place in the past, the correct expression is, "You had better have studied your lesson instead of playing, as you did." "Have studied" is here the perfect infinitive, just as it is in "should have studied."

An interesting circumstance in connection with this proper use of "had have" is that even Jespersen was led astray by it to the extent of including a line of Tennyson's in which it appears, in his list of examples of the improper "had have." The line is from *Becket* III, 3:

> She had safelier have slain an archbishop.

This is really an example of the "had better" idiom, with "safelier" in place of "better," and if the "have" had been omitted, it would have been incorrect. I am glad to say that Dr. Jespersen has very readily admitted this in a personal letter, in which he states that the quotation should have been put down as an example of the "had better" idiom. His frank admission of the mistake is in refreshing contrast to the attitude of many lesser men, who seem to feel that they must maintain the pose of infallibility, and when they cannot refute the reasoning of one who questions a statement of theirs, simply ignore the communication.

Yet Tennyson himself was not always careful to use "have" where the sense demands it in constructions of this kind. In *The Voyage of Maeldune* he has the following:

> Each of them liefer had died than have done one
> another a wrong.

"Liefer" is the comparative of the word still in colloquial use in expressions like "I had as *lief* (often incorrectly called "leave") go as stay." "Had liefer" is an idiom of the "had better" type and like the latter should be followed by the infinitive. It should be here, "had liefer *have* died," as indeed the poet recognizes himself, since he continues with "than *have* done." If this "have" is correct, there should be another before "died."

Most amazingly, there is another error in the line—the use of "each" with "one another." We do not say, "Each did one another a wrong," but "*They* did one another a wrong," or "Each did the other (or another) a wrong." All in all, the line is an excellent example of the fact that even a great writer may go sadly astray in his use of English—which ought to be a source of encouragement to us common folk, who sometimes feel perhaps unduly humiliated over our mistakes.

"Might could" and "used to could"

Some mistakes arise from an effort to supply an actual deficiency in our language, for English, like all other tongues, has some imperfections. It is not uncommon to hear people say, "I might could go," or "I used to could see better than I do now." The correct expressions are, of course, "I might be able to go" and "I used to be able to see better," or "I could see better formerly," or "I was once able to see better," or something similar. The auxiliary verb "might" is to be followed by the infinitive (without "to"), and the verb whose present tense is "can" and past tense (indicative and subjunctive) is "could" has no infinitive. The one who says "might could" or "used to could" is mistakenly endeavoring to substitute the past tense "could" for the missing infinitive. Neither has "can" a past participle, and that is why we cannot say, "He has could," but must make it, "He has been able." And it is the absence of the infinitive again that makes it possible for us to say, "I shall can," (unless canning fruit is under discussion), and requires us to make it, "I shall be able."

Likewise "shall," "will," and "may" have neither infinitives nor past participles. "Must" and "ought" have only the present tense of the indicative, though "must" was formerly, and is still occasionally, used as the past. "Ought" originated as the past subjunctive of "owe," but is not now so considered.

Most of these verbs in German have a complete conjugation. A German, for instance, can say not only "I must," but also "I musted," "I shall must," and "I have musted"— that is, the German equivalents for these expressions, of course—whereas an English-speaking person can say only "I must." For the past, he must substitute "I had to" or "was compelled to" or "was obliged to," and for the future, "I shall have to," and so on. It is in the use of such verbs that the study of our sister-language German throws a great deal of light upon an obscure point in English, since it enables us to see our language as it once was. The study of Latin is likewise of value in the understanding of English grammar, but not upon this particular point.

"Most" for "almost" and similar errors

The number of reasonably well educated people who think that "most" can be correctly substituted for "almost" is surprising. In fact, it would appear at times that almost everybody (not "most everybody") thinks so. A simple rule for guidance is that when the meaning "nearly" may be substituted, the word to be used is "almost." "Most of the people have gone," is correct, but not "Most all the people have gone." It should be "almost all." In ordinary conversation the mistake is not so serious, for then we may imagine that in the mind of the speaker who says "Most all," the word is spelled with an apostrophe, " 'most," to indicate that he realizes it to be a mere shortening of "almost." But to use "most" without the apostrophe in place of "almost" is really a sign of ignorance.

Another thing that is surprising is the number of people who do not know that the verbs corresponding to "embroidery" and "laundry" are "embroider" and "launder." Many women will say, "After this is 'embroideried,' it will have to be 'laundried.' " The correct words in such a sentence are "embroidered" (pronounced "embroidurd") and "laundered" (pronounced "laundurd").

"I was sorry to hear about you being sick"

A rather more serious matter, though one still open to some dispute, is the error involved in such a sentence as, "I was sorry to hear about *you* being sick." It will be evident,

I think, to the large majority of readers that "you" in this sentence should be replaced by "your." "About your being sick" certainly sounds much better. Yet just as certainly it is correct to say, "I saw *you* crossing the street." Indeed, no one would think of saying, "I saw *your* crossing the street."

The reason for the difference in usage is that the two words ending in "ing"—"being" and "crossing"—are not of the same kind, though they have the same appearance. In the first sentence "being" is a noun—a verbal noun, called a gerund—used as the object of the preposition "about." What one is sorry to hear about is the sickness—the "being sick." But in the second sentence "crossing" is an adjective, describing "you." "Whom did you see?" "I saw you, and saw you (as you were) crossing the street."

The general rule is that the possessive form of a noun or pronoun is to be used before the verbal noun, or gerund, that ends in "ing." Examples of the correct use are:

> They regretted *his refusing* to come. The *boy's staying* out late was a source of worry to his mother. *Its being* false makes a great difference. Many Democrats were disturbed over the *President's proposing* to enlarge the Supreme Court.

Examples of the use of the participle, which does not require the possessive of the noun or pronoun, are:

> We heard the *train coming*. He felt the *water rushing* past. They caught sight of *him, swimming* in the distance.

Sometimes it may be a little difficult to decide which form of expression should be used. In one of our better magazines a few years ago appeared a sentence of this sort: "The newspaper published a picture of their receiving a check." The point is a rather delicate one, but it seemed to me then, and still does, that it would have been better to say, "of them receiving a check." The question revolves around whether the picture was of the receiving or of the men as they received the check. The act of receiving is a somewhat indefinite process that could hardly be shown in a photograph, but there would be no difficulty in making a picture of the men as they were in the act of receiving the check.

Sometimes either form may be used, though with different meanings. We may say, "I am surprised at him playing," or "I am surprised at his playing." The first means, "I am surprised that he played," that is to say, "I thought he was too sick to play," or "I didn't know that he knew how to play." But the second means, "I am surprised at how well (or how poorly) he played."

Two things must be frankly admitted, however. The first is that good writers have not always used the possessive form before the gerund, when logic seemed to call for it; the second, that sometimes it is impossible to do so, as in the case of the word "this," which has no possessive. We say, "I am sorry to know of *its* being true," but we cannot very well say, "I am sorry to know of *this's* being true." We simply have to leave it at "of this being true," and if we are sticklers for accuracy, we can tell ourselves that "this" is a peculiar word in which the possessive has the same form as the nominative, just as in Latin *civis* may be either nominative or genitive. "These" likewise has no possessive.

Among the good writers who have not used the possessive with the gerund on occasion, is Irving, who wrote "a doubt as to *Shakespeare having been born* in her house." Tennyson has "pardon *me saying*," and Charlotte Brontë, "*hear of me being discovered*." Nevertheless, I feel sure that the large majority of readers will agree that it sounds better to say "*Shakespeare's* having been born," "pardon *my* saying," and "hear of *my* being discovered."

A question which arises in connection with the use of the gerund is whether we should say, for instance, "I was surprised at its being *he*," or "at its being him." While there is some ground here for dispute, the better opinion seems to favor "its being he" on the ground that we say—or should say—"It was he."

"I should have liked to have been there"

We often hear statements like "I should have liked to have been there." While it is barely possible that the one who says such a thing really means it, the chances are very strong that he simply means and should say, "I should have liked to be there," though another way of expressing the same thought —not as logical, but in good use—is "I should like to have been there."

A somewhat similar mistake, heard occasionally, is, "You ought to have made him *gone*," where it is obvious that "made him *go*" is the reasonable wording.

"No sooner . . . when"

"I had no sooner sat down *when* he came and sat beside me." "He had no sooner started *when* he turned and came back." Such sentences should have "than" in place of "when," and are, once more, the result of confusing two methods of expressing the same thought. "I had *hardly* (or *scarcely*) sat down *when* he came and sat beside me" is correct, and so is "I had *no sooner* sat down *than* he came . . ." but when we take "no sooner" from one sentence and combine it with "when" from the other, the result is disastrous to the principles of congruity, even though the meaning is still evident.

"Feel badly"

Certain mistakes obtain such currency among cultured people that they often pass unrecognized and carry with them no stigma of social inferiority, as others do. Among them is "I feel badly" for "I feel bad." Indeed there is at least one book on the use of English enjoying a considerable reputation which vigorously defends the use of "I feel badly" on the following grounds. It is generally admitted that it is correct to say "I feel well." "Now," says the author, "since we use the adverb 'well' with 'feel,' we should also say 'feel badly.' " The fallacy of this argument is that in the expression "I feel well," the word "well" is not an adverb, but an adjective, as the author might have ascertained from a dictionary. And one can soon see whether or not "I feel badly" is correct by considering whether he would say, "I feel gladly," and, "I feel sadly." Obviously the natural—and correct—forms are "feel glad" and "feel sad." What objection is there, then, to "feel bad"?

It would seem that our reluctance to say, "I feel bad" arises from the fact that we are prone to associate the word "bad" with moral badness—a legitimate association, to be sure, but not the only one. "I feel bad" really means "I feel myself to be in bad health," or "in bad spirits." Notice that it has two opposites—"I feel well," in reference to health, and "I feel good," in reference to spirits.

Although "to feel well" has only one meaning—that is, to feel oneself in good health—"to look well" has two, the other one pertaining to general appearance. "You look well in that hat," means that you make a pleasing appearance in it. It should be noted that "well" is likewise an adjective in such a sentence, though its meaning is different from that in "to feel well."

"I expect he was here yesterday"

Most English textbooks teach that the word "expect" properly refers to the future and that consequently it is right to say, "I expect he will be here tomorrow," but wrong to say, "I expect he was here yesterday." The word they usually urge in place of "expect" in a sentence referring to the past is "suppose," though sometimes they suggest "think." Fowler, however, defends the use of "expect" in this manner. According to him, what is in the mind of a person who says, "I expect he was here yesterday," is "I expect that when the truth is revealed, it will be found that he was here yesterday." While I have the greatest respect for Fowler's scholarship and for his common sense, somehow I cannot help feeling that this is a far-fetched explanation. It seems to me that "suspect" is really the appropriate word in such a sentence, and that "expect" is substituted for it from a mistaken feeling that "suspect" must not be used except where it is a question of an evil action of some sort—much the same feeling that makes many of us incorrectly prefer "feel badly" to "feel bad."

Of course, when we say that we suspect a man, we mean we suspect him of doing something wrong. But the situation is different when the word "suspect" is followed by a clause introduced by "that." Suppose, for instance, that an anonymous gift of a large sum of money to a college has been announced by the authorities, and that Mr. Smith is an alumnus of the college, of large means and generous disposition. Would it not be perfectly natural for some one to remark, "I suspect it was Mr. Smith who gave the money"? It is quite true, of course, that "suspect" is more often used in its bad sense, but that happens because human beings generally conceal their bad deeds and make their good ones known, so that there is not so much occasion to suspect the latter.

It does not seem to me that the textbook advice to replace "expect" by "suppose" or "think" when it refers to the past, is good. "I suppose he was here yesterday" does not express the thought that most people have in mind. And "think" is too strong. "I daresay" would do very well, but not many Americans would naturally use "I daresay" in conversation.

A difficult sentence

Sometimes we find a real difficulty in expressing our thoughts in language that is correct and yet simple. Consider this sentence, for instance: "She sent me a present that I didn't know what it was." Some readers may have received presents of this kind, but the objection to the method of telling about it is that the word "that" has no construction, as the grammarians put it. The really logical way of putting it is to leave out "it" and say, "She sent me a present that I didn't know what was," but I am quite sure no English-speaking person would think of saying it in that way. Indeed I know of no way of completing the sentence that is both graceful and correct when we begin with "She sent me a present that—" We might say, "She sent me a present of such a sort that I didn't know what it was." Here "that" is simply a conjunction, whereas in the first one it is a relative pronoun without any use. We might also say, "She sent me a present of whose use I was ignorant," but that sounds a trifle stilted. Some would solve the difficulty by simply saying, "She sent me a present, but I didn't know what it was."

I once heard a woman say, "She's the type of visitor that you can't do anything else while she's around." Here is the same difficulty—namely, that the relative pronoun "that" has no construction; yet it is more easily remedied. The sentence is a confusion of "She's a visitor of such a type that you can't do anything else (than entertain her) while she's around," and "She's the type of visitor that prevents you from doing anything else . . ." both of which are correct.

I trust this discussion of errors has made it clear that they are not all of the same seriousness. Some suggest ignorance and a low order of social culture, and are to be avoided at all costs, if one cares for the good opinion of his fellow men. Others are more or less current among people of high social standing. It is well to avoid these expressions also, but the situation is not so pressing. Millions of Americans will find enough of the more serious sort in their own speech to demand all their attention.

An eighteen-year-old boy, a junior in an American high school, recently won the five-thousand-dollar prize in an essay contest on the subject "How Can America Stay out of War?" After he arrived in New York to receive the prize, however, a strange fact came to light. It was discovered that the essay bore a strong resemblance to one written by a university president and published in a magazine a few months before. Confronted with the evidence, the boy readily admitted that he had copied largely from the article, but calmly pointed out that the conditions said nothing about the necessity for originality in the essay. Here is his account of the matter, as given word for word in a newspaper:

> "My history teacher gave us this subject *How to Keep America out of War* as part of our class-work. My brother and me have been boarding at Mrs. Blank's place all winter on account of it's right cold on our farm and the roads get bad. I see where I have to get me some material to write that essay and I asked Mrs. Blank did she have any-thing and she had this magazine. She gets it all the time. I looked it over and I reckoned I might get some stuff out of it, and I did. It was filled with a lot of words that was too big, and I took them out and put in words I thought of. I didn't think at the time I'd get anywheres with it. Thought it was a good-enough piece, but I was sure they'd be bet-ter ones than that. I didn't think it was so hot."

The boy who uttered these words was a junior in high school, who according to his own statement given else-where in the article, was weak in mathematics, but "did pretty well" in English. His history teacher rated him as "probably the brightest boy we have ever had in school." Yet his English, as exemplified in his statement to the news-paper, is almost that of an illiterate. Nobody expects a schoolboy to talk like a book, and his characterization of the essay that he copied as "not so hot" is a piece of harmless slang at his age. But surely no one would have thought him affected if he had said, "My brother and I have been board-ing," instead of "my brother and me," or put "words that *were*" instead of "words that *was*," or changed "on account of" to "because," or substituted "there'd" for "they'd," not to mention the correction of other glaring crudities in the statement.

One can well believe that the boy did not deliberately set out to be dishonest, and it is quite probable that he had the ability to use good written English in his school compositions. If he had put his statement into writing, it would no doubt have been far better expressed. But his speech is fairly typical of that of tens of thousands of his fellows in high school, scattered all over the country, even of many college students, and—incredible as it sounds—of some college professors. In our efforts to extend the benefits of higher education to everybody, we are rapidly building up in this country a large body of supposedly educated people unlike any other set of educated people the world has ever seen, in that they cannot—or do not—speak their native language correctly. Is this to continue, or shall we Americans demonstrate to an incredulous world that the great mass of our people, along with their rapid absorption of the minor elements of culture, can acquire what is perhaps its major element and certainly its major evidence—a mastery of our mother tongue?

WORD-ORIGINS
FALSE AND TRUE

XVIII

The flood of misinformation that is constantly being poured out concerning the English language extends even to the matter of the origins of English words—a subject which misstatements and exaggerations can hardly render more curiously fascinating than it already is.

The authors of these false derivations seem to go out of their way to invent far-fetched explanations of words whose origin ought to be evident to an intelligent person and can at any rate be readily learned by referring to any complete dictionary. It is frequently published in newspapers and magazines, for instance, that the word "news" originated from a custom of early newspapers of printing at the top of the first page a diagram showing arrows pointing north, east, west, and south, in order to indicate that their news came from everywhere. These compass-points were designated by the initial letters N, E, W, S, and from their combination came the word "news," according to the story. I cannot help wondering whether the people who put such a weird tale into print really believe it themselves.

In the first place, the letters in such a diagram, if made into a word at all, which is unlikely, would naturally come in

the order NWES, since it would look like this: $W \stackrel{N}{+} E$. In the second place, the words "news" actually means "the things that are new," as common sense would indicate, and as all the dictionaries testify. It was originally plural, and people asked, "What *are* the news?" not "What *is* the news?" as they do today. It seems a little odd for an English adjective to be pluralized, but it was apparently done after the order of the French *les nouvelles*.

"Sirloin" and "nowadays"

And then there is that other fanciful little story about the origin of "sirloin," which is no doubt familiar to most of my readers. According to it, King James I of England one day ate a cut of beef which he liked very much, and learned upon inquiry that it was a piece of loin. He thereupon drew his sword, touched the remainder of it, and said, "I dub thee Sir Loin," after the manner, of course, of conferring knighthood on a man. Both the *Century* and the *Oxford* dictionaries specifically deny this story, which fact will probably not, however, keep it from being published over and over again, as time goes on, for few people ever question any statement about English which they see in print, and as the newspapers are read more than the dictionaries, most of them will never see the truth about it. If our lexicographers know the facts in the case, the "sir" in "sirloin" is simply a corrupted spelling of the French word *sur*, meaning "on" or "over." The sirloin is the cut over the loin.

A friend sent me a newspaper clipping recently, in which among some true and interesting statements with regard to the derivation of words, the assertion was made that "nowadays" is simply a corruption of "in our days." This is an ingenious etymology, but unfortunately not true—at least not believed by the men who make it their business to find out where our words come from. They say that "nowadays" is, as one would naturally expect, a combination of "now" and "a" (meaning "in") and "day," with the adverbial ending "s" found on words like "towards" and "backwards." Incidentally, the tendency now seems to be toward omitting the "s" from the two latter.

"Fore!", "spit and image" and "Hobson's choice"

In one of those newspaper features which exploit the incredible or the unusual, there appeared the statement that the cry of "Fore!" used by golfers to warn those on the course ahead of them that they are about to hit the ball originated from the habit which many of them had of counting "One! Two! Three!" as they made practice swings and then hitting the ball on the count of "Four!" But the new *Webster* gives the much more simple, reasonable explanation that "Fore!" is a contraction of "Before!" and means, of course, "Look out before!"

I can sympathize with those who are misled by these false stories of etymology, for I have been similarly taken in. We sometimes hear it said that a child is the very spit and image (or spittin' image, or spit image) of one of his parents. I came across what seemed to be a very plausible explanation of this strange expression in a newspaper article—namely, that it originated with Negro "mammies" in the South in an effort to say "spirit and image." Impressed with its ingenuity, and taking for granted that the expression was really Southern, I proceeded to repeat the explanation in a talk on the radio. Fortunately, one of my listeners questioned it, and when I consulted the *Oxford Dictionary*—as I should have done in the first place—I discovered, to my surprise, that the expression is not Southern at all, but was used in England in the seventeenth century, and originates from the belief more or less prevalent in various parts of the world that the saliva of a human being contains, so to speak, the very essence of him.

All complete dictionaries give the origin of words, but the *Oxford* is remarkable in that it gives for every word and expression a quotation of the passage in which it first appears in English literature, along with the date and the name of the source and author. More than that, it does this for *every meaning* of every word, and in addition gives further quotations, each with its date, illustrating the use of the word by writers at intervals on down to recent times. In discussing the use of "none" in an earlier chapter I mentioned that King Alfred used it as a plural in the year 888. This piece of information I obtained, as the reader has doubtless surmised, from the *Oxford*.

To one who is interested in the history of words, this monumental work, which took more than fifty years in preparation and required the services of thousands of volunteer readers in addition to its regular staff of editors, is invaluable. But two words of caution are necessary as to its use. First, its pronunciations and its opinions on matters of usage are British, rather than American. Second, the reader must be careful not to infer, as some mistakenly do, that the various words were not used in English before the date of the quotation giving their first appearance in literature. Most of them came first into the spoken language, and there is not any way to tell how long they had existed in it beforehand, or whether they had not been previously used in some written document which has not come down to us.

The expression "Hobson's choice" means no choice at all. It originated, according to the dictionaries, some three hundred years ago from the custom of a livery-stable keeper named Hobson, who lived in Cambridge, England. In order to keep certain of his horses from being used more than the others, he required the customer always to take the horse that stood nearest the door, depriving him thus of any choice in the matter. Yet on a national radio program a year or two ago the statement was made that the expression arose from the feat of the late Richmond Pearson Hobson in sinking the collier *Merrimac* in Santiago Harbor during our war with Spain in 1898. Oddly enough, the conductor of the program, who gave out this piece of misinformation, stated clearly the meaning of the expression—no choice at all —emphasized the fact that Lieutenant Hobson *volunteered* for the task—that is to say, chose it freely—and still apparently failed to see that his false derivation involved a contradiction. But I have often noted that the minds of otherwise intelligent people cease somehow to function when a point of English is the issue.

"Date"

But let us look into the history of a few very common English words, and see whether we may not find some true stories to match these fanciful inventions. The word "date," for instance, means one thing to the student of history, another to the grocer, and still a third to the young people. There is an obvious connection, of course, between the first and third meanings, but how did it all come about?

To begin with the "date" of the grocer has no connection with the other two. It comes from the Greek word *daktylos*, a finger, and the name is applied to the fruit because of its resemblance to the human finger—a short and stubby finger, to be sure. *Daktylos* went from Greek into Latin, and then into French, where it was shortened to "date" and handed over to English.

The "date" that refers to time is, however, a contraction of the Latin word *datus*, meaning "given," the past participle of *do, dare, dedi, datus*, which causes so much trouble to beginning Latin students, because they all want to say *davi* for the perfect instead of *dedi*. The reader has doubtless noticed at the foot of legal or official documents words such as, "Given under my hand and seal at so-and-so on such-and-such a day." This is an old form coming down from the middle ages, when it was always written in Latin and began therefore with the word *datus*, or more accurately with another form of it, *data*. *Data* was changed into *date* by the French, from whom we took it, and the word first meant both the time and the place, as it still sometimes does when we speak of a letter or other document, though usually now it means only the time, often merely the year, of an event.

The way in which the young people have transformed the meaning of "date" is remarkable. It is not difficult to see how it comes to mean what in more formal English is "engagement" or "appointment," but they do not stop here. Having these appointments is called "dating" and the one with whom the appointment is made is called a "date," as well as the appointment itself. "Bring your date over to my house," is a way of putting it which shows the extreme flex-

ibility of the English language when it is handled by those
bent on expressing their thoughts in as few words as possible.

Reading dates and numbers

A few words may be appropriate here on the reading of
dates. Columbus discovered America in the year 1492.
The shortest, crispest way to read this date is "fourteen
ninety-two." If more formality is desired, it may be "fourteen hundred and ninety-two." If there should be any reason for extreme formality, it might be "one thousand, four
hundred and ninety-two." There is never any reason for
saying, "fourteen and ninety-two," for such a way of reading the date has neither the merit of brevity nor that of
formality. The same principles, of course, apply to all dates.
The year 1910 is either "nineteen ten" or "nineteen hundred
and ten," not "nineteen and ten."

It is very much to be regretted that textbooks on arithmetic and teachers of the subject now usually instruct pupils
to read a number like 253 as "two hundred fifty-three."
That is not English. The English custom is to say, "two
hundred *and* fifty-three," and there is no good reason why
it should give way to this uncouth substitute. Of course, its
meaning is just as clear. So is the meaning clear if we say,
"Here is a basket of apples, pears, oranges," but who wants
to omit the "and" in such an expression?

The arithmetic texts urge this barbarity on the ground
that it is of assistance in the reading of decimals. They wish
the pupil not to use the word "and" except to mark the
place of the decimal point. They would therefore have him
read a number like 435.692 as "four hundred thirty-five and
six hundred ninety-two thousandths," rather than "four
hundred *and* thirty-five and six hundred *and* ninety-two
thousandths." It is quite true that their method would avoid
confusion in cases like that of the two numbers 400.005 and
.405, both of which under the ordinary plan would be read
"four hundred and five thousandths." But such a difficulty
can be avoided without changing the English method of
reading numbers. By far the best way of reading decimals
is that used by practically all scientists or mathematicians

who deal frequently with them. Under their system, a number like 435.692 is read "four three five point six nine two." 400.005 would be "four naught naught point naught naught five," and .405 would be "point four naught five." What could be simpler?

"Helpmeet," "coach," and "pig in a poke"

But to return to our derivations. A wife is sometimes referred to as a "helpmate" and sometimes as a "helpmeet." Both terms are now in good standing, but one originated in a mistake and the other in a mistaken effort to correct the first. The eighteenth verse of the second chapter of Genesis, as given in the King James Version, reads: "And the Lord God said, It is not good that the man should be alone; I will make him an help meet for him." "Meet" is here used in the old sense of "suitable, fitting," and the suitable help that Adam was to have was, of course, Eve. But in some way the words "help" and "meet" were run together, some people began to speak of Eve as Adam's "helpmeet" and the term was extended to all wives. Others, to whom "helpmeet" sounded strange, decided that it must be a corruption of "helpmate," and proceeded to use that word, which now is more common than the other, and deservedly so, for it expresses very well the idea in the verse of Scripture, even though it is of mistaken origin.

Why should a football coach be called a coach, when that is really the name of a carriage? The answer is that he makes it easier for the players to learn the game, just as riding in a carriage is easier than walking. The term "coach" was first applied not to a teacher of athletic sports, however, but to a private tutor in subjects like Latin and mathematics. One who engaged such a tutor was said by the other college students to be riding in a coach, because he could cover the ground faster than they. This is exactly the reason why students of the present day designate as a "pony" or "jack" the little book in which they find their Latin or German or French already translated for them, and which saves them— illegally—the trouble of digging it out for themselves.

It should perhaps be added that "coach" as the name of a vehicle came to us through the French and the German from *Kocs*, the name of a village of Hungary where coaches were first made.

Most people readily recognize that a handkerchief is simply a "hand kerchief," for "kerchief" is still used as a separate word. There are few who know, however, that the syllable "ker" is a corruption of "cover" and that "chief" means head, so that a "kerchief" is simply a "cover-head," a derivation that in view of the current fashion among American women of tying peasant-kerchiefs over their heads, does not seem so strange after all. When women began to carry pieces of cloth similar to kerchiefs in their hands, they were naturally styled "hand kerchiefs," and when men took up the fashion, and carried them in their pockets instead, the expression "pocket handkerchief" came into use. We have then the remarkable situation that a pocket handkerchief is, by derivation, a covering for the head to be carried in the hand and put into the pocket.

There is an old saying, "Don't buy a pig in a poke," which means little to most people. In the Southern mountain regions, however, it would be perfectly intelligible, for there a sack or bag is regularly called a "poke," another word which comes to us from the French, as may be seen by its similarity to the French *poche*, meaning "pocket." And this English word "pocket" is nothing but a diminiutive of "poke." In other words a pocket is a "poke-ette," a little poke or bag. "Pouch" is the same word in a different form, and a poached egg (not "porched" egg, as some strangely imagine) is so called because the yolk, in poaching, becomes enclosed in a sort of pouch or pocket formed by the white. But the "poach" that has to do with taking game or fish illegally on private grounds and "poke" that means "thrust" or "prod" are entirely different words, of Germanic origin.

There is some similarity in sound between the words "boulevard" and "bulwark," but apparently none in meaning. Yet the two are different forms of the same word. "Bulwark" comes from the old German "bolwerk," which the French also took and turned into "boulevard," retaining the original meaning of "rampart" or "fortification."   But in the course of time the old fortifications of French cities were torn down, and in their stead broad streets used largely for pleasure driving were constructed, so that the word "boulevard" came over into English meaning a street of this kind.   But with the advent of the automobile a new turn has been given to the word.   When we now say that a street has been "boulevarded," it means that those who are driving on it have the right of way at intersections, while drivers on cross streets must come to a stop before entering it.   This is, in a way, a return to the original meaning, for the boulevard acts as a sort of protection or bulwark to those who are on it.

"Mr. and Mrs." and "Ma'am"

The abbreviation "Mrs." is from "mistress," though it is, of course, not pronounced "mistress," but "missiz" or "mizziz."   The latter is the almost universal formal pronunciation in the South, though the editors of our dictionaries seem never to have heard of it.   In rapid or careless speech in that section it is frequently shortened to "Miz." "Miss" is likewise a shortened form of "mistress," but it should be noted that it is not considered an abbreviation and consequently does not require a period after it, as do "Mr." and "Mrs."   "Mrs." was at one time used for unmarried as well as married women, and it is only in comparatively recent times that it has been limited to the latter.

"Mistress" is the feminine of "mister," which is itself a corruption of "master."   "Master" came to us from the French, who took it from the Latin *magister*, which was used as a general title for people holding high positions. And the root of the word *magister* is the syllable "mag," meaning "large," found also in the Latin *magnus*, which has come down to us in "magnify," "magnitude" and "magnate."   In other words, the "magister," like the magnate, was the "big shot," as the slang phrase puts it today.

Like the abbreviations we have been discussing, "sir" and "madam" are tokens of respect, and like them they go back through the French to the Latin. "Sir" is ultimately from the Latin *senior* meaning "older," which we have taken over without change as the English "senior." "Madam" is the French *ma dame*, meaning "my lady," and comes from Latin *mea domina*. *Domina* is the feminine of *dominus*, "master," and likewise kin to *dominari*, "to dominate" or "rule over."

"Madam" is of course often abbreviated simply to "ma'am" (preferably pronounced "mam," not "mom.") Children formerly were taught to say "Yes, ma'am" and "Yes, sir" to their parents and to older people in general, and that custom still obtains largely in the South, but elsewhere the tendency is to leave those forms to servants or those of inferior position. Oddly enough, "Yes, sir" is often considered good form when "Yes, ma'am" is frowned upon. A Canadian pupil told me that in Canada (at least in his section of it) pupils answered "Here, sir" when a man teacher called the roll, but simply "Here" when it was called by a woman. He added that they felt that something was lacking in the latter instance and often were uncomfortable about it, but simply could not bring themselves to utter the word "ma'am." All this seems very strange to one reared in the South, where men and boys regularly use "ma'am" in addressing ladies—the term "lady" including all women of any social standing.

"Yes, ma'am" and "No, ma'am" are sometimes rather inelegantly abbreviated to "Yes'm" and "No'm." It is interesting to reflect that this "m" sound is added to the words by some people today in the United States because the Romans in Italy two thousand years ago used the word *domina* for the mistress of the household. Julius Caesar took the Roman arms and the Latin language into France, which he called *Gallia*, about fifty years before the birth of Christ. The Celtic people whom he conquered there finally adopted Latin and changed *domina* to *dame*. Then the descendants of a band of Norwegians who had settled in France and learned the French speech carried it to England under William the Conqueror in 1066, the word *madame* was taken over into English, changed to "madam," contracted to "ma'am," brought to this country some six hundred years later, and finally still further shortened in the speech of some till the single letter "m" is all that is left of the stately Latin *domina*. And yet, now as then, it is essentially the same symbol of respect.

"Pants," "bunk," "flower," "check"

The English language has many words which come from the classic Greek, but few would ever suspect that the colloquial "pants" is one of them. Its history is very curious. The accusative plural of the ancient Greek word for "all" was *panta*, the word for "lion" *leon*. The Greeks combined the two into a man's name, Pantaleon, meaning "in all respects a lion." This name was handed down to the Romans, who in turn gave it to the Italians. In the course of time a very holy man by the name of Pantaleon became after his death the patron saint of Venice. Many Venetian children were named after him—so many in fact that "Pantaleon" came to stand for a Venetian about as today "John Bull" stands for an Englishman. Then in Italian comedies there came to be a stock comic character in the form of a Venetian, called Pantaleon of course. To make him funnier he was dressed in a costume in which the breeches and stockings were made all in one piece—a new thing in those days. These garments came to be called *pantaleone* from the name of the character—just as bloomers were named after Mrs. Bloomer—the word passed over into French as *pantalon*, was taken into English as "pantaloons," and finally abbreviated, especially in America, into "pants." From Greece to Rome to Venice to France to England to America—from about 2000 B.C to nearly 2000 A.D.—an adjective meaning "all," part of a man's name, of a saint's name, of a comic character's name, and finally the term for an ordinary garment—such is the condensed history of this little everyday word.

These words are being written in Asheville, North Carolina, in the county of Buncombe—the only county, to the best of my knowledge, whose name has become a part of the English language. According to the new *Webster*, it originated from a remark made by Felix Walker, who from

1819 to 1821 was a representative in the United States Congress for the district in which the county is located. While he was speaking, other members of the house impatiently demanded a vote on the question at issue, but he persisted, saying that the people of his district expected it, and he was bound "to make a speech for Buncombe." The *Century* and the *Oxford* tell the story in somewhat different form, but at any rate it became a common saying in Congress, that a member who was speaking with obvious insincerity or for the effect it would produce on his constituents was speaking for Buncombe. From this it was only a step to calling any pointless or foolish talk "buncombe." The world seems to have been waiting for the word, for it spread with rapidity. In England the spelling is usually "bunkum," and the slang "bunk" is merely an abbreviation of the word, which seems destined to last as long as English is spoken and human nature remains what it is. But let us devoutly hope that the amount of buncombe put forth about the use of our language will at least diminish as the years go by.

Though the two are quite similar in sound and spelling, it will surprise most people, no doubt, to learn that "flower" and "flour" are in reality one and the same word. The original spelling was "flour," but the meaning "flower." What we now make our bread with was then called "meal," but the finer portion of it came to be known as "the flower of the meal," just as we now speak of "the flower of the family" or "the flower of the army," meaning the finest member of the family or the finest soldiers of the army— presumably because the flower is the finest part of the plant. When it became possible to grind all the "meal" to the fineness of the best portion of it, it was all called simply "flour," and the term "meal" gradually restricted to a coarser substance, such as corn-meal. Later the spelling for the blossom was changed to its present form, but the bread-making substance kept the older one.

We get the words from the French *fleur*, which in turn is derived from the Latin *flos*, *floris*, meaning "flower," from which we get directly "floral," "flourish," and the girl's name "Flora." Notice that the English word "blossom" is in its first syllable quite similar to the Latin *flos*. There is in fact a connection between the two, though not so direct as that between *flos* and "floral," or even that between *flos* and "flower." Our word "blossom"—and also "bloom"—comes down from Old English, sometimes called Anglo-Saxon, which, as readers will recall, originated in Germany, not England, and is rather closely kin to modern German, in which, as evidence, the word for "flower" is *Blume*.

The ancient Germanic language from which much of English and nearly all of German is derived was itself a descendant, or branch, of a still older language, which our scholars call Indo-European, and Latin, as we have seen, is another branch of the same parent-tongue. English "blossom" and "bloom" represent the Germanic (or Teutonic) version of the original Indo-European word for "flower," and *flos* is the Latin version of it. The two versions separated possibly five or ten thousand years before the birth of Christ, when the ancestors of the Romans left the common Indo-European home and migrated to Italy. They stayed apart from that time till about seven hundred years ago, when the Norman-French under William the Conqueror brought the Latin version to England, and side by side "blossom" and "flower" exist in English speech today.

When the word "check" is mentioned, many people will instantly think of that meaning which was in the mind of the man who said that to him the most beautiful three words in the English language were, "Enclosed find check." But the word has a strange variety of apparently unrelated meanings. If your brakes fail to check your car properly, you drive into a repair-shop and ask the mechanic to check your brakes. After the work is done, you may reach into the pocket of your checked suit—if your fancy runs to suits of that kind—and take out your check-book to pay for it. You get a check for your baggage or your hat, and you check off the items on a list by placing a check-mark by the side of each.

And yet none of these widely-differing meanings is the original, which can be found only in the game of chess. When a chess-player has so arranged his pieces that one of them threatens to capture his opponent's king on the next move, he calls out "Check!" The king is then said to be "in check," and if the opponent cannot get him out of check on the next move, the game is lost. The checking piece serves as a restraint on the king's motions, for he cannot, ordinarily, move in its direction. Hence "to check" means fundamentally to restrain or hold back. So, naturally, we say the brakes check the car. Your baggage-check restrains the railroad from giving your baggage to anybody else. The bank check is so called because the name was first given to what we now call the stub, the part that remains in your check-book, shows you how much you have drawn out, and hence restrains you from over-drawing your account. A checking list restrains you from attending to the same item twice or overlooking any item, and very naturally the mark which you place by each item as it is attended to is called a check-mark. A piece of cloth that has the pattern of a checker-board—or chess board—is said to be checked, and that accounts for the checked suit.

But to start with, the word "check" is a corruption of the Persian word *shah* meaning "king," and when the player calls out "Check!" he is really crying "King!"—that is to say, "Look out for your king!" One of the most interesting developments in the use of this word is in connection with the automobile. To check a part of your car means to go over it carefully, in order to restrain it from the possibility of improper functioning. Notice the wonderful condensation of meaning which we pack into the word in this use. We drive into a battery service-station and say, "Please check my battery," which is to say, "Please investigate the condition of my battery, and do whatever may be necessary to make it continue to function properly." And so for busy Americans the title of an ancient Persian king has become a time- and breath-saving word, packed with practical meaning, thanks to the common sense and vivifying genius of the English language.

THE SPEECH
OF THE SOUTH

XIX

ROUGHLY speaking, the speech of the United States may be divided into three varieties—Eastern, Western, and Southern. Of course there are sub-varieties in each of the three, besides an almost incredible amount of variation among individuals, so that the subject of the speech of any section is one that is likely to be somewhat difficult to discuss. It would be ridiculous to think that all Easterners talk alike, or all Southerners, or Westerners. In fact no two persons have exactly the same speech, and when we speak of a certain thing as being characteristic of Western speech, for instance, what we really mean is that a greater proportion of the people of that section will be found to have this speech trait than is true of other sections. Southerners in general speak more slowly than Easterners or Westerners, yet I personally know several native Southerners who rattle away like an express train.

Our dictionaries have practically always been published in the East and usually edited by Eastern men. Consequently they have very naturally taken Eastern usage for the most part as the standard and ignored that of the West and the South. Educated and cultured people nearly always feel instinctively that the speech with which they are familiar is the only true English and that all other varieties are ignorant or wilful perversions of it. In recent years our lexicographers have become more liberal and have made an honest effort to do justice to all sections, yet it is nonetheless true that the Eastern influence still prevails in the dictionaries and in English textbooks generally.

Southern speech and the Negro

Southern speech, especially, has been the subject of much misunderstanding on the part of the people of other sections, most of whom are firmly convinced that its peculiarities are the result of corruption by contact with the Negro. The idea seems plausible, for during many generations Negro nurses have been employed to take care of Southern children. Furthermore, the typical Southern speech is found in the lowlands, the former slave-holding districts, where Negroes are abundant, and not in the mountainous sections where they are scarce or even in some instances entirely lacking. Southern mountaineers sound their *r*'s very plainly, and so in general do Southerners of the lower classes—usually the descendants of non-slaveholders—whereas the lowland Southerner who has had more contact with the Negro is likely to turn "doctor" into "doctuh," "here" into "heah," "art" into "ah-ut," and so on. But unfortunately for the theory of Negro influence, the cultivated people of Southern England, to whom Negroes are curiosities, do very much the same thing. Incidentally, expression teachers in the United States now generally instruct their pupils not to sound a final *r* unless it is followed by a word beginning with a vowel. In "Doctor Smith," the title would be pronounced "Doctuh," as in the South, but in "Doctor Allen," the *r* is given its full sound, according to this theory. Considering these things, I think we shall have to conclude that the Southern Negro has gotten his dropping of the *r* from the Southern white man, instead of the reverse.

The Southern "long i"

Another characteristic of Southern speech is the omission of the final ee-sound that properly goes with a long *i*. According to some Northern writers, a typical Southerner would render, "I had a nice time," as, "Ah had a nahce tahme." Those really familiar with Southern speech will, of course, recognize this at once for the exaggeration that it is, but there is no doubt that it does signify a tendency that really exists. In some words with long *i*, particularly *I* and *my*, when they are unemphatic, the cultured lowland Southerner does omit the ee-sound or make it very faint, but when the word is emphatic, he will sound it as clearly as the average person from other sections. He may say, "Ah haven't seen you for a long time," but he would never dream of saying, "Not Ah," for "Not I." On the other hand, Southerners of the lower classes and Southern mountaineers—the very ones who have never had Negro nurses or other close contact with the Negro—do for the most part regularly omit this final element of the long *i*, regardless of whether the word is emphatic or not, and incidentally produce a sound that it is impossible to indicate in ordinary print. It is the first element of long *i* without even a trace of the second. It is not the broad *a* as in "ah," but comes nearer being the so-called "intermediate *a*," that many mistakenly think is the only correct sound for the *ask*-words, as was mentioned in a previous chapter. But, however that may be, it is evident that here again is a peculiarity of Southern speech for which the Negro is not responsible.

"Carry" for "take"

It always amazes people from other sections to hear a Southerner use "carry" in the sense of "take" or "escort." A Southern boy speaks very naturally of "carrying" a girl to a party, but it will not do to infer from this that he is expecting to transport her bodily in his arms. He will either walk by her side, accompany her on the bus or street-car or taxi, or call for her in an automobile, which may range from a model-T Ford to a Rolls-Royce, according to circumstances and his financial condition, just as a Northern boy might do. Yet this use of the word "carry" is not an invention of the South, nor is the Negro responsible for it, either. It is simply the old English usage, which may be found, for instance, in the King James Version of the Bible. The *Century* gives one meaning of "carry" as "take or escort," and so did the first edition of the *New International*, issued in 1908, though the new second edition marks that meaning as "now dialectic."

"I am going to buy me a hat"

Another example of the survival of an old English expression in the conservative South is seen in the statement, "I am going to buy me a hat," where in other sections it would be, "I am going to buy a hat," or if it were felt necessary to specify the one for whom the hat was intended, "I am going to buy myself a hat." Non-Southerners look askance at this use of "me." Yet Shakespeare in *Macbeth* represents Lady Macduff as saying, "Why, I can buy me twenty at any market." And since he puts the speech into the mouth of a member of the nobility, it is obvious that this use of "me" was in good standing in his time. Or are we to assume that the Bard of Avon picked it up from his Negro "mammy" during his childhood on his father's plantation at Stratford?

"You-all"

But the most striking characteristic of Southern speech is the use of "you-all" as the plural form of "you" whenever it is desired to make it clear that more than one person is referred to. It distinguishes the Southerner from the non-Southerner with much more accuracy than the Mason and Dixon line, for except in the most remote mountain districts— where "you-uns" is substituted—it is the instinctive custom of every native Southerner, white or black, illiterate or highly-educated, cultured or uncultured, and the expression is not so used anywhere else in the English-speaking world except where it has been carried by Southerners. The usage is one of the most amazing linguistic phenomena and at the same time one of the most misunderstood.

Non-Southerners—many of them, at least—have acquired the grotesque notion that "you-all" is used in the South to refer to one person or more than one indiscriminately. With insignificant exceptions this is entirely false, as every Southerner is eager to testify and as Northerners who have lived in the South for any length of time will substantiate. The expression was invented to be used in the same way and for the same purpose as "you people," or "you folks," is used elsewhere. It would have no point otherwise. The Northern misunderstanding is caused chiefly by the fact that Southerners, being so conscious of its meaning, frequently use it in speaking *to* one individual, though they mean the phrase to include both him and those associated with him. I recall hearing a Southern boy once say to another, "Did you-all catch any fish last night?" and reflecting at the time that a non-Southerner who might have happened to hear it would instantly have seized on it as an example of the use of "you-all" in the singular. But it was nothing of the kind. The boy meant, "Did you and those with you catch any fish last night?" At least that is what I assumed. The only other possible assumption for me, after fifty years' residence in six Southern states, would have been that the boy had suddenly gone crazy and was beginning to lose his command of language, or his ability to distinguish one person from more than one.

Mr. Al Jolson gave all Southerners who heard him an opportunity for a hearty laugh, though he was not being intentionally funny, when one evening in a radio play he took the part of Negro youth and proposed to his sweetheart in these words: "Will you-all marry me?" Bigamy is not entirely unknown among the colored race, any more than among the white, but surely this is the first time a plural proposal was ever made. Mr. Jack Benny and Mr. Eddie

Cantor are two others among the hosts of Northern come-
dians who labor under the delusion that "you-all" is used in
the South as a singular. While one would naturally hesitate
to oppose such distinguished linguists, it ought to be remarked that if their belief is true, we have the incredibly
pitiful situation of millions of Southerners living all their
lives in sad misunderstanding of one another's speech.

Perhaps one foundation for this wide-spread mistaken
notion of the use of this expression may be found in the fact
that Southerners always say "you-all" in buying goods in a
store, even though it might be a small country store with
only one salesman. Here, of course, "you-all" refers to the
firm, the establishment. "Have you-all any eggs?" is the
Southern way of putting it. Might not the same question
elsewhere be, "Have you people any eggs?" The only thing
that makes the Southerner wonder is that people from other
sections interpret "you-all" as singular just because there is
only one visible person to whom it is addressed, when they
would not dream of interpreting "you people" as a singular
if used under the identical circumstances.

The only other foundation for this strange delusion is that
very, very rarely "you-all" is used by Negroes in addressing
a white person, or by very ignorant white people to one of
higher position, as a sort of polite plural, just as the French
use *vous* to one person when they are not on familiar terms
with him. This, of course, is how "you" itself came to be
used as a singular, when it is really the plural for "thou,"
and the phenomenon is one that occurs in many languages.
But this polite use of "you-all" to refer to one person is so
extremely rare that most Southerners have never even heard
it. I have been fortunate enough to have had one opportunity to hear it in my fifty years of life in the South, the
speaker being a Negro bell-boy in a small hotel who was
addressing a white guest whose name he did not know.
Inquiry among my pupils has discovered two Southerners
who have heard negroes use the expression in this way and
one who has heard it so used by white people in the mountains of West Virginia. And to give the reader all the

evidence in my possession, let me add that I have heard on fairly good authority that some white people in the Ozark mountains use "you-all" in the singular—whether for politeness or not, I cannot say—but if they really do so, Southerners from any other region would be utterly at a loss in conversing with them.

But Southerners, strangely enough, sometimes defend the use of "you-all" on mistaken grounds. Many of them will tell you that it is to be found in Shakespeare and in the Bible. To prove their point they will cite from the one such lines as in Antony's speech in *Julius Caesar:*

> You all do know that on the Lupercal
> I thrice presented him a kingly crown . . .

Or from the Bible:

> The grace of the Lord Jesus Christ be with you all.

But these are instances not of the Southern "YOU-all," which always has the emphasis on the "you"—unless in rapid speech it is abbreviated to "y'all"—but of the standard English expression "you ALL"—emphasis on the "all"—which is current wherever English is spoken. Though the Southern expression comes from the other, there is a wide difference between the two. "YOU-all," the Southern idiom, is, as I have said, merely "you" in the plural. "YOU-all come over to my house," does not mean, "I am insistent that every one of you come," but is merely an invitation extended to the group. If the speaker wants to make it clear that he desires *everyone*, he either shifts the emphasis and uses the standard English expression "you ALL," or says "all of you," or sometimes even "all of YOU-all."

It may be remarked that in writing letters Southerners do not ordinarily spell "you-all" with a hyphen, though it would be better if they did so, since it would distinguish it from "you ALL." The fact that the two expressions have in the past looked exactly alike in writing and in print has made it almost impossible to trace the history of the Southern idiom by examining correspondence and literature. Consequently nobody seems to know just when or why "you-all" originated.

Two or three things become clear as we ponder over this problem. In the first place it very obviously originated in the southern portion of the United States, for it is used nowhere else. The time of origin must have been certainly in the eighteenth century, for if we set it any later, there is no way in which to account for its spread over the entire section, since phrases of this sort do not spread with the rapidity of modern slang or anything like it. And, oddly enough, I think we shall have to hold the Negro responsible for its origin, though he did not invent it. But in the early days of slavery it must have been highly important for the planter in giving instructions to his workers to be able to make a clear distinction between "you" in the plural and "you" in the singular, and it was important to do so in the simplest words possible, for the Negroes knew no other kind. What simpler word is there than "all" to express the meaning? Can we not imagine the owner saying, "Now, Bill, you look after the mules, and Tom, and Joe, and Jack, you—all—chop cotton"? Might he not thus have fallen into the habit of indicating that the word "you" was plural by adding an unemphasized "all," and finding it simple and useful, might he not have extended its use to conversation with his family and friends? I am inclined to believe that this is what actually happened and that the usage spread all over the South with the exception, as I have said, of the remote mountain districts—that is to say, those farthest removed from the slave-holding sections, which would naturally be the last to get it.

If this theory is true, we have at last a genuine example of the influence of the Negro on Southern speech, though not in the way that those who speak of that influence generally mean. It is possible perhaps that the softer tone-quality of the Southerner's voice has been to some extent brought about by unconscious imitation of his black servant and friend. That I leave for others better qualified to discuss. But I can find no evidence of any other linguistic influence. There seems to be an instinctive feeling among people of a higher culture that fights strongly against the adoption of the speech-habits of a lower one, no matter how closely they are brought into contact with them. Southern children with the gift of mimicry or the dramatic instinct sometimes take up for a brief period an expression or pronunciation of a Negro nurse, but ordinarily they drop it even without the parental urging they are sure to get.

"*I should like for you to be there*"

It is very common in the South to hear expressions like "I should like for you to be there," "I should hate for him to leave now," and "I don't intend for him to see me," in each of which, it will be noticed there is a combination of an infinitive and its subject (sometimes called an "infinitive clause") introduced by the word "for" and used as an object of a verb. It is this "for" that makes the Southern usage different from that of other sections, and its use in such expressions has been severely criticized as being a needless intrusion. But "for" is here an expletive, just as it is in sentences like the Biblical "It is easier for a camel to go through the eye of a needle . . ." or "For you to say that is absurd." Though "for" in such sentences was originally a preposition with the pronoun as its object, it is now merely a sign of the appearance of this so-called infinitive clause. It has no other meaning, and ought to be generally recognized as an expletive. The grammarians have been slow in so recognizing it, though they do not question the correctness of the usage. The only difference in the Southern idioms and the illustrations of standard usage which I have quoted is that in the former the word "for" introduces a combination of infinitive and subject which is used as the *object* of a preceding verb, whereas in the latter the combination is the *subject* of a verb (or perhaps taken as in apposition with the subject "it" in some instances). The Southern usage, then, is merely an extension of the other, not a grammatical atrocity concocted by the ignorant. It has, by the way, some vogue in other sections, and, indeed, may not have originated in the South, though it is in such frequent use there that to many Southerners it sounds as unfinished to say, "I should like you to be there," as it would to say, "You to talk that way is absurd."

"Evening" for "afternoon"

Much surprise and some amusement is expressed by visitors to the South over the Southern custom of using "evening" in the sense of "afternoon," particularly in the expression "Good evening," which may be heard at any time after the noon hour. Yet the new *Webster* is authority for the statement that the same usage is found locally in England, and the conversation between Mercutio and the nurse in Act II, Scene 4, of *Romeo and Juliet* would indicate that in Shakespeare's day "Good evening"—in its shortened form "Good den"—was the regular salutation after twelve o'clock. It seems probable that "evening" originally designated the entire time from noon till midnight, just as "morning" was, and still is, used for the time from midnight till noon.

But if people from other sections are surprised at the Southerner's transformation of the afternoon into evening, the Southerner is surprised by the still more remarkable transformation of afternoon into night which takes place among pupils and teachers in various parts of the North, notably in Ohio, where the time after school is always referred to as "night," even though school may be dismissed in the middle of the afternoon. A story in a boy's magazine, for instance, contained the expression "that night at football practice," though the practice evidently took place in the afternoon, as usual. An Ohio schoolteacher employed in an Alabama high school had a habit of saying to pupils whom she wished to "keep in" as a punishment, "You'll have to come to see me tonight," meaning, of course, "You'll have to report to my room after school." But when she used the formula in Alabama, she was surprised to hear one boy to whom she addressed it reply, "Excuse me, Miss Smith, but I have a date for tonight."

No Ohio person with whom I have talked has been able to explain this strange usage, but the probability is that it originated many years ago when schools, especially in the country, held till four or half past in the afternoon, at which time it is really dark in midwinter in the Northern states.

Is Southern speech slovenly?

The charge of slovenliness is frequently brought against Southern speech, and it must be admitted that a common fault with speakers of the section is an indistinctness of utterance, which is caused by a failure to bring out the consonants clearly, particularly those on the ends of words. On the other hand, though the average Southerner is inclined thus to be careless with his consonants, he is in many instances more careful of his vowels than the average speaker of other sections. In an earlier chapter the comment has been made, for instance, that pronunciations like "dooty" for "duty" and "nooze" for "news" are almost unknown in the South.

As a futher illustration consider the two verses quoted below, the one an answer to the other, which appeared in newspapers published in Ohio and New York respectively:

Reality

Too bad, dear, that romance is over so soon.
Though it does not exactly concern us,
It is touching to think lovely brides of last June
Are now shoveling coal in the furnace.

But sadder by far, though it's none of our doin',
That turn of the wheel, cruel, malicious,
That has him that led her to the altar last June
Now sweeping and washing the dishes.*

There is ample internal evidence in these verses that they were not written in the South. I do not believe that it would

---

* Reprinted with the permission of Ed Scanlan, *Buffalo Evening News*.

ever occur to a Southerner that "furnace" is an acceptable rhyme for "concern us" or "dishes" for "malicious." It is obvious that these newspaper poets must have been familiar with the pronunciations "furnus" and "dishus," whereas in the South the vowels in these final syllables are always brought out clearly.

It is apparent also that the writer of the last stanza pronounced "cruel" in one syllable—"crool"—for the two-syllable pronunciation, "cru-el" that is regularly used in the South will not fit in the meter. I don't believe I have ever heard a Southerner say "crool" or "pome" (for "poem"), both of which atrocities are very common elsewhere, though, to be sure they are certainly not representative of the best speech in any section. These pronunciations originate, I believe, in an effort to say "cru-ul" and "po-um," and the Southerner avoids them because he does not turn the "e" into "u" in this way. Nor does he say "schoo-ul" for "school" and "mew-ul" for "mule," as some Northern people do, though once more let me say that I am not trying to represent these as the approved pronunciations in the North.

"Mary," "Sarah," "various" and so on

In the South words like "Mary," "Sarah," and "various" still maintain their original pronunciation with a long *a* in the first syllable—"May-ry," "Say-rah," "vay-rious"—and are not turned into "Merry," "Serrah," and "verrious," as seems to be the current style elsewhere, and it will probably be a long time before Southerners yield to what seems to them an unseemly change and, especially, a maltreatment of the grand old Biblical names of Sarah and Mary. But there is one proper name in which Southern usage has altered the sound of the vowel, contrary to its general tendency—"Alexander," in which the first "a" is turned into a short "e." An ignorant Southerner once put down his initials as "E. Z." and when asked what the letters stood for, replied, "Ellick Zander," which gives a very good idea of the Southern pronunciation.

A shibboleth

The old Testament tells of a battle in which the Gileadites defeated the Ephraimites, who fled. As the victors pursued and caught scattered fugitives, it was sometimes difficult to tell them from their own men, so that as a test they required them to pronounce the word "shibboleth." If they pronounced it as spelled, they were proved to be Gileadites, but if they said "sibboleth," they were revealed as Ephraimites. If such a shibboleth should ever be needed in our country to distinguish Southerners from Northerners, I would suggest the following sentence:

> Mrs. Alexander Cooper's daughter Mary was at school Tuesday.

Nearly all Southerners would read such a sentence as follows:

> Mizziz Ellexander Cooper's ("oo" as in "cook") daughter Mayry was at school (one syllable) Tyuesday.

Practically all Northerners would say "Missiz Al-exander Cooper's ("oo" as in "coo") daughter Merry," and some of them would say "schoo-ul" and "Toosday." Some Ohioans pronounce "Cooper" in the Southern fashion—possibly other Northern people do so—but I have never known a Southerner who pronounced the word as it is commonly pronounced in the North. Southerners likewise pronounce "hoop" and "coop" with the sound of "oo" in "cook," though just why there should be a sectional difference in the pronunciation of these particular words is a mystery. There are a number of people who pronounce "roof," "room," and "hoof," with the "oo" as in "cook," but, as far as my observation goes, that is an individual, not a sectional, matter.

Words like "moral," "authority," and "Dorothy"

In the South short "o" before an "r" followed by a vowel retains its regular sound as in "not," and does not turn into "aw" as it does in the speech of many people who live in other sections. For instance a Southerner would read the question,

> "By what moral authority did Dorothy gather
> Florida oranges in the forest?"

in this way:

> "By what mah-ral authah-rity did Dah-rothy
> gather Flah-rida ah-ranges in the fah-rest?"

and never in this way:

> "By what mawral authawrity did Dawrothy
> gather Flawrida awranges in the fawrest?"

On the other hand, "on" in the South is practically always pronounced "awn," never "ahn." Incidentally, "awn"—or something very much like it—seems to be more or less common over the country as a whole, though our dictionary-makers are apparently unaware of it.

"Grease" and "greasy"

A story is told of Theodore Roosevelt that as a school-boy he attempted once to recite that old favorite which begins:

> At midnight in his guarded tent
> The Turk lay dreaming of the hour
> When Greece, her knee in suppliance bent,
> Should tremble at his power.

According to the story, which may be apocryphal, the future president got as far as the third line and stuck. He stood there repeating "When Greece, her knee—when Greece, her knee,—" until his teacher called out from the back of the room, "Well, grease her knee again, Theodore, and maybe she'll go."

Southerners will have some difficulty in appreciating this story fully, not from lack of humor, but because the verb "to grease" is pronounced in the South not "greece," but "greeze." When grease (pronounced "greece") is applied to a car by the Southerner, he refers to the operation as "greezing," and the condition of his hands after it is over as "greezy," not "greecy." According to the new *Webster*, the same usage prevails in England, but not generally in other parts of the United States. It is, of course, in line with English usage to pronounce the verb with a "z" sound. We make the same distinction between the noun "use" and the verb "to use" (pronounced "uze"), and likewise between the noun "abuse" and the verb "to abuse" (pronounced "abuze"). A similar change in consonant sounds separates "bath" from "bathe," "wreath" from "wreathe," and "grass" from "graze." In defense of the Southern prounuciation of the adjective, let me quote the opinion of a Northern friend, who himself says "greecy," that somehow "greezy" sounds a great deal greasier than "greecy."

The words that begin with "wh-"

In words like "what," "when," and "white" the "h" is sounded in the South—sounded easily and naturally without effort or special instruction—except perhaps by some speakers in certain localities, as in the vicinity of Charleston and in Louisiana, where the French influence is strong. Mr. H. L. Mencken's flat statement in his book *The American Language* that Americans do not naturally sound the "h" in these words must have been made without due investigation. It is certainly far from the truth in the South, and I cannot believe that it represents the situation in the North with accuracy. I tested the matter one summer by asking each of the seventy-nine pupils in my summer-school classes to read aloud the following sentence—not revealing to them my purpose:

When did he come, what did he do, and why did
he leave?

The pupils were drawn from various Southern states, with a
slight sprinkling from the North, and every one, without
exception, sounded the "h's" in the three words quite clearly.
This "wh" sound seems peculiar to English, and few foreigners ever master it. In Anglo-Saxon the "h" was written
first, and that spelling really represents the sound. We write
"what," "when," and "white," but we say "hwat," "hwen,"
and "hwite." For the benefit of readers who do not naturally sound these "h's" let me say that the secret consists in
blowing, just as one would in order to blow out a candle,
immediately before the utterance of the word. Blow and
say "wat," and the result is "what." Blow and say "wen,"
and the result is "when."

Of course, in rapid speech, where the word is unemphasized, the omission of the "h" passes without notice. But
when the "wh" word is made prominent, the failure to sound
the "h" is very noticeable, and, I may add, rather painful to
those accustomed to hearing it and sounding it themselves.
Take this sentence, for example—and for practice also, if you
need it:

Why do whales whimper and whine when they
are whipped?

Surely it suffers greatly when transformed into:

Wy do wales wimper and wine wen they are
wipped?

A strange circumstance in connection with the pronunciation of these words, however, is that "why" when used as
an exclamation is always pronounced without the "h," even
by those who would sound it otherwise. For instance, in
"Why, John!" the sound would be "wy," but in "Why did
you do that?" the "h" would be heard. What the reason is,
I cannot say, but it is a fact of usage, supported by the
authority of the new *Webster*.

One's opinion of Southern speech, as of other things, will depend largely on whether he judges it by the best or the worst. At its worst the speech of the South is a dreadful thing, but at its best it has an admitted charm that is not surpassed by that of any other part of the English-speaking world. Southerners would do well to model their speech upon that of the most cultured people of their own section, rather than to make the unnatural effort to imitate those of another. And, of course, the same principle applies to the natives of any section. But let each of us strive to diminish rather than increase the points of difference, to soften the elements peculiar to his section rather than to emphasize them. In this way, we may finally arrive at a genuine standard of American speech, which, as some one has finely said, shall "combine the melody of the South with the vigor of the West and the precision of the East" into one surpassing version of our mother tongue.

BRITISH ENGLISH

XX

WHEN Rudy Vallee was giving a series of broadcasts from London in the summer of 1937, he had on one of his programs an excellent English actor, Charles Laughton, who in the course of telling a story had occasion to speak of a man and a girl. When he did so, he added, as if in explanation, "—that is, a *guy* and a *dame* to you, Rudy," thus nobly upholding the British tradition of assuming or pretending to assume that slang is standard usage in America, and of comparing it—by implication, at least—with formal British English. Now it is of course merely human nature to pick out the worst of the other man's family, crowd, party, section, nation, or race and compare it with the best of our own. We rather expect the British—some of them, at least—to take it for granted that slang or colloquialisms of a low order are truly representative of American speech, but the astonishing thing is that they are aided and abetted in this by some Americans.

I heard an American once exemplify the difference in the speech of the two countries by the statement that Americans say "dumb" for the British "stupid" and "calamity-howler" for the British "pessimist"! Just when did "stupid" and "pessimist" go out of use in America? "Dumb" is fairly common on the colloquial level, but "stupid" is still the regular term in dignified speech, and "calamity-howler" is certainly not nearly so common as "pessimist" in the United

States. But why this eternal comparison of a low level of American English with a high level of British? Suppose for once we take them both on a high level—the language of books.

Fortunately for the purposes of such a comparison, we have the testimony of the best of witnesses—unintentional, to be sure, but so much the better—that stout Britisher, Fowler. In his admirable *Modern English Usage* he has a discussion of the difference in the American and British ways of spelling words like "honor," "favor," and "labor" (British: "honour," "favour," "labour"). In the discussion occurs this very illuminating statement:

> Our first notification that the book we are read-
> ing is not English, but American, is often nowa-
> days the sight of an "-or."

A moment's reflection is necessary in order to catch the full significance of such a statement—namely, that on the literary level the differences between American English and the British variety are so slight that an ardent Britisher, a world-famous authority on the use of English, who would naturally be extremely sensitive to such matters, can read an American book for some time without discovering that it *is* American, and that when the discovery is made, it is often brought about by a mere matter of spelling.

And yet a number of Americans are busily engaged in attempting to show that there is an "American language" so different from English—that is, British English—that it deserves an entirely different name. What becomes of such a theory in the face of a fact like that revealed by Fowler's unintended testimony? Of course, it may be argued with truth that when we leave the literary level and come to the conversational, the differences in the speech of the two countries become greater. No one will deny that. But even in the free and easy speech of everyday life these differences are surely not great enough to justify the term "the American language," unless indeed one chooses to use the word "language" in a sense in which no student of languages employs it. There are differences quite noticeable in the speech of the various sections of the United States, yet the very ones who tell us that "American" is a different language from "English" insist at the same time that these sectional differences are not great enough to justify even the use of the term "dialect" in describing them. In this they are quite right, but their reasoning is rather inconsistent.

Where is this matter of naming languages to stop? If there is really an American language—as distinct from the English language—might we not by going just a little further speak of the New England language, or the Middle Western language, or the New York language, or the Virginia language? Indeed, no two individuals speak exactly alike. In a certain sense each of us has his own language. Why not then the Roosevelt language and the Al Smith language (as heard over the "raddio")? A strong case could certainly be made for the magazine *Time* language, and a still stronger one for the Gertrude Stein language. My, how our list of languages does grow! How shall we ever communicate with each other any more?

"*Honor*" *or* "*honour*"

But let us return to Fowler. His entire passage concerning the spelling of words like "honor" is so interesting that I should like to give more of it, beginning before the quoted sentence and including it. Remember that he is an Englishman writing for Englishmen.

> The American abolition of "-our" in words like "honour" and "favour" has probably retarded rather than quickened English progress in the same direction. Our first notification that the book we are reading is not English, but American, is often nowadays the sight of an "-or." "Yankee" we say, and pride ourselves on spelling like gentlemen; we wisely decline to regard it as a matter for argument. The English way cannot but be better than the

American way; that is enough. Most of us do not come to the question with an open mind.

After this ironic chiding of his countrymen, Fowler goes on to show that the American way is the better in this instance, that the British have already adopted it in some words, and that they should do so in the others.

"Leftenant"

There are, of course, many minor differences between British and American speech, some of which have been commented upon in previous chapters. A British pronunciation which seems entirely without reason to Americans is that of "leftenant" for the word which they spell, like us, "lieutenant." It is said that this originated when the word was first introduced from the French. At that time it was common to give the letter "u" the shape of "v," as indeed one may still see it in public monuments, and when "lieutenant" was first introduced into English, the spelling was "lievetenant," the "v" standing for "u." But it came to be pronounced mistakenly "leave-tenant," and this was shortened later to the present-day British "leftenant," which will probably persist as long as the British temperament remains what it is—as long, indeed, as "Cholmondeley" is called "Chumly" and "Beauchamp" is turned into "Beecham."

"Derby," "Berkeley," and "clerk"

In England the words "Derby," "Berkeley," and "clerk" are pronounced "Darby," "Barkly," and "clark," as is probably now known to most Americans. This is merely a relic of the time when "er" followed by a consonant or coming at the end of a word was regularly pronounced "ar," just as it now is in both England and America in the word "sergeant." "Star," "start," "smart," and many others used to be spelled with an "e" before the "r," but the spelling has been changed to fit the pronunciation. This explains why the abbreviation for "university" is "varsity," and also why in the mountains of North Carolina the service-berry is called the "sarvice-berry." And our proper name "Clark" was originally "Clerk."

Slops

My most amazing personal contact with British English came when I inquired of the wife of an English friend concerning the condition of her husband, who had been sick, or ill, as the British always put it, for some time. "Oh," she answered, "he's better, but his throat is in such bad shape that he can't eat anything but *slops*." After the first shock of such a statement, it dawned upon me that by "slops" she must mean liquid or semiliquid food, and a consultation of the dictionary revealed that as one definition of the term. It is quite possible, of course, that it is so used in some parts of America, but I should not like to accuse any American I have ever known of eating slops, which it may be well to explain for the benefit of British readers usually means in the United States either table refuse fed to hogs or water that has been used for washing and is ready for the sewer.

British grammar

It is commonly said that educated Britons are on the whole more careful with their grammar than Americans of the same class, and this is very probably true, especially if the term "educated" is interpreted to include all those who have attended college. But anyone who imagines that British grammar is impeccable would do well to look over Fowler's *Modern English Usage* and note the multitude of examples of the erroneous use of English which his sharp eyes have gathered from the newspapers, magazines, and books of England.

The men who are prominent in the political life of England have much more frequently been drawn from the upper and more highly educated classes than those of

America, and one would naturally expect their use of the
language to be better. That may be true also, but my confidence in it has been sadly shaken by some recent examples
of it that have appeared in the press. Here, for instance, is
a sentence taken from a British note to Mussolini:

> His Majesty's government is so convinced of the
> accuracy of this estimate of the work of the League
> that they feel that no useful purpose would be
> served by re-opening the question.

One question, however, that His Majesty's government
might have re-opened with profit is whether they wished to
consider the word "government" as singular or plural. It
may be either, for here it means the prime minister and his
associates, and is consequently one of those collective nouns
that, as we have seen, may be taken either way. But it is
hardly consistent to make it both singular and plural in the
same sentence, as is done in the statement, "His Majesty's
government *is* so convinced . . . that *they feel*. . ." It
should be, I think, *"are* so convinced that they feel," but it
might logically read, "is so convinced that *it feels."*

Some time ago a high British official gave up his office,
and the letter that presented his resignation contained the
following sentence:

> My only object in joining the National Govern-
> ment was because I felt sure the coming together of
> all political parties was the only chance of putting
> this country through the crisis.

This must be another instance of the famous British custom
of "muddling through." It is not difficult to see what the
sentence means, but to reconstruct it so that it *says* what it
means is a different matter. It will take more than one
change in the wording. "Object in joining" should apparently be "reason for joining," but even then one cannot
properly say, "The reason for joining is *because* I felt sure
. . ." any more than one could say "The object is *because* I
felt sure . . ." We must change "because" to "that" in order

to avoid this error that all the schoolbooks warn us of, and then we have a fairly decent sentence: "My only reason for joining the National Government was that I felt sure, etc." Or, if the word "object" was really what the gentleman had in mind, he might have made it: "My only object in joining the National Government was *to aid in* the coming together of all political parties, *which* I felt sure, etc."

But two possible excuses may be offered for the poor handling of our language by this particular statesman. In the first place, he was writing under the influence of some emotion, and in the second, it is a fact that he rose to his high position from the ranks of labor without the advantages of the education which most Britishers in such offices possess. I should have been inclined to lay more emphasis on this latter excuse if I had not also come across a piece of rather slovenly English on the part of another British statesman who has all the traditional educational equipment—a graduate of one of the famous private schools which the British strangely call "public" schools, a graduate of a university, and holder of six honorary degrees from other colleges and universities. Here is an extract from his speech in Parliament:

> His Majesty's government have made it clear that under no circumstances will interference by Italy with the existing regimes in Egypt and Palestine be tolerated, and any attempt *to do so* will be considered as an unfriendly act.

The fault is with the phrase "to do so," which does not fit with the noun "interference." The reading should be, "any attempt to interfere," or simply "any attempt at it." If "to do so" is to be used, there should be some verb-form to which it may refer. It would be possible, for instance, to say, "Italy will not be allowed *to interfere*, and any attempt to do so will be considered as an unfriendly act."

"Shall" and "will"; "should" and "would"

But there is one matter in which the cultured speakers of Southern England certainly are more accurate than most of those in America—namely, the observance of a distinction between "shall" and "will" and a similar one between "should" and "would." Indeed there is, I think, no other part of the English-speaking world where these distinctions are generally observed by the great body of educated speakers, and it is therefore really a matter of doubt whether they can rightfully be considered genuine universal rules of English. They are recorded, however, in practically all our grammars, and are observed by many careful speakers in the United States—more often still by writers. Educated people should certainly be familiar with them. If, having attained this familiarity, they do not see fit to observe them, they have at least the advantage that the failure to do so cannot be attributed to ignorance on their part.

The future tense in English

The Teutonic languages, of which English, as the reader will remember, is one, had no future tense, but used the present instead, as English continues to do in some instances. For example, we say, "I will tell him when (or if) I *see* him tomorrow," in which sentence the verb "see" is clearly present *tense* though it just as clearly indicates future time. Eventually, however, English built a future tense—or, to be more accurate, a substitute for it—by the use of the words "will" and "shall" followed by the infinitive (without "to") of the verb in question. This future tense is given below for the verb "go" in accordance with the rules laid down in the grammars and actually observed by most cultured speakers in Southern England and by many elsewhere.

Future tense of "to go"

I shall go	we shall go
you will go	you will go
(thou wilt go)	
he, she, it will go	they will go

Notice that "I" and "we" are followed by "shall" and all other subjects by "will." This is the simple future, which expresses merely what is going to happen, without any regard to the wish or effort of the speaker. But if the speaker means to *make* it happen, the situation is reversed, and we have the following:

> To show desire, promise, or determination
> of the speaker, let him say:
>
> | | |
> |---|---|
> | I will go | we will go |
> | you shall go | you shall go |
> | (thou shalt go) | |
> | he shall go | they shall go |

There is nothing very odd about all this, nothing that is not generally observed by the average intelligent American, except the use of "shall" after "I" and "we" in the simple future, for which most of us substitute "will," which according to the theory should not be used except to show that our wills enter into the matter. For instance, the technically correct form is "I shall be glad to see you," not "I will be glad to see you," for by these rules that would mean, "I want to be glad, I will make an effort to be glad," whereas gladness is expected to come of its own accord. Hence, "I shall be sorry," rather than "I will be sorry," and "I am afraid I shall be hurt," rather than "I will be hurt." But, of course, "He will be glad," "they will be glad," and "you will be glad." The Irish have never observed these rules, and there is an old, old story of an Irishman unable to swim who fell into the river, and cried out, "I will drown; nobody shall help me," when, of course, what he meant was, "I shall drown; nobody will help me." I have always doubted, however, that he really said, "Nobody shall help me," because it is quite uncommon to hear "shall" used in place of "will." The mistake—if it is really a mistake—is nearly always the other way.

It will be evident that in a great many sentences it is possible to use either "shall" or "will," with a slight difference in meaning. "I shall be at my office tomorrow" and "I will be at my office tomorrow" are both correct. The first means "I am expecting to be there, in the ordinary course of events I shall be there," whereas the second is very likely a promise— at any rate the speaker means to indicate that he has made up his mind to be there.

"Should" follows the same rules as for "shall," and "would" those for "will." Consequently, it is considered correct to say, "I should like to see you," rather than "I would like," because we have again the expression of a feeling, which is supposed to come of its own accord. Hence, "I should be sorry, or angry, or happy," not "I would be sorry, etc." On the other hand, "He would like to see you" and "They would be sorry to see you leave" are correct, for here the subject is no longer "I" or "we."

Of course, the "should" that means "ought to" is always "should," regardless of its subject, and after "if" it is likewise used with "you," "he," and "they," as well as with "I" or "we." And "would" can be used with any subject in the sense of "was accustomed to," as in "We would sit and sing for hours at a time."

In the interest of accuracy, there are two more things that should be mentioned with regard to the use of these words. In asking a question, it is considered correct to use the verb that you expect the one to whom the question is addressed to use in his answer. On this principle, one would ask, "Shall you be sorry to see him go?" because the answer would be, "I shall be sorry," or "I shall not be sorry." A similar principle holds in indirect quotations. You hear some one say, "I shall be sorry to see him go," and you may report it by saying, "He says he shall be sorry to see him go," or "He said he should be sorry." This is not a requirement, however, for it would be correct also to say, "He says he will be (or, said he would be) sorry."

And it should be remembered, too, that "shall" may be used in the sense of prophecy, as in the Biblical "it shall come to pass," or in a somewhat similar use after "when" and other conjunctions of time.

A summary of the situation

I do not pretend that the brief statements just given cover the subject of the use of "shall" and "will," for many learned and lengthy monographs have been written about them. Our grammars frequently record these rules as if they were ironclad, and Fowler seems to be perfectly certain that cultured Britishers observe them in spite of the fact that he gives example after example—all drawn from British sources, presumably—in which they are *not* observed. I have one more of the sort to add—or rather two, taken from the speech of a British statesman already referred to—the "public"—school and university graduate. In addressing Parliament he said on one occasion, "I would like to say at the start," and on another, "I would like to tell the House." In both cases "would" should have been "should" according to the technical rules we have been discussing.

And it may relieve the minds of some Americans to know that the greatest scholar we have ever had in the White House, Woodrow Wilson, formerly president of Princeton University and an author of repute, a user of masterly English, did not observe these distinctions. When he was a candidate for re-election, he received one day a telegram from a man who claimed to represent many others stating that unless Wilson made certain changes in his policy, he and his friends would not vote for him. Wilson, who knew his man, immediately shot back this tart reply: "I would be very much mortified to have you or anybody like you vote for me." I don't think that the one who received the telegram had any doubt as to its meaning, but the rules we have been discussing call for "*should* be very much mortified."

Woodrow Wilson was only one among millions of educated and cultured Americans who have used "will" and "would" where the rules call for "shall" and "should." Poutsma, a British authority on the use of English, has this to say:

Most non-English Britishers utterly fail in their attempts to conform to the rules laid down by the English grammarians (for "shall" and "will"). . . . But it may also be doubted that the true-born Englishman, even when he constantly moves in educated circles, strictly observes the rules, even in his considered utterances.

The situation is one clouded with uncertainty and very distressing, as uncertainty nearly always is. The English-speaking people ought really to come to some agreement on the matter. If the rules are reasonable and helpful, if they assist us in making important distinctions that cannot otherwise be made, let us by all means observe them. Otherwise let us accept "will" and "would" for the simple future after "I" and "we" as well as after other subjects, and say no more about it. The distinguished American grammarian Curme thinks that it would be a distinct gain to do so. What does the reader think?

"Pure" English

There is some talk in America and rather more in England about the necessity for keeping the English language "pure." Indeed there is in England a "Society for Pure English," and I recall reading in a British magazine the statement that the "purest" English in the world was that spoken by the officers of the British army. Exactly what this means, I must confess I do not know, for I am always a little bewildered when people begin to talk about "pure" English.

Pure water, for instance, is that which contains no foreign substance, and I can see that when English-speaking people adopt idioms or modes of speech which are characteristic of foreign languages, their English may be said to be impure. I have heard that some people in Pennsylvania say, "How long are you here?" meaning "How long have you been here?" In doing so they are obviously using a German idiom, and in this respect their English is not pure. And I have also noted with some distress that many Americans have broken away from that principle of good taste which has heretofore prevented English-speaking people of refinement from interlarding their conversation with ejaculations involving the use of the name of God. But whether this is due to contact with people of other nationalities, who exclaim *Mein Gott!* or *Mon Dieu!* or *Madre de Dios!* on slight provocation and with no more sense of speaking profanely than English-speaking people have when they say "Good gracious!" or whether it is just a phase of our wonderful progress out of Victorian delicacy into coarseness, I do not know. Yet I am sure that it is not things of this sort that people are referring to when they express a fear lest the purity of the English language be corrupted.

Those who apply the term "pure" to English apparently mean to designate by it a speech that is free from error of any sort, faultless, perfect, if such a thing is possible; and they have ample dictionary warrant for applying the word in that sense to a language. Nevertheless it seems to me to be unsuitable and misleading, when applied to English particularly, for it indicates in the first place that there is an absolute standard by which the purity of one's speech can be judged. I have no doubt, for instance, that the British Society for Pure English would instantly classify any English as impure which contained "Americanisms," and that it would classify as an Americanism any word or meaning of a word or phrase or turn of speech which is used in the United States and not in England—or better, not used by "the right people" in England. Even if the word or phrase originated in England, if it has died out there and is still used in America, it is an Americanism to Englishmen, and hence for many, a thing to avoid—if they can. The fact that it may be used by two-thirds of the English-speaking people, including some as highly cultured as any that may be found in England, has nothing to do with it.

Not all Englishmen, of course, are so uncompromising. Their most able scholars have long recognized the right of Americans to introduce new words and new meanings for old ones into the language, and, of course, to preserve a word or a meaning that has died out in England. There are signs also that the time is not far distant when Englishmen as a whole will be willing to judge an American usage on the basis of its intrinsic merit rather than its place of origin or preservation. Whatever hastens the recognition of the fact that the language is a common heritage of the two peoples will ultimately be to its benefit and the benefit of all who speak it.

But the second reason why the term "pure" is not suitable for application to English is its history. Much of the strength and beauty of our language is due to the way in which for the past thousand years it has borrowed with the greatest freedom from every language with which it has come in contact. Starting as a rude yet vigorous variety of German, it was polished and enriched by contact with the French, drew copiously from the sonorous and stately Latin, adapted the terms of the classic Greek, and took what it needed from Celtic, Danish, Dutch, Spanish, Italian, Hebrew, Arabic, and many others. "Pure" is hardly the term to apply as a compliment to such a language. Yet, with a genius for language-making never surpassed, the English-speaking people have taken these heterogeneous elements and woven them into one fabric that we recognize instantly and unmistakably, not as German or French or Latin or any other of its component parts, but as English—good English, always ready to be made better, always eager to seize the best wherever it may be found, defeating every attempt to strangle its freedom—our world-encircling, living, growing mother tongue.

ENGLISH SPELLING

XXI

THE vagaries (pronounced "vaGAries," remember) of English spelling are well illustrated by a clever bit of anonymous verse that begins:

> When the English tongue we speak,
> Why is "break" not rhymed with "freak"?

The author then calls attention to the incongruity of the pronunciations of "sew" and "few"; "horse" and "worse"; "beard" and "heard"; "cord" and "word." "Cow," he says, ought to rhyme with "low," but it does not. Neither does "shoe" rhyme with "foe." "Hose," "dose," and "lose" make a curious set, since they all end in "ose," but no two are pronounced alike. "Goose" and "choose," "doll" and "roll," "home" and "some" are three pairs which ought to rhyme, but do not. Another strange set of three is found in "comb," "tomb," and "bomb," and still another in "blood," "food," and "good." "Pay" and "say" rhyme, but "paid" and "said" do not. "Mould" and "could" are a curious pair, and "done," "gone," and "lone" and their weird set of triplets, which look alike, but do not sound alike. And the poem concludes wistfully, "Is there any reason known" for all this?

Now, the answer to this plaintive question is yes. There is a reason for every peculiarity of pronunciation and spell-

244

ing in English, and a great many of the reasons are known to the scholars. We call "l-o-s-e" "lose," for instance, because we have been unconsciously influenced by the fact that "l-o-o-s-e" is pronounced "loose." "Said" is pronounced "sed" rather than "sayed"; because it is so often spoken rapidly in expressions like "said he," or in other connections where it is unemphatic, that its vowel sound has been shortened. And a close examination would doubtless reveal the reasons for many of the anomalies asked about in the verses and for hundreds which it does not mention. "Tongue," for instance, is good Anglo-Saxon and was originally spelled "tung," the present spelling being due to the efforts of Norman-French scribes, who did the official writing in England for a long time after 1066. If you should ask a modern Frenchman unfamiliar with English how he would spell "tung," he would very likely answer without hesitation "t-o-n-g-u-e."

English-speaking people are so accustomed to our peculiar spelling that many of them do not realize that there are languages in which the spelling always agrees with the sound —or nearly so. Some years ago I noticed in a newspaper "query box" a very amusing answer to the question of a correspondent who wrote:

> I have been told that in German schools little or no attention is paid to spelling after the second grade. Can you tell me whether this is true?

To which the editor gravely responded:

> We have no definite information about the course of study in German schools, but we are sure that the Germans would not neglect so important a subject as spelling.

Phonetic spelling

The fact is that German spelling agrees so nearly with the sound that children need very little instruction in it. This

is, of course, true of every language originally. The reason
a language gets into the unphonetic state of English or
French is that the pronunciation changes while the spelling
remains the same. Some languages, however, seem able to
keep the pronunciation fairly well fixed or to change the
spelling to fit it, so that they do not get into the situation of
English, which is strikingly revealed by the following
sentence:

> The rough cough and hiccough plough me
> through.

Here we have five pronunciations for the ending "ough"
—"uff," "off," "up," "ow," and "oo." "Hiccough," by the
way may be spelled "hiccup," and should always be pronounced in that way. The name is derived from the sound
of a hiccup, and the spelling "hiccough" comes from the mistaken notion that it is a kind of cough.

A great many well-meant efforts have been initiated to
make English spelling phonetic, but only slight progress has
been made in that direction. For more than thirty years
The Literary Digest used spellings like "tho," "thru," and
"slipt" with scarcely any net effect on other publications or
on the spelling of the general public. Such forms still look
odd, and they therefore offer a slight distraction to the
reader and become a small but real hindrance to the ready
perception of the thought.

There are many powerful arguments on the side of sim-
plifying English spelling and making it as nearly phonetic
as possible. If such a condition could be attained, it would
save a great deal of time in school, for that now spent—with
rather poor results—on spelling could be devoted to other
things. It would relieve millions of English-speaking people
—or better, English-writing people—of a great deal of trouble
and worry and enable them to put their attention more on
the higher elements of writing and less on the mechanics of
it. The abolition of silent letters would save a great deal of
white paper, printers' ink, and type-setters' time—and might

conceivably even throw a few of the latter out of work, in which case it would, no doubt, meet with some opposition.

But I hardly think it is yet time for the printers' unions to become alarmed, for there seems little prospect that our spelling will soon become phonetic, or even be greatly simplified. The old order is too strongly fixed. We have become accustomed to it, and to introduce any extensive changes now would bring about a state of chaos and confusion that would disorganize the writing and printing of more than one generation. It might be argued that the changes could be introduced gradually—indeed that was the plan suggested by the Simplified Spelling Board—but that would only prolong the agony and mean that for several hundred years English spelling would not look quite natural to anybody.

An interesting question likewise arises as to *whose* pronunciation is to be used when we set about adapting English spelling to pronunciation. If each person is to use his own pronunciation, we shall have an intolerable confusion in spelling, but if anybody thinks that the people of any given section of the English-speaking world are going to submit tamely to having words spelled as the people of another section pronounce them, he fails to realize the stubbornly individualistic spirit of those who speak the English language.

Besides, the adoption of a phonetic system, as far as it can be applied to English, would not solve entirely the problem of incorrect spelling. Every teacher knows, or should know, that it is not the strikingly unphonetic words that cause the most trouble. Take the word "thousand," for instance, and consider the sound of the last syllable. Does anybody pronounce the "a" in it as he would if it were simply the word "sand"? Practically nobody,—except in singing—for it is what we call an obscure vowel, having the sound of the "u" in "but" spoken very rapidly. The word "thousand" would be pronounced in practically the same way as now, if it were spelled "thousond," "thousend," "thousind," or "thousund." Take "defendant" and "dependent," and see whether you can discover any difference in the sound of the last syllable of each, as you ordinarily pronounce them.

I am aware that the theory exists that English-speaking people should cease to obscure these vowels in the unaccented syllables of so many words, and should bring them out plainly, as is generally done in French, German, and other languages. Many years ago I knew a young woman who insisted on saying "sev-en" and "elev-en" rather than "sev'n" and "elev'n," because she felt it was wrong to slight the last "e" in the words, as people ordinarily do—and, of course, as the dictionaries approve, though she did not know it. I have often wondered why she picked out these two words and overlooked the thousands of others in which vowels are obscured or almost omitted. A great deal of the peculiarity that marks almost any foreign accent in English is due to this practice of bringing out the unaccented syllables more plainly than English-speaking people generally do. I wonder that any English-speaking person thinks that the foreign way of speaking our language is better than that developed through the centuries by those to whom it is a native tongue. Our method, indeed, is open to abuse. When carried to an extreme, it is likely to result in an indistinctness of utterance that is always a fault, but skillfully handled, it gives a unity to our longer words that is quite desirable, since it makes easy the grouping and placing of emphasis that are essential to good reading and speaking. But English is more difficult to handle skillfully than the other languages, for he who would speak it so as to give full play to all the vigor and beauty of which it is capable, must be careful to avoid on the one hand a fatal slovenliness of enunciation and on the other an overprecision that is so uncharacteristic of our speech as to be painful to the listener.

Another objection to phonetic spelling is that it would increase the confusion between words of similar sound but different spelling, such as "would" and "wood," and "to," "too," and "two." I suppose all three of the latter group would be spelled "too," which would bring about some odd situations. For instance, there is the story of the railroad conductor whose train stopped at a certain station at two minutes before two o'clock and left at two minutes after two. When a passenger asked him once how long it would be there, he answered, "Four minutes. From two to two to two two." Under the phonetic system, this would read: "Too too too too too too."

There are likewise three words in English whose pronunciation is the same as "you." The other two are "yew" and "ewe," and oddly enough, none of the three is phonetically spelled. If the phonetic system should be adopted, we should have to spell them all, I suppose, either "yoo" or "yu"—perhaps simply "u." This would be rather strange, but it would at least prevent mistakes like that of the young minister who was reading to his congregation a passage from the Bible referring to a "little ewe lamb," and rendered it as "the little e-wee lamb."

And there are four words in English pronounced "rite," the other three being "wright" (a workman), "write," and "right." All four may be combined in the sentence, "Can the wright write 'rite' right?" which under the phonetic system would be, I take it, "Can the rite rite 'rite' rite?" That is not strictly phonetic, of course, but we must leave the silent "e" on the end of "rite," to show that the "i" is long, unless we invent another letter to stand for that sound —and to make English strictly phonetic, we should need many new letters.

In short, the situation is simply this. English spelling deserves nearly everything bad that has been said about it. It is illogical, unreasonable, even whimsical, vexatious, and time-wasting—but there is nothing we can do about it except to learn it. A misspelled word looks illiterate, even though it is perfectly true that some people with very able minds had great difficulty in spelling correctly. The practical business man is as deeply offended by the poor spelling of his stenographer as the literary esthete would be—perhaps even more so.

The good speller is the one who remembers how the word

looks. But the poor speller cannot do this, and his only hope is to study the words that trouble him until he retains their spelling by sheer force of repetition. His task is difficult, but fortunately not as difficult as it seems at first. He will find that there are probably only a few hundred words at most to which he will need to devote much attention. Some are so simple that any literate person can spell them. Others are so uncommon that he will probably never have occasion to use them in writing, and if he should, he can refer to the dictionary. *But the really important thing is to know that he does not know how to spell a word when he does not.*

Many people go through life misspelling words without realizing it, for their friends who receive their letters are too polite to tell them about it. It was with a shock that I once came to the realization that the word I had thought of for years as "mushroon" was—and is—really "mushroom." Somehow when the wrong spelling once becomes fixed in one's mind, he may read the word a thousand times in print and always seem to see it spelled as he mistakenly thinks it is.

Some spelling tests

I have given a number of spelling tests on the radio and have received many comments from listeners such as "I had been misspelling that word (or those words) all my life and didn't know it," or "I thought I was a good speller till you started giving those tests." Some listeners have absolutely refused to believe that a certain word was spelled as I gave it till they had confirmed it by the dictionary.

The revival of interest in old-fashioned spelling bees—or spelling matches, as the term generally goes in the South—is an encouraging sign, and much of the credit for it must be given to the radio. I am giving below some lists of the words that I have found most difficult for radio audiences, arranged in the form of three tests of twenty words each. All the words are in fairly common use at least, and consequently are such as educated people should know how to spell. For the first test I have selected what I believe to be the twenty most difficult words—or better, the most difficult twenty words, for that way of putting it is somewhat more reasonable, though neither is entirely satisfactory—that can be found in English among those in ordinary use. If you have a friend who thinks he is a good speller, give them out to him. If he spells them all correctly, he is one in ten thousand, perhaps one in fifty thousand. If he does not miss more than three, he may congratulate himself.

Test No. 1

consensus	exhilarating
dissension	iridescent
corroborate	appellation
erysipelas	guttural
sacrilegious	colonnade
supersede	tranquillity
desiccate	phlegm
liquefy	kimono
ecstasy	villainy
innuendo	subpoena

I have omitted from this list three words which are usually included in lists of this sort. They are:

plaguy
vilify
chaperon

My reason for not including them is that there is some dictionary warrant for the spellings "plaguey," "villify," and "chaperone," and in a test of this kind there must be no room for doubt as to the correctness or incorrectness of a word.

The second test contains some words that will undoubtedly be more troublesome to certain readers than some in the first test. Nevertheless I do not think that it is quite so difficult.

Test No. II

occasion	abscess
accommodate	committee
necessary	conspicuous
separate	effervescent
assassinate	penitentiary
privilege	hyacinth
hypocrisy	chrysanthemum
noticeable	dentifrice
vacuum	gherkin
malign	picnicking

Three words in this test call for comment. "Noticeable" requires the "e" after the "c," to keep it from being pronounced "notikable." For the very opposite reason the "k" is inserted in "picnicking." If it were omitted, the natural pronunciation would be "picnising." "Vacuum" has two "u's" in succession, in spite of the fact that the *Century Dictionary* says that "u" is never doubled in English. Two other words in which it is doubled are "residuum" and "menstruum."

Test Number III is probably as difficult as Number II. Indeed I should not be surprised if some readers find it more so.

Test No. III

annihilate	sergeant
tyranny	beneficent
repellent	anoint
dissipate	repetition
rarefy	questionnaire
synagogue	siege
fuchsia	omission
battalion	diphtheria
soliloquy	conscientious
embarrassment	shell-less

Words that end in "less," such as "wireless," do not ordinarily require the hyphen, but it must be inserted in "shell-less" in order to keep three "l's" from coming together, since it is a rule in English that a letter is never "tripled." Notice that "questionnaire" has two "n's," while "millionaire" has but one. Both words, by the way, should be accented on the last syllable—except when, as in the preceding sentence, they are brought together in contrast. In that case the first syllable is emphasized, since that is the one in which they differ. Similarly we speak of "the sane and the INsane," though the word is ordinarily pronounced "inSANE."

One's knowledge of spelling ought also to include the names of places and persons that are frequently met with, so perhaps a test on proper names will not be out of place among the others. It is equally divided between places and persons.

A test on proper names

Philippines	Macaulay
Filipino	Thackeray
Massachusetts	Ben Jonson
Tennessee	George Eliot
Mississippi	O. Henry
Cincinnati	Kosciusko
Czechoslovakia	Anne Boleyn
Buenos Aires	Gandhi
Chautauqua	Disraeli
Chile	Tutankhamen

Two supertests

And now for the benefit of possible spelling professionals, so to speak, who may scorn the foregoing tests as too easy for experts, I present below two "supertests," which I trust will be difficult enough to satisfy them. We leave the field of ordinary words, of course, and I include only ten in each. For most people this should be enough.

Supertest No. I

psittacosis (pronounced "sittaKOsis")
eleemosynary ("ellyMOSinary" or "ellyeeMOSinary")
synecdoche ("sinNECKdokee")
metonymy ("meTONimy")
ptarmigan ("TARmigan")
psyllium ("SILium")
gnostic ("NOStic")
gnomon ("NOmon")
prestidigitator ("prestiDIJitator")
gneiss ("nice," a kind of rock)

Supertest No. II

bdellium ("DELLium")
phthisis ("THIGHsis")
caoutchouc ("KOOchook" or "KOWchook")
mnemonics ("neMONics")
schizophrenia ("SKIZoFREEnia")
pterodactyl ("TERoDAKtil")
cirrhosis ("siROsis")
hendiadys ("henDIGHadis")
giaour ("jour")
syzygy ("SIZijy")

"Giaour" is noteworthy in that it has four different vowels in succession—the only English word, to the best of my knowledge, of which this is true. It is Turkish in origin and use, meaning "infidel" or "unbeliever"—that is to say, an unbeliever in Mohammedanism, a Christian, for example. "Syzygy," probably the most curious word in English, is a term used in astronomy and other sciences.

It is not always the longest words that are the most difficult to spell. "Incomprehensibility," for instance, would not be troublesome to anyone except one who had never seen it. It is this lack of familiarity that often causes a good speller to miss a rather simple word in a match. It is amazing how many perfectly good words there are in the dictionaries that are entirely unfamiliar even to well educated people who happen not to have gone deeply into the particular subject to which they belong.

Some technical terms

Here, for instance, is a definition from the *Century Dictionary:*

> PTEROPTOCHIDAE: A South American family of formicarioid passerine birds, typified by the genus *Pteroptochus*, with tracheophonous mesomyodian syrinx, taxaspidean tarsi, operculate nostrils, and ten primaries.

If the reader should desire to find out the meaning of some of these terms, and should look up "taxaspidean," for example, here is what he will find:

> TAXASPIDEAN: having that modification of the scutelliplantar tarsus in which the plantar scutella are contiguous, rectangular, and disposed in regular series.

This, of course, makes the whole matter perfectly clear. Once and for all we understand that the Pteroptochidae are a South American family of formicarioid passerine birds, typified by the genus *Pteroptochus*, with tracheophonous mesomyodian syrinx, operculate nostrils, and cutelliplantar tarsi in which the plantar scutella are contiguous, rectangular, and disposed in regular series. But to do the *Century* justice I ought to say that after characterizing the birds with this formidable array of epithets, it adds that they are wrens that live in the rocks.

Old Samuel Johnson had a celebrated definition of "network" in his famous dictionary, which ran: "anything reticulated or decussated at equal distances, with interstices between the intersections." When reproached for using big words to define a simple idea, he answered that if we set out to define big words by a means of smaller ones and those by others smaller than they, we finally reach the very smallest, and the only way in which we can define *them* is by using the big words over again. If the reader will attempt to give a definition for a word like "is" or "in" or "of," he will soon see what the good doctor was driving at.

The longest word in English

Considerable interest attaches to the question of what word in the English language is the longest. There have been many candidates for the honor, the latest of which is one purporting to be the name of a disease. It contains forty-five letters, and according to the newspapers, has won recognition by the Puzzlers' League. Here it is:

pneumonoultramicroscopicsilicovolcanokoniosis.

It is supposed to signify an inflammation of the lungs caused by inhaling very small particles of quartz dust from a volcanic eruption. It does not seem to me that this, however, is an actual word, for I cannot imagine anyone's actually using it. It is really six words in one, put together after the fashion of some terms in organic chemistry, which may be called words, in a certain sense, but which really show the chemical composition of the substance they denote, and are more on the order of formulas.

The longest word recorded in the new *Webster*, so far as I know, is:

honorificabilitudinitatibus,

which has twenty-seven letters, but is open to the objection that it is not really English at all, since it is the dative (or ablative) plural of a medieval Latin word, and would not be recorded in an English dictionary at all, except that Shakespeare has one of his characters use it, in the play *Love's Labor's Lost*, merely to show off his supposed learning.

Furthermore, the *Standard Dictionary* gives us one of twenty-eight letters:

antidisestablishmentarianism,

which is a genuine English word and has actually been used to convey a meaning. This is to the best of my knowledge the longest legitimate English word recorded in a dictionary, though I have heard that a derivative of it was once used that is still longer. It is said that an English bishop, speaking in the House of Lords, uttered the phrase "antidisestablishmentarianistically speaking" and thus set a record by using a word of thirty-four letters, though, so far as I know, it has never been recorded in a dictionary. It seems, however, to be properly formed, and, of course, all words have to be used by some one before they *can* be recorded in the dictionaries, so I see no reason why we should not admit it.

Let us take the word apart, to get at its meaning. "Antidisestablishmentarianistically speaking" means "speaking as an antidisestablishmentarian." The prefix "anti" means "against," so that an antidisestablishmentarian is one who is opposed to disestablishment. Now the word "disestablishment" means little to most Americans, but a great deal to Englishmen, for the Church of England—represented in this country by the Episcopal Church—is said to be "established" —that is to say, it has for ages been the official church of that country, supported partly at least by the government. This seems an unnatural situation to most of us, no doubt, but to many Englishmen it appears the most natural and proper thing in the world, and a good many years ago when it was proposed to disestablish the Church of England in Ireland, where most of the people are Catholics or Presbyterians— and in Wales, where most of them are Congregationalists, Methodists, or Baptists—there was more or less opposition. Those opposing were naturally called antidisestablishmentarians.

But, some may say, since "anti" and "dis" are both negative prefixes and nullify each other, why not leave both off and call them simply establishmentarians? The answer to this is that the proposal was not to establish the Church in Ireland and Wales. It was already established, and those in opposition were trying to prevent its disestablishment. Therefore when the good bishop spoke in the House of Lords, he could properly say that he was speaking antidisestablishmentarianistically.

We have carried our analysis of this enormous word down to its basis "establish," and I wonder whether we might not go a little further. "Establish" means "to make stable or firm," and comes from the Latin *stabilis*, which in turn comes from *stare*, "to stand." Notice that we have in English the words "stop," "stay," and "still," all likewise beginning with "st" and all indicating a cessation of motion. The German word for "stand" is *stehen*, and the Greek is *histemi*, both containing this "st." In fact, the word for "stand" in fourteen of the languages of the great Indo-European family, to which English belongs, contains the combination "st."

In pondering over this very striking circumstance, an idea has occurred to me, which I should like to present to my readers, with the warning, however, that it may be only my fancy. But does it not seem likely that ages ago when the original Indo-European language was just beginning to be formed, when two of our ancestors were roaming the forest in hunting or warfare, one of them would warn the other of the approach of game or of the enemy by making a hissing sound such as might now be represented by the letters "st," and that on hearing it the one warned would naturally *stop*, take his *stand*, and *stay still?* And is it not possible, then, that this simple hissing sound is the ultimate basis of these words, of the Latin *stare*, the German *stehen*, the Greek *histemi*, and all the others of similar sound and meaning? No man, I suppose, can answer such a question definitely, and I present it only as a theory which seems not unreasonable. If it should not be true, the truth is doubtless just as remarkable. It may appear a far cry from this instinctive hissing sound of a savage to the "antidisestablishmentarianistically" of the bishop. But some such journey has obviously been taken by all the tongues of the civilized world, and its accomplishment is one of the greatest triumphs of the human mind. The development of languages from their primitive forms to the wealth of vocabulary by which they express the most delicate shades of thought and feeling is an amazing process, and nowhere is its history more amazing than in our English speech.

THE LIVING
ENGLISH SUBJUNCTIVE

XXII

Not long ago, in an ably written book on the teaching of English, I encountered the statement that in order to find examples of the use of the subjunctive—other than those of the "if I *were*" type—it is necessary to go to the classics. This is only a slightly extreme way of putting what is taught in nearly all school grammars of the present day. There is a general impression among textbook writers and teachers of English that, as far as ordinary speech and writing are concerned, the subjunctive is either dead or rapidly dying. Even the usually keen-sighted Fowler says in his *Modern English Usage* that it "is moribund except in a few easily specified uses."

Yet in the very book in which the reader is referred to the classics for examples of the subjunctive, there were numerous instances of its use which the author obviously failed to recognize. Furthermore, it is not at all unusual to find subjunctives in newspapers, in magazines with no pretensions to literary style, and even in the language of ordinary conversation. Far from dying, it appears to be actually gaining ground in certain uses which the textbooks commonly ignore, or treat with gross inadequacy, and which Fowler does not even mention in his four-page discussion of the subjunctive in *Modern English Usage*.

If the reader is skeptical of the truth of the statement just made, I ask only that he *watch* closely as we continue our discussion, that he *examine* with particular care the verbs of this paragraph. I urge that he *let* nothing escape him, for I prefer that he *be* convinced with his own eyes, and it is important, of course, that he *exercise* great care lest he *be* deceived. I would not for an instant propose that he *take* my word for it, since it is vital in matters of this sort that each *form* his own opinion. As I desire that he *be* completely satisfied, I insist that he *be* not too hasty to abandon his former beliefs. Heaven *help* him in his efforts! And I close the paragraph with the request that the reader *observe* that every one of the italicized verbs in it is a genuine subjunctive and that not one is of the type found in "if I were."

Furthermore, there is nothing abnormal or unnatural about any of them, though it is, of course, unusual to find so many in so brief a space. All are in the present tense, third person singular, and consequently are easily recognized as subjunctives either by the fact that they do not end in "s," as the indicative would, or that "be" is used instead of the indicative "is." Similar subjunctives may be found in the columns of any newspaper, and if the reader is still skeptical, I suggest that he search (there's another!) the first page of his favorite journal tomorrow. If he does not find more than one, his experience will be different from mine.

By reference to our third paragraph it will be found that seven of its subjunctives occur in clauses introduced by "that" after the verbs "ask," "urge," "prefer," "propose," "desire," and "insist." But there are many other verbs that may be followed by such a clause with its verb in the subjunctive. Notice the following sentences:

> I move that he *be* admitted to membership.
> I suggest that he *return* tomorrow.
> He demands that it *be* done immediately.
> I am anxious that he *get* it at once.

Still other verbs of this kind are "require," "recommend," "order," "beg," "stipulate," "specify," "direct," and "advise."

And it should be noted that nouns of similar meaning may be followed by the same construction, as in the example toward the close of our second paragraph: "with the *request* that the reader *observe*.

We also had the subjunctive used in the second paragraph after the expressions "it is important" and "it is vital." Here are other examples after similar expressions:

> It is urgent that it *get* here tomorrow.
> It is best that he *retire*.
> It is desirable that it *be* done at once.

And subjunctives may likewise be found after "it is necessary," "it is fitting," "it is essential," "it is advisable," "it is sufficient," and others of the same general type.

It is these numerous and important uses of the present subjunctive in clauses beginning with "that" which Fowler, by some incredible oversight, fails utterly to take into account in his article on the subjunctive. One who ignores them as he does, might well think that the subjunctive is dying, but their vigor is compelling evidence to the contrary. Indeed, it seems to me that this is one use in which the subjunctive is actually *gaining* ground today. It would be possible to use a verb phrase with "should" in most of these expressions instead of the simple subjunctive, but more and more the latter is being used. For instance, we can say correctly and do sometimes say, "I insist that he *should go* at once," but it is becoming exceedingly common to hear, "I insist that he *go* at once." Later in this chapter I shall have more to say about this "should"—and perhaps I had better add just here for the encouragement of readers not familiar with the subjunctive that I shall attempt a thorough explanation of the matter before we have finished. Just now, however, I am addressing myself chiefly to those who know something of the use of the subjunctive in other languages, but labor under the current mistaken notion that its uses in English are so insignificant that they deserve only very scant attention.

As those who have heard him on the radio will readily testify, Mr. Walter Winchell's speech would hardly be called classic or stilted. While he apparently "sees all and knows all," it is doubtful whether he would admit any acquaintance with the subjunctive, if taxed with it. Yet he once made the following statement in one of his gossip columns of the air: "It was only natural that he *get* in a cab and *go* home to his wife." I am sorry not to be able to satisfy my readers as to what happened when the gentleman arrived at home, but the truth is I was so fascinated by Mr. Winchell's use of the two subjunctives that I failed to follow the remainder of the story. Here again "*should* get . . . and go" might have been used, but the simple subjunctive actually was used.

And consider the following sentence from the magazine *Time*, which certainly never lets itself be bound by pedantic rules and could not possibly be accused of attempting to perpetuate the speech of the past: "Also a request went to the Pan American-Grace Airways that the 40-passenger *Pan American Clipper be* held at the President's disposal in case he . . . *decide* to return home by air." The first subjunctive, "be," is of a very common type already discussed, but the second, "decide," follows "in case," after which the use of "should decide" would be very common. Is not *Time's* use of the simple subjunctive here significant of the growing tendency I have spoken of?

Numerous examples of the subjunctive may be found in every issue of *Time*, of which the following are typical:

> . . . Colonel Edward Green, whose mother, miserly Hetty Green, specified that the family fortune *remain* intact.
>
> Lest President Augustin Justo *feel* left out, Franklin Roosevelt hastened to invite him also to the White House.
>
> Father Mussolini ordered that they never *be* mentioned again in this connection, lest they *get* swelled heads.

Newspaper examples of the subjunctive are likewise very abundant, but I shall quote only one—a sentence from an Associated Press dispatch, which is a little unusual:

Two truckloads of Christmas mail arrived today for Edward, Duke of Windsor, though he was represented as wishing only that the world *forget* him.

Notice once more that the simple subjunctive "forget" is here used in place of "would forget."

And lest some of my readers think that the subjunctive appears only in writing, let me give a few instances of it that I noticed and recorded in the course of a few days' listening to ordinary conversations:

I am insisting that she *do* it.
They would prefer that I *work* straight on through.
It was just destined that he *get* that ticket.
I am determined that my daughter *be* able to take care of herself.

In none of these instances was the speaker a person of unusual education or literary inclination.

Aside from its vigorous and growing use in these clauses beginning with "that," the present subjunctive has two other uses in which it is very much alive and which are illustrated in our third paragraph. One is after "lest," as in "lest he *be* deceived," and in "lest they *get* swelled heads" in one of our quotations from *Time*. The other is in the expression of a wish, as in "Heaven *help* him in his efforts."

"Lest," of course, is largely a literary word, one not ordinarily heard in conversation. On the other hand, there are many common phrases abundant in everyday speech in which a wish is expressed by means of the subjunctive. "God *bless* you," for instance, means "I wish that God may bless you." And to go to the other extreme, "The devil *take* you!" "Plague *take* you!" and "*Confound* you!" are all examples of evil wishes expressed by the subjunctive. In the Lord's prayer we have three instances of this type of the subjunctive in "Hallowed *be* thy name," "Thy kingdom *come*," and "Thy will *be* done." Other examples are: "The saints *preserve* us!" "God *grant* it!" "God *save* the King!"

"Long *live* the King!" And another instance, which is not usually recognized, is found in the sentence, "Somebody *close* the door," which really means, "I wish that somebody would close the door." This needs to be carefully distinguished from the imperative, which we find in the command, "Close the door." "One of you *hold* his hands" contains a similar instance of this frequently unrecognized subjunctive.

The impression that the subjunctive is dying comes partly from the failure to realize that these uses of it which we have been discussing are genuine subjunctives, and partly from the fact that its use after "if," "unless," "although," and "until" has actually declined within the past hundred years or so. It was formerly common to see and hear such clauses as "if he *come*," "unless he *go* at once," "though he *do* so," and "until it *be* proved." But now for many years it has been standard usage to say, "if he *comes*," "unless he *goes* at once," "though he *does* so," and "until it *is* proved," in all of which the indicative is used. Undeniably the subjunctive has lost ground here. *Yet even here the change seems to have reached its limit, and usage is now stationary.* The subjunctive may be, and often is, still used after these four conjunctions, especially when the element of doubt is emphasized. It is not unusual to hear "If it *be* true," "though it *be* true," "unless it *be* done," and so on, and under the proper circumstances such subjunctives carry with them no air of affectation or antiquity. Major Bowes, for instance, said in his "Amateur Hour" one evening, "It will save much embarrassment if such requests *be* not made."

Furthermore, there was never a real justification for the English use of the subjunctive in ordinary conditions such as, "If he come," when there is no great degree of doubt about the matter. Neither German, French, nor Latin uses the subjunctive under similar circumstances, though all these languages use the subjunctive in general rather more freely than English. Since it served no good purpose, it is well that this use has passed away, but its passing has not affected the true uses of the subjunctive.

So far we have been discussing only subjunctives in the present tense, though, to be sure, they often refer to *future time*. But the past subjunctive is also used very freely, far more so than most of us realize. Of course, everybody who knows anything at all about the subjunctive knows that "were" is subjunctive in the expression "If I were you," and also in "I wish he were here." This is the *past* subjunctive, and yet it refers to *present* time. The meaning is, "If I were you now," and "I wish he were here now." In English—as in Latin and German—we use the past subjunctive when we want to make a supposition that we know to be untrue or a wish that is impossible of fulfillment, even though it is the present time that we have in mind. This seems very curious, but it is undeniably a fact, as the reader can see for himself. The reason, no doubt, is that the past seems more unreal than the present.

Now let us consider for a moment the following sentence, which doubtless has been spoken thousands of times by older people who were attempting to give advice to younger ones:

> If I *were* you and *had* your opportunities and *knew* what I know now, I would certainly take advantage of them.

In this sentence, everybody that is fairly familiar with the subjunctive will agree that "were" is a subjunctive in the past tense, expressing an unreality in present time. Now the question arises, what are "had" and "knew" in the sentence? There can be but one answer: "had" and "knew" are also past subjunctives. To be sure, they look exactly like past *indicatives*, but they fulfill the functions of subjunctives, and as a matter of history, *they actually are subjunctives that have changed in the course of years till they look like indicatives, though they were originally quite different from them.*

But some one may ask, "If they look exactly like past indicatives, why not call them so? Why attempt to maintain a distinction that does not now exist, even if it once did?" Let me answer that by two questions. First, if you call "had" and "knew" past indicatives, how are you going to explain the fact that they are connected with the unquestioned subjunctive "were" by the co-ordinating conjunction "and" and that they obviously have the same function as "were"? Second, if you call "had" and "knew" past indicatives, how will you explain the fact that your past indicatives refer to present time? No, the best explanation is the true one that the verbs are really subjunctives that look like indicatives. There is no use, of course, in trying to explain that to very young students, but the question is not likely to arise with such.

For all verbs except the verb "to be" the past subjunctive looks exactly like the past indicative, but can be almost infallibly distinguished from it by the golden rule that the past indicative shows past time, while the past subjunctive shows present or future time. In "He told me that yesterday," "told" is past indicative, but in "You wouldn't believe it if I *told* you," it is past subjunctive, for it means, "If I should tell you now or in the future." Notice that the thought in this use of the subjunctive may also be expressed by "should" or "were to." We may say either,

> "If he came now, it would be too late," or
> "If he should come now, it would be too late," or
> "If he were to come now, it would be too late."

The only difference in these sentences is that the use of "should" makes his coming seem a little more improbable than in the first, and the use of "were to" seems to make it still more improbable. Notice also that in such sentences as "If he came, it would be too late," we are not expressing an actual unreality or impossibility, as in "If I were you," but an improbability. This is a second use of the past subjunctive. A third one—though essentially the same as the first—is that after "as if" and "as though," in sentences such as, "He looks as if he were sick," which is only a shortened way of saying, "He looks as he would look if he were sick."

But before we go further, we must answer the impatient question that will certainly arise in the minds of many readers, "Well, just what *is* the subjunctive, after all?" It is not easy to frame a simple answer to such a question, but I shall do my best. The subjunctive is the form of the verb that the speaker uses to show that he is expressing simply an idea in his mind—not an actual fact. It may actually *be* a fact, but the use of the subjunctive shows that he is not *thinking* of it as a fact. And he may show this by some other means than the use of a special form of the verb, but when he does use a special form for that purpose, the verb is said to be in the subjunctive mood. There are two other moods in English—the indicative and the imperative. The indicative is merely the ordinary way of speaking, and the imperative gives a command or request, as in the sentence, "Close the door, Henry."

The subjunctive in English was originally so unlike the indicative that it was possible to tell the two apart at a glance, but the language has so changed that today some forms of the two moods are exactly alike, as has already been pointed out. If they were all alike, we could dismiss the subjunctive and forget about it, but there are still some differences, and no person can speak English well who does not recognize them. These differences are greater in the case of the verb "to be" than in other verbs, but they exist in nearly all. Here is a comparison of the present and past indicatives of this verb with the same tenses of the subjunctive:

> Present Indicative: I am, you are, he is, we are, you are, they are.
> Present Subjunctive: I be, you be, he be, we be, you be, they be.
> Past Indicative: I was, you were, he was, we were, you were, they were.
> Past Subjunctive: I were, you were, he were, we were, you were, they were.

Notice that after "we," "you," and "they," the past indicative and the past subjunctive are both "were," and consequently cannot be told apart except by their use. The past subjunctive of other verbs is exactly like the past indicative. Indeed, it is permissible under certain circumstances to use "was" after "I" or "he" instead of "were" as the past subjunctive of "to be," though that is usually not advisable. It is a serious mistake, for instance, to say, "If I was you," for "If I were you." Yet sometimes when we want to make a supposition especially vivid, even though we know it is not true, we use "was." "Even if he *was* here," we say, "he couldn't do anything about it." Such a use of "was" should be regarded not as an indicative, but as a past subjunctive formed like a past indicative, as is the regular way of forming it for verbs other than "to be." And another instance of this use of "was" as a past subjunctive is found in expressions like "It is high time he was here," in which few would use the regular past subjunctive "were."

It has been so impressed on the consciousness of educated people that "if I were" and "if he (or she, or it) were" are the correct forms that many mistakenly feel that it is always incorrect to use "was" after "if." This is probably why so many say, "He asked me if it *were* true," when it should be, "He asked me if it *was* true," for in this sentence "if" means "whether," and the statement made is what is known as an "indirect question," which does not use a subjunctive in English, though it does in German and Latin. If it were correct to say, "He asked me if it were true," it would also be correct to say, "He is asking me if it *be* true," which, of course, nobody thinks of saying. And very few would have a tendency to say "He asked me *whether* it *were* true." It is only when "if" is substituted for "whether" that we want to use the subjunctive, and this tendency is obviously brought about by the frequency of the "if I were" combination. Yet it is quite true that some very respectable writers have used "were" in these indirect questions where "was" is the logical word.

Some time ago a lawyer of considerable ability and prominence in his profession asked me to decide an issue which had arisen between him and his secretary over the matter of the use of "was" or "were" in a sentence which ran substantially as follows:

> We ask the court to hold that if there was (or were?) such a deficit, it occurred on or before September 1, 1930.

The lawyer contended for "was," the secretary for "were." The lawyer was right, for the reference is to past time and what is being considered as a fact. The use of "were" would indicate present time and an unreality. If there were no deficit, it would not occur on or before any date.

So much for the subjunctive of "to be" in the past and present tenses. For a verb such as "go," the present indicative and the present subjunctive are as follows:

> Present Indicative: I go, you go, he goes, we go, you go, they go.
> Present Subjunctive: I go, you go, he go, we go, you go, they go.

The only difference is in the third person singular, where the subjunctive has "go" instead of the indicative "goes." By the way, the simplest rule for forming the present subjunctive of any verb in any form is merely to take the infinitive and drop the "to." This applies to "to be" as well as the others. What could be easier?

The past subjunctive of "go" is "went" in all forms, exactly like the past indicative, of course.

It is possible also to have subjunctives in the perfect and past perfect tenses. The perfect is merely a combination of the word "have"—never "has"—with the past participle. It has scarcely any use in present day English, but here is an example from the King James Version of the Bible: "If the salt *have lost* his savor, wherewith shall it be salted?" (Notice also the use of "his" for "its," which was common at one time. "Its" was just beginning to be used when the King James Version was made.)

The past perfect subjunctive is exactly like the past perfect indicative; that is, it is formed with "had" and the past participle. But it shows simple past time—not past perfect. In the sentence, "I had been there a long time when he came in," "had been" is past perfect indicative, but in "If I had been there, I should have seen him," it is past perfect subjunctive, and, like the past subjunctive, shows an unreality. It is also used in a wish that refers to the past, as "I wish I had been there." It is needless to add that such a wish is impossible of fulfillment.

English grammars do not ordinarily give a future or a future perfect subjunctive, probably because of the fact that neither of these tenses occurs in the subjunctive in Latin. Text-book grammar has always been more or less modeled after that of Latin. But if we say that "I shall go, you will go, he will go," and so on, is the future indicative of "go," we can as reasonably say that "I should go, you would go, he would go," and so on, is the future subjunctive. And as the future perfect indicative is "He will have gone," so the future perfect subjunctive would be "He would have gone." But the grammars do not usually record matters thus.

In fact, school grammars generally pay very little attention to the common and important words "can," "could," "may," "might," "must," "will," "would," "shall," and "should," except to call them auxiliary verbs, and to show the use of "will" and "shall" in the future. Older grammars used to say that—except "will" and "shall"—they were used to form the "potential" mood of other verbs, but we hear little of that now.

These verbs are peculiar in that they always need the infinitive (without "to") of another verb to complete their meaning, though this infinitive may sometimes be understood. But they are also peculiar in the fact that they have no infinitives of their own, nor have they any past participles, though they once had both and the corresponding verbs in German still have them. "Must" has nothing but a present tense. "Can," "may," "will," and "shall" are present indicatives, while "could," "would," "should," and "might" are sometimes past indicatives, but more often past subjunctives.

Notice the different meanings of "could" in the two follow-ing sentences:

> He could not go yesterday. ("Could" means "was able.")
> He could go today. ("Could" means "would be able.")

This difference is due to the fact that in the first sen-tence "could" is past indicative, while in the second it is past subjunctive. Of course at one time the two forms were different. However, they can still be distinguished from each other by the golden rule that enables us to distinguish any past subjunctive from a past indicative—namely, as we keep repeating, that the past subjunctive shows present or future time. Readers may recall the incident I told of in an earlier chapter concerning the physician who inquired of a Negro, "Could I use your telephone?" and after the Negro's answer, "Yes, you may," felt greatly rebuked and humiliated because of what he considered his mistaken use of "could." What he was using, however, was the past subjunctive, and its effect in this instance was to make his request seem more polite. This is sometimes called the "sub-junctive of softened statement," and another instance of it may be seen in the question, "*Might* I be of help to you?" which is a little more deeply courteous than "May I be of help?" though the latter, is of course a polite form in itself.

"Might" is nearly always a past subjunctive, though it would be a past indicative in the sentence, "Mother said we might go," meaning "Mother said that we had permission to go," where it obviously refers to the past. "Should" and "would" are likewise usually past subjunctives. The "should" that means "ought" is a subjunctive, and "ought" itself is the past subjunctive of "owe," though we now think of it as a present indicative. It is possible, especially in poetry to substitute "were" for "would be" and "had" (subjunc-tive) for "would have" in expressions like "It *were* better to go at once" and "Had he been here, we *had* been glad."

And in a previous chapter I have spoken of the use of the past subjunctive "had" in expressions like "had better."

Some cautions are needed against the numerous false conceptions that surround this rather mysterious subject. One is that any expression of doubt is in the subjunctive. This is not at all true. When we say, "I doubt that he is coming," both verbs are in the present indicative. It is true that the idea expressed by a verb in the subjunctive is usually more or less doubtful, but that is because the subjunctive represents, by the definition, an idea in the speaker's mind, rather than an actual fact. And, as was stated, this idea—or the fact that it is an idea—may be brought out in other ways. When we say, "I think perhaps he will be late," we express an idea that may or may not prove to be a fact and we show also that there is more or less doubt about it, but we do these things by the use of the word "think" (an indicative) and the adverb "perhaps," not by using a subjunctive.

Another misconception is the notion that "I may go" is subjunctive, because it expresses a mere probability. But "may" is here present indicative, and the sense of probability comes from the meaning of the word "may." Yet in "May he come soon!" "may" is a present subjunctive, evidently expressing a wish. And my judgment is that in a purpose clause, such as, "He studies in order that he may learn," "may" is a subjunctive, or at least a descendant of an original subjunctive. "Let him come soon," expresses the same idea as "May he come soon," but "let" is imperative (with subject "you" understood), as it also is in "Let us go."

Different languages use the subjunctive under different conditions, and its use in any particular language must be learned by contact with that language itself. Yet those who have become familiar with the subjunctive in Latin, French, or German will more readily understand it in English. For most Americans, the greatest value of the study of a foreign language is the light that it throws upon our own, and if the teachers of foreign languages realized (a past subjunctive) that fact more clearly, their instruction would be more valuable and at the same time more interesting to their pupils, who would not only learn a great deal about their native tongue that they could not get in any other way, but would also make more rapid progress in the foreign language.

There are many people who ridicule the idea that the study of other languages is of great benefit in obtaining a knowledge of English—or rather they argue with a great show of common sense that it would be more reasonable to devote *all* one's time to English without wasting any on the foreign tongue, and thus learn still more about it. This *sounds* like the height of wisdom, but the truth is otherwise. Nothing is understood so well when studied by itself as it is when compared with something else of the same kind. And English, in particular, has lost so many of its grammatical forms that the significance of those which remain cannot be thoroughly grasped without the study of a language like Latin, which retains them all, or nearly all. And German, being more closely kin to English in its grammar, throws a light on some points which Latin leaves dark. French is not so valuable for a knowledge of grammar, but has contributed so many words and phrases to English that some familiarity with it is indispensable to a mastery of our language.

But a thorough understanding of the English subjunctive will not be easy to acquire even for one who has encountered it in other tongues. Let not the reader who has no knowledge of foreign languages be discouraged, then, if he finds that some—or even much—of what has been said in this chapter remains obscure to him. We have been dealing with the most difficult subject in English—one obviously not fully understood by some who write English textbooks. It would be too much to expect those with little or no linguistic training to master it without considerable effort.

Much the same situation exists, of course, with regard to all the finer points of English grammar and usage. They are not matters to be touched on in elementary school and high school and then laid aside, but are worthy, on the contrary, of continued, serious study by mature and intelligent men and women. The materials for such a study lie constantly before us. And the study itself is not only absorbing and fascinating, but it has the added advantage of leading us toward what is at once a highly cultural and an intensely practical goal—the mastery of our mother tongue.

CHANGES, PAST
AND FUTURE

XXIII

FASHIONS come and go in language, as in clothes, and new styles in speech are frequently set in motion by the usage of some person of high station at a moment when the attention of a nation or perhaps of the world is centered upon him. "At long last," began the Duke of Windsor to the eager ears of waiting multitudes, and the rather unusual phrase is fast becoming a commonplace. When Grover Cleveland was president he used the expression "innocuous desuetude" in a public speech, and for years "innocuous desuetude"—which means simply "harmless disuse"—was a favorite locution with many people, some of whom perhaps were not entirely certain of its exact meaning.

It was Theodore Roosevelt who introduced "the strenuous life," and older people can recall that during and after his administration they heard the word "strenuous" till they were sick of it. Woodrow Wilson's "Make the world safe for democracy" was quoted, re-quoted, turned around into "Make democracy safe for the world," and changed over and over into "Make so-and-so safe for something else," until the obvious fact that the Versailles treaty had made the world rather unsafe for democracy sent that expression into Cleveland's innocuous desuetude. And then Warren Harding for some unknown reason selected the very rare "normalcy" for use in his phrase "return to normalcy," and that word has been threatening ever since to displace the formerly much more common "normal" and "normality." Next came the "new era" and "just around the corner," then "the forgotten man" and "the new deal." In fact, a pretty good review of the history of our country could be made with the help of these catch-words alone.

Worn-out phrases

Nearly all such expressions pass out of use before many years have gone by, for their basis is different from that of those trite phrases which seem to have immortal life, because they always sound beautiful or clever to those who hear them for the first time and to those whose appetite for them never seems to be dulled, even by a thousand repetitions. A few of the hundreds of possible examples are:

> All nature seemed at rest. . . . The tree stood like a lone sentinel. . . . Too full for utterance. . . . A sadder, but wiser man. . . . Which would be laughable, if it were not tragic. . . . But that is another story. . . . It's a small world, after all. . . . Tired, but happy. . . . More sinned against than sinning. . . . Conspicuous by his absence. . . . The psychological moment. . . . Do justice to a dinner. . . . Last but not least. . . . As luck would have it. . . . The proud possessor. . . . A long-felt want. . . . In the last analysis. . . .

There is nothing seriously wrong with any of these. In fact, if they had not had merit, they would not have been overworked. Any one of us is likely to use some of them, or others equally trite, in conversation without any great harm, and it would be strange if none crept into our writing. But their constant use, or particularly their use with the feeling that we have said something remarkably apt and clever, is a sign that our minds have gone to sleep.

"He needs no introduction"

There is another expression that I should like to place on the forbidden list, though I do not recall having heard anyone else offer objection to it, and my aversion may be the result of mere personal prejudice. But I cannot help wondering why three persons out of five seem to consider that a very clever way to introduce a speaker of any prominence whatever is to say, "He needs no introduction." And why, after saying that, do two of the three proceed to make the needless introduction longer than a necessary one should be? The most appropriate introduction of my experience was made in three words by the president of a teachers' college in North Carolina. The speaker, Josephus Daniels, was delayed in arriving, and the audience had been waiting in the auditorium for him for fifteen minutes, when the two men came out on the stage. As the applause subsided, the president stepped forward, holding the speaker by the arm, said, "Here he is!" and the introduction was over. Under the circumstances, nothing could have been better or more effective, though, of course, in an ordinary situation such unusual brevity would have been unseemly.

"Very real"

And after the needless introduction has been finally completed, how often does the speaker begin, "I wish to assure you that it is a very real pleasure to be with you tonight." Why *"very* real"? When I hear a speaker use this phrase, I cannot help thinking that the pleasure or the advantage or the privilege that he is talking about is not real after all and that he is merely trying to persuade his audience and perhaps himself that it is real by putting the word "very" before the adjective. Incidentally, how much more real is something that is very real than something that is merely real? The fact is that "very" has been so overworked that it has almost ceased to have any significance. Indeed, under some circumstances we actually use it to lessen the force of the word it is applied to. "How are you feeling?" we ask, and the answer comes, "Oh, very well, I suppose." Here it is obvious that the speaker is really not feeling well and uses the word "very" to indicate it, though logically it should mean that he is feeling better than usual.

"Pinch-hitter"

I wonder sometimes whether our Congress might not be persuaded to pass a law imposing a fine of not less than five hundred dollars, or six months' imprisonment, at the discretion of the judge, on any person called on to speak in place of another who begins his address by describing himself as a pinch hitter. Because of the crowded conditions of our prisons, I suppose the fine would be preferable, and indeed as a producer of revenue, it would doubtless equal or surpass the income tax. What is a pinch hitter, anyway? He is a player who in an emergency—or "pinch"—is sent in to bat for another *because he is a better hitter than the one he replaces.* What shall we think, then, of the modesty of a substitute speaker who says that he is pinch-hitting for another man? I heard one speaking in place of General Hugh Johnson so describe his rôle and then go on to show his knowledge of baseball by entering upon an elaborate comparison in which he referred to General Johnson as a Babe Ruth. A man who can pinch-hit for a Babe Ruth must be good. But, of course, the speaker, far from meaning to compliment himself, was trying to be very modest, and was merely using words inaccurately, as we are all likely to do at times.

It is not unusual for speakers or writers to attempt to win the favor of their listeners or readers by showing their familiarity with popular sports. In that case, however, they would do well to make sure that it is not their unfamiliarity which they are revealing. Here is an extract from an article by a rather well known writer, who is evidently making in it a great effort to put himself on the level of the masses, with somewhat ludicrous results:

If one's language clearly expresses his thought, is it really important that his vocabulary and grammar be perfect?

I do not believe so. Suppose I say, "In the first game of the world series the Yankees beat the Giants 8 to 1 because Lefty Gomez breezed 'em by the batter so fast he blasted the Giants out of the box in the sixth—even Lou Gehrig." If you know baseball you get what I mean.

If the writer had known baseball, he would have known that Lou Gehrig is a Yankee, not a Giant, nor do I think he would have spoken of a pitcher's blasting the batters out of the box, for that is what batters are usually said to do to a pitcher. At any rate, it is rather peculiar to speak of "blasting" by means of "breezing," for there is a considerable difference between a blast and a breeze. And the oddest thing about the matter is that the grammar of the illustrative sentence is quite good, though it is supposed to be an example of the opposite sort. Is it possible that the writer is unable to use bad grammar, even when he makes a deliberate effort to do so? And those who think the subjunctive is dying in English are asked to note his use of "be" in the first sentence, and reflect that here is an instance of its use by a writer in the very act of decrying the importance of grammar.

Is good grammar important?

But is it really important that one's grammar and use of words—which is what I judge he means by vocabulary—be perfect? Well, we live in an imperfect world, and it is a little too much to expect perfection in anything from a human being. But if he means to ask whether it is important that one's grammar and use of words make a reasonable approach toward perfection, it is like asking whether it is important that one's clothing be clean, pressed, and in good style and taste. The answer to that question, of course, depends on who is doing the answering. A great many people would say yes. Others would say no, and would point out that as long as the clothing covers the body, it is fulfilling its main function, so that it really doesn't matter much what it looks like. And not all the people who take that attitude are tramps; some are quite respectable, and make good, decent citizens.

A traveler in a remote backwoods section spent the night with a family in a log cabin, and when he awoke the next morning set about making his usual civilized toilet, or as much of it as the limited facilities of the household would permit. The little boy of the family watched him intently as he shaved, brushed his teeth, combed his hair, and so on, and finally when, after much time and effort, everything was complete, he asked very earnestly, "Say, Mister, ain't you a lot of trouble to yourself?" What the traveler answered is not recorded, but the only correct answer to the boy's question is yes. It is a good deal of trouble to live in civilized fashion, but most of us think the result is worth it. It is some trouble also to use good English, and a great deal of trouble to break bad habits of speech. Let the reader decide for himself whether the result is worth the trouble, but let him be assured that when once he has found the better way, he will never willingly go back to the old.

Worn-out quotations

Our great writers have put some things so aptly that circumstances are continually arising in which certain quotations from them seem appropriate. But even the words of the great, though they wear better than most, can lose something of their freshness if too often repeated, especially if the matter that calls them forth is something trifling. It is a very remarkable fact that in a list of such hackneyed quotations which Fowler gives, there are found no less than seven from *Hamlet*, namely:

A consummation devoutly to be wished.
Metal more attractive.
My prophetic soul!
There's the rub.
To be or not to be.
Pity 'tis, 'tis true.
More in sorrow than in anger.

He might well have added:

Method in his madness.
Something rotten in Denmark.

And there are many more from that remarkable play that are very frequently heard—sometimes from people who do not realize that they are quoting Shakespeare. One of my pupils told me that she had always thought that "something rotten in Denmark" was slang. (The full quotation, by the way, is "Something is rotten in the state of Denmark," and the other is, "Though this be madness, yet there is method in't.")

It is a striking proof of the genius of the man who is generally considered to be our greatest English writer, and perhaps the greatest writer of the world, that more than three hundred years after his death, so many of his lines should still be household words. It is easy to see at least one reason why *Hamlet* is called his masterpiece. No single work of any author has furnished us with so many quotable lines, those given above being only a small part of the entire number. And I trust no reader will feel that he must never quote any of those which Fowler has classified as "hackneyed," or the two which I have added to his list. Sometimes there is nothing else so appropriate. A great deal depends on the make-up of one's audience, and still more on the manner in which the quotation is rendered. To utter in a gathering of educated people a line that has been familiar to them all from childhood, with an air of acquainting them with a brilliant discovery, is only to make oneself tiresome and to arouse resentment among one's listeners. About the only better method of reflecting on their intelligence is to add every now and then, "if you see what I mean." But there is a way in which even an old line may be made to take on new life, a way of delicately implying that what is familiar to the speaker is likewise familiar to his audience.

But it is important, of course, not to misapply or to mix one's quotations. The most startling case of this sort that could well be imagined was that of a clubwoman who was preparing a paper on the subject "Woman." Readers will recall—if I may be permitted to use the method of delicate implication that I have just recommended—the passage from Scott's *Marmion* that runs as follows:

> O Woman! in our hours of ease,
> Uncertain, coy, and hard to please;
>
> .   .   .   .   .
>
> When pain and anguish wring the brow,
> A ministering angel thou!

And there is one rather more familiar from Pope:

> Vice is a monster of so frightful mien
> As to be hated needs but to be seen;
> Yet seen too oft, familiar with her face,
> We first endure, then pity, then embrace.

(After delicately implying this familiarity with literature, it is usually likewise advisable to give your quotations in full, for fear the implication may, in the case of some, be false.)

In some manner these two passages—though they are not in exactly the same meter—became mixed in the mind of the club-woman, and the result was that her paper began in this amazing fashion:

> O Woman! In our hours of ease,
> Uncertain, coy, and hard to please;
> But seen too oft, familiar with her face,
> We first endure, then pity, then embrace.

Quotations concerning women seem especially liable to perversion. When I was a young high-school teacher, a school girl, whom we will call Susie Smith, came to me once Friday afternoon, asking for one on that subject, to use in answering the roll call in her literary society. The only thing I could think of at the moment was the words of an old toast: "Woman! Without her, man is a savage." In repeating it for the girl, I happened to think of a story of how it had once been purposely changed by some man to read: "Woman without her man is a savage," and very foolishly told Susie about it, warning her, however, to be sure not to render the line in that way. What happened was, of course, what any experienced teacher might have foreseen. I attended the meeting of the literary society that afternoon, and when the secretary called out "Susie Smith," was both highly amused and somewhat mortified to hear Susie recite glibly, "Woman without her man is a savage."

Women's English

I have heard that in some languages there are certain words that are used exclusively by men and others used exclusively by women. While this is, of course, not true in English, there is nevertheless a slight tendency in that direction. "Horrid," for instance, is seldom used by men, and "dainty" has a decidedly feminine connotation, though men sometimes use it. In general, women's choice of words will be in favor of the more specific and concrete as against the general and abstract. I once heard two little girls at play, engaged in an imaginary telephone conversation. "Well, I'll slip on a fresh dress and come right over," said one to the other. How differently a boy would have put it. In the first place, of course, it would never have occurred to him that a change of costume was necessary for going anywhere, but if it had, he would never have spoken of "slipping" on a "fresh" garment, but of "putting" on a "clean" one. Yet the girl chose the more deli-

cate "fresh" and the more specific "slip." As a boy, I used
to wonder why my mother would ask me to slip upstairs
for her, to step across the street, to run up to the grocery,
but never simply to "go" anywhere.

Yet in at least one respect men seem to have control of
our language. I have already mentioned that in the absence
of any specific indication to the contrary the word "he"
means both "he" and "she," according to the grammarians,
the lexicographers, and the courts of law. The implication
of this usage is, of course, that the normal, natural human
being is male, the female being only a sort of peculiar sub-
species. But when it comes to celestial beings, we have a
peculiar situation. In the Bible angels are always referred
to as "he," there being apparently no ladies among them.
But in modern America they are usually thought of as feminine and referred to as "she." On the other hand, the deity
is in English, as, I believe, in nearly all languages, designated
by the masculine pronouns. Though it is absurd to think
of God as possessing the specific characteristics of either
sex, we have become so accustomed to this use that anything else sounds a little ridiculous, as is shown by the story
of remarkable exhortation made by a woman who was a
leader in the cause of woman suffrage in its early days, when
the movement was weak and its ultimate success doubtful.
A defeat in an important state election had just been suf-
fered, and a group of ardent workers had gathered to con-
sole one another and to consult as to the next step. The
atmosphere was somewhat gloomy, but the leader was un-
daunted. "Let us put our trust in God, sisters," she exclaimed. "*She* will bring us through safely."

The effect of literature on language

But let us return to the question of quoting from the
works of our great writers. The actual quoting may be,
and sometimes is, overdone, but the stocking of the memory with fine passages from pieces of great literature is a

splendid practice, and it is unfortunate, I think, that our schools do not require as much of it as they once did. One of the glories of the English tongue is its literature. And even though in general the language of our great writers is too formal and dignified for use in ordinary daily conversation, its presence in the mind of the speaker affords an excellent background and serves as a constant restraint against the temptation to let our free and easy colloquial speech degenerate into the crude language of illiteracy. He who desires a genuine mastery of English would do well to steep himself in the writings of those men and women whose works are the shining lights in its history.

I think that one reason for the decline in the practice of memorizing passages from literature was that too often the pupil had no clear understanding of the meaning of the selection and was permitted—or even taught—by the teacher to recite it in such a way as to obscure the meaning effectively for himself or a listener. A favorite passage, for example, has always been Portia's speech from *The Merchant of Venice* beginning:

> The quality of mercy is not strained.

I wonder how many thousands of students have memorized this fine passage without realizing that here "quality" is used in its older sense of "essential nature," that "strained" means "forced," and that the general meaning of the line is that people cannot be made merciful by compulsion. Yet the failure to realize these things detracts much from the sense and consequently also from the beauty of the whole passage. A few lines further—still speaking of mercy— Portia continues:

> It is an attribute to God himself;
> And earthly power doth then show likest God's
> When mercy seasons justice.

For many years, both as a student and a teacher, I read these last two lines in this way:

And EARTHLY power doth then show likest GOD'S
When MERCY seasons JUSTICE.

But from Curry's *Foundations of Expression* I learned my
mistake. They should be read:

And EARTHLY power doth then show LIKEST God's
When mercy SEASONS justice.

To me the transformation was remarkable, and I felt that I
had never realized fully what Shakespeare meant till I read
the lines in the right way.

Every teacher of English literature should be a good
reader and should read aloud very frequently to his class.
Many of our students profess not to like poetry, and the
reason is very commonly that they have seldom or never
heard it read properly. Never to have the poetry read
aloud in the classroom, or to permit the untrained and un-
gifted student himself to butcher it, as is sometimes done,
is a travesty on teaching and a crime against English literature. But the teacher who loves poetry himself and has
the ability to present it properly will never need to com-
plain of lack of appreciation on the part of his pupils.

I have spoken already of the influence of the King James
Version of the Bible on our speech and have mentioned
specifically that our present-day use of the word "talented,"
as in the expression "a talented man" comes from the parable
of the talents. Oddly enough another parable has served to
give many people a false impression of the meaning of a
word. If you should ask the first ten people you meet the
meaning of the word "prodigal," the chances are that more
than five of them would say something like "repentant," and
their answers would be based on memories of the parable of
the Prodigal Son. But the son in this parable would have
been just as prodigal if he had not repented and gone back
to his father, for "prodigal" means "spendthrift" really.
Yet so much has its use in the parable affected our understanding of its meaning that the new *Webster* says that the

noun "prodigal" is often used in the sense of "a repentant waster."

One of the strangest perversions of meaning that I have ever seen in print appeared in a poem published in a daily newspaper. This was the line:

> And the minstrel plays on his *culverin*.

Now a culverin is an old-fashioned cannon, which could hardly be played upon by a minstrel, and I was greatly puzzled to know at first how the poet could have made such a mistake, for it was on the whole a very good production. Finally the solution dawned upon me. In Macaulay's spirited poem *The Battle of Ivry* these lines occur:

> Hurrah! The foes are moving. Hark to the mingled din
> Of fife and steed and trump and drum and roaring culverin.

It is not difficult to see how one unfamiliar with the word would get the notion from this that a culverin is a musical instrument.

"Flout" and "Flaunt"

Perhaps this is as good a place as any to mention the confusion that exists in the minds of many between the words "flout" and "flaunt," though so far as I know it has no basis in any passage of our literature—unless, indeed, the Republican national platform of 1936 be counted as literature. To flaunt is to wave or display impudently; to flout is to treat with contempt. When the Republicans accused President Roosevelt of "flaunting" the Supreme Court, they evidently meant that he had flouted it. But "flaunt" is often mistakenly used for "flout" in this way. In addition to the similarity in the sound of the two, there is the fact that waving something impudently in somebody's face is one method of flouting him, and this, I think, is largely responsible for the confusion.

Mistakes of this kind are frequently brought about by the unconscious combination of two words of similar meaning into another that unfortunately has quite a different one. The man who remarked that it is very beautiful in April to see the trees beginning to put on their new summer "garbage" was obviously thinking of the words "garb" and "herbage." Probably not many readers in these days of the automobile know that a martingale is part of the harness of a horse. Neither did the reporter who saw in the police records that a man had been arrested for stealing a martingale, and set out to write a human interest story on the meanness of a man who would deprive the rightful owner of a poor little songbird. Well, a martin is a bird, and a nightingale is a bird, so why shouldn't a martingale be a bird also? Yet, unfortunately for the reporter, it wasn't. It might be added in this connection, to anticipate another possible confusion, that though a martin is a bird, a marten is a beast.

However powerful the influence of great writers and men of high position may be upon the development of the language, it should be remembered that this influence exists simply because the great mass of intelligent people approve their usage and follow their example. It is a case of leadership, not dictatorship. Sometimes indeed the people refuse to follow, take things into their own hands, and bring about changes which are bitterly fought by writers and scholars, who are usually conservative, and often like to stick by the old way of saying things, even though it may not be the best. I have already mentioned an example of this, namely, the use of the word "but" in the sense of "except," in which the literary usage that regards it as a conjunction is giving way before the popular usage that makes a preposition of it.

"Recipe" and "receipt"

Another example is the change in the meanings of the words "recipe" (pronounced "RESipee") and "receipt," which has taken place within the present generation, though it is not yet quite complete. The *Century Dictionary*, published in the nineties, defines "recipe" as a set of instructions for compounding a medicine and "receipt" as directions for preparing and cooking food. But the new *Webster*, issued in 1934, says that now "recipe" is the term generally used in cooking, and that medical formulas are usually called "prescriptions," leaving "receipt," of course, to mean the act of receiving or a written statement acknowledging the payment of money or the delivery of goods. This change has come about gradually and in the face of the authorities, but it seems to be on the whole a desirable one.

The passing of the double negative—that is to say, the illogical piling up of negatives to increase the negative force —which, as I have mentioned, was once in the best of use, has been brought about, I believe, by leaders and people combined. But it still persists with the children and the ignorant. Indeed, in some instances literary usage itself has not fully settled.

The use of "or" and "nor"

A great many people find themselves at a loss to know exactly when to use "or" and when "nor," and unfortunately our textbooks often treat the subject either inadequately or incorrectly. They all say very properly that it should always be "neither . . . nor" rather than "neither . . . or," as, for instance, in the sentence, "I have *neither* time *nor* money for such things." But what shall we do when we substitute another negative, such as "no," "never," or "not" for "neither"? Shall it be "I have no time *or* money," or "no time *nor* money"? The answer is that in older usage "nor" was generally preferred, but today the normal usage is "or," with "nor" as a possibility under certain conditions. If the lack of money is an afterthought, or if it is desired to lay special emphasis on it, "nor" may be used, though it is better in that case to place a comma before it and regard it as introducing a condensed independent clause. "I have no time, nor money," is correct, but the thought in it seems to be, "I have no time for such things, nor have I any money for them." This, of course, differs only in emphasis from

"I have no time or money." The same principle permits the use of "nor" after "not" or "never" under similar conditions.

Turning nouns into verbs

One way in which our language is constantly changing is through the turning of nouns into verbs, which it does with great freedom, though not every attempt at such a change meets with success. Just now a strong effort is being made, as we have mentioned already, to establish "to contact" in the sense of "to make contact with" and "to proposition" for "to submit a proposition to." And the noun "audition" is no sooner brought into use by the radio than we begin to hear sentences such as, "He was auditioned yesterday." Librarians often speak of a book as being "accessioned," meaning that it has been formally made a part of the library and entered in what they call the "accession book," in which phrase the noun is called on to do duty as an adjective. Whether such verbs will ever come into the general use of careful speakers, remains to be seen. Many oppose them bitterly, and perhaps with reason, but we must remember that the verb "to progress" was fought vigorously, especially in England, when it was first formed from the noun "progress."

Both "summer" and "winter" are now in very good use as verbs. People say, for instance, "We shall winter in Florida or California and summer in Maine or in Asheville." We also hear the verbs "to week-end" and "to Sunday," but it seems to many that this is carrying the thing a little too far. Such verbs sound strange to them, just as they did to the farmer who got a letter from his brother in the city, describing at some length how he spent his time and concluding in this way: "Last Saturday we breakfasted at home, and then motored over to the beach, where we Sundayed." The farmer thought the matter over a little, decided that two could play at that game, and wrote an answer that ran about like this:

Dear Jim:

This morning I got up when the clock fived, and muled out to the corn-field, where I gee-hawed till dark. Then I muled back home, suppered, rocking-chaired, and piped in front of the fire for an hour, staircased up to my room, and bedsteaded till the next morning when the clock fived again.

The result of a remarkable double transformation of noun into adjective and adjective into noun is seen in the word "kindling" as used in such expressions as "Kindling for sale." Here, it is of course, a noun, as matters stand. Yet "kindling" in this use is merely a shortened form of "kindling wood," in which it is an adjective. But "kindling wood" means "wood for kindling," and therefore we see that after all our adjective "kindling" is really a verbal noun, or gerund, that has been turned into an adjective. So the grammarian, when he sees the sign "Kindling for sale," thinks of the word "kindling" as a noun that has been made from an adjective that is really a noun that is derived from a verb. Ordinary people just think of it as the name of something to start a fire with.

"The house is being built"

The changes that we have been discussing so far in this chapter, like most changes in language, concern the use and meaning of words. Many readers will doubtless ask what other changes there could be, for most people think of a language as a mere aggregation of words. Now, to be sure, words are an essential part of every language, but fundamentally a language is a way of putting words together. In other words, it is a grammar, as we said in an earlier chapter, when we spoke of the fact that English is classed as a Teutonic language largely because of its Teutonic grammar, in spite of its preponderance of words derived from the Latin. An illustration of just what this statement means may be in order. Consider the sentence:

Gradually increasing hostility separates ancient enemies.

Every word in it is derived from Latin, but it is held together and made to make sense in an Anglo-Saxon—that is Teutonic, or Germanic—way, just as much as the following sentence in which essentially the same thought is expressed by means of Anglo-Saxon words:

Slowly growing unfriendliness sunders old foes.

In both sentences we have the addition of the Anglo-Saxon ending "ly" to turn an adjective into an adverb, and of the Anglo-Saxon "ing" to make a present participle from a verb. We have likewise the English ending "s" used for two entirely different purposes in both sentences—one to show that the verbs "separates" and "sunders" are in the third person singular of the present indicative, and the other to form the plural of "enemy" and "foe." Furthermore the order of words—the same in both sentences—is Teutonic, not Latin.

Since grammar is so fundamental an element of a langauge, it is not surprising that changes in it come rarely and slowly. The last addition of importance to English grammar may be found exemplified in the simple sentence:

The house is being built.

The average person will scarcely see anything very striking about such a sentence, but to a grammarian it is exceedingly interesting. Grammarians are a queer tribe, but I am inclined to think that they get more pleasure out of life than most people. What interests them in this particular sentence is the fact that it is only within the lifetime of many people now living that it has finally and unquestionably become good English.

About the year 1890, Richard Grant White, a writer of some ability and the author of several works on the use of English, devoted thirty pages in one of his books to an effort to prove that the expression "The house is being built" contains one of the most atrocious pieces of bad English that could be imagined. Many readers will wonder, no doubt, how else the thought could be expressed. Yet up till about the time of our Revolutionary War, or a little earlier, the English-speaking person who wanted to convey that thought said, "The house is building," or earlier, "is a-building" or "in building." About 1750 our present method of forming the progressive passive—for that is what "is being built" is—began to come into use, being devised obviously to avoid the ambiguity of the older usage when it occurred in such sentences as "The boy is whipping," where it might mean either that the boy was being whipped, as we now put it, or that he was whipping some one else.

The advantages of the new method are so obvious that one would think it would have made rapid headway, but the fact is that it was bitterly fought by many people of education and culture, who rather foolishly felt that the English language was being ruined by such innovations—only they couldn't very well say "was being ruined," for that was the very thing they were fighting, and they probably said "was ruining" or "going to ruin." But in the end the conservatives either gave in or died off, and Richard Grant White's thirty-page outburst seemed to be all that was needed to settle the matter irrevocably against him. Today there are comparatively few people who know that the correctness of an expression like "The house is being built" was ever called in question, though the older usage may still be seen occasionally.

"Due to" as a preposition

It is not likely that we shall soon see another important grammatical change or addition in English. But other changes are occurring under our very eyes, some of which might, in a way, be considered grammatical. For instance, the expression "due to" has in the speech of many become a compound preposition, and is used to connect a noun with a verb, though "due" is properly an adjective and ought always to modify a noun. For example, in the unexceptionable sentence, "The postponement of the game was due to rain," the adjective "due" modifies the noun "post-ponement," and is itself modified by the prepositional phrase "to rain." But in the sentence, "The game was postponed, due to rain," which we often hear, though the authorities are generally opposed to it, there is no noun which "due" can modify, and it is evident that "due to" is used as a compound preposition in the sense of "because of," taking "rain" as its object, and forming with "rain" a phrase modifying the verb "was postponed."

I think the origin of this usage is due to ("due" here modifies "origin") the use of sentences such as, "He made a failure, due to lack of effort." In this "due" may be, and orig-inally was, considered to modify "failure," but it may also be taken as part of the compound preposition "due to," be-ginning a phrase which modifies the verb "made." Those who interpret it in this way naturally take another step and say, "He failed due to lack of effort," in which there is no way at all of considering "due" as an adjective. The new *Webster*, though very liberal in many ways, condemns this new use of "due to" as erroneous, and it is undoubtedly very offensive to many careful writers and speakers. I join with them in hoping that it will not prevail, but I fear it will. After all, it has as much justification as "owing to," which is well established as a preposition. The next twenty years should see the matter settled, either with "due to" fully ap-proved for prepositional use or definitely relegated to the speech of those whose speech-habits carry little weight.

Who will make the decision?

The decision in this case and the decision in all future changes of our living, growing language will be made not by the scholars, the grammarians, and the lexicographers, but by the great body of intelligent English-speaking people, most of whom I fear are not as well qualified as they ought to be for their great privilege and responsibility. Many who feel that they are eminently fitted for such a task are so im-bued with the idea that the particular form of English spoken

by the people of their little section or group is the only
"pure" English, so lacking in breadth of vision and common
sense that their narrow views present a pitiful contrast to the
scope and sweep of the vigorous language which they vainly
assume to guide, and to govern with the petty falsities of
rules evolved from the depth of their imaginations or repeated parrot-like after others.

On the other hand, far too many of those who have the
grasp of mind and soundness of taste and judgment which
would fit them admirably for the task are without the
knowledge of our language, its real rules, its history, achievements, and possibilities, that is essential for the purpose. English-speaking people are often strangely unaware of the
excellencies of English, even apologetic for it, and at the
same time largely ignorant of foreign tongues. The two
conditions naturally go together, for, as has been pointed
out, a mastery of English is impossible without some knowledge—the more the better—of German and French.

Each language, of course, has some point or points of
superiority, and it would be foolish boasting to claim that in
every respect English excels all the others. But if we put
the matter on the basis of adaptability to all the worthy pur-
suits of life at the same time—to use in business, to social in-
tercourse, to science, to literature in the form of both prose
and poetry—it has no serious rival. More than eighty years
ago a German, Jakob Grimm, known to scholars as one of
the greatest linguists of the world and to children as collector
—with his brother Wilhelm—of *Grimm's Fairy Tales*, made
this prophetic statement:

> English has a veritable power of expression such
> as perhaps never stood at the command of any
> other language of men. . . . Its highly spiritual
> genius and wonderfully happy condition have been
> the result of a surprisingly intimate union of the
> two noblest tongues in modern Europe, the Teu-
> tonic and the Romance. It is well known in what
> relation these two stand to each other in the Eng-

lish tongue, the former supplying the groundwork, the latter the spiritual conceptions. In truth the English language, which by no mere accident has produced and upborne the greatest and most predominant poet of modern times—I can, of course, mean only Shakespeare—may with all right be called a world-language, and like the English people, appears destined to prevail with a sway more extensive than its present over all portions of the globe. For in wealth, good sense, and closeness of structure, no other language at this day spoken deserves to be compared with it—not even our own German, which is torn even as we are torn, and must rid itself of many defects before it can boldly enter the lists as a competitor with the English.

This prophecy is today being strikingly fulfilled, for English is now spoken by almost two hundred millions of people in various parts of the earth, while German, which ranks next to it among the European languages, has not half as many speakers. Furthermore, English is rapidly displacing French as the international language, and the time is apparently not far distant when a knowledge of it will be considered essential to the education of a man of any nationality. More and more it is coming to be taught as the first and most important foreign language in the schools of the world. A distinguished Japanese vistor, Doctor Kagawa, is authority for the statement that ten million of his fellow-countrymen now speak English and that it occupies a prominent place in the course of study of Japanese schools. All over the earth millions of foreign students are digging eagerly into the difficult mysteries of the speech that seems so simple and natural to us. Many of them will never master it perfectly, of course, but will always speak it with an accent that betrays to others their nationality or the speech of their early childhood, just as millions of Americans are never able to break away from the misuse of English acquired through ignorance or carelessness in the first few years of their lives.

Yet I heard not long ago the amazing story of how one foreign-born woman got rid of this foreign accent—heard it from her own lips, and questioned her closely about it. I can vouch for the fact that no one who listened to her would ever suspect that English was not her native tongue, though the truth is that she came to America from Denmark at the age of seventeen, with no knowledge of our language.

Her father was a man of means, but soon after their arrival he was swindled out of his money by rascally Americans. On this account the daughter conceived a violent hatred for the United States, a hatred which extended even to the English language, which she vowed she would never learn. But in this time of great distress she and her family found comfort and much practical help from Americans belonging to a religious denomination, whose teachings they subsequently embraced. Then the girl began to study English, and mastered it very well, except for the fact that she spoke it with a decided Danish accent, which stamped her at once as a foreigner. This accent persisted for twelve years, till at the age of twenty-nine she had the following almost incredible experience.

Seated one evening on a bench in a St. Louis park, she was idly watching the folds of the American flag floating over a government building near by, when there came over her the thought of what that flag stands for—freedom of speech, freedom of religion, freedom of the individual to make his own way and be judged for himself rather than for his ancestors. A great love for America and Americans swept over her—a love so strong as to include even the rascally Americans who had swindled her father. She went home much uplifted, and went about her duties as usual on the following days, but noticed that whenever she spoke, people looked at her strangely. Finally, on the third day, a good friend asked her, "What has become of your Danish accent?" and she realized suddenly that it had been gone since that miraculous moment in the park.

Account for this remarkable happening as you will, it is clear that in some way she suddenly caught the underlying idea of our language—the spirit of English—in that outburst of emotion which must have made her feel toward the speech of America as if it were her own mother tongue. And we who speak English, not, indeed, with a foreign accent, yet poorly and meanly, in manner ill befitting the beauty and vigor of the language we have inherited from our ancestors —may we, too, come to know the miracle of a transformation in our speech, the happy outgrowth of a deep and abiding love for our mother tongue.

INDEX